Design and

D0514147

Design and Creativity
Policy, Management and Practice

Edited by
GUY JULIER AND LIZ MOOR

Oxford • New York

English edition
First published in 2009 by
Berg
Editorial offices:
First Floor, Angel Court, 81 St Clements Street, Oxford OX4 1AW, UK
175 Fifth Avenue, New York, NY 10010, USA

Berg is the imprint of Oxford International Publishers Ltd.

Library of Congress Cataloging-in-Publication Data
A catalogue record for this book is available from the Library of Congress.

British Library Cataloguing-in-Publication Data
A catalogue record for this book is available from the British Library.

ISBN 978 1 84788 307 0 (Cloth)
978 1 84788 306 3 (Paper)

Typeset by Avocet Typeset, Chilton, Aylesbury, Bucks.
Printed in the UK by the MPG Books Group

www.bergpublishers.com

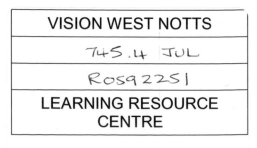

Contents

Illustrations

Acknowledgements

Many of the ideas for this book were initially discussed through two workshops, under the title of 'Counting Creativity: Understanding the Systematization of Design Practices'. These events were funded through the Arts and Humanities Research Council's 'Nature of Creativity' workshop and seminar programme of 2006–7, and were hosted by the Design Council, London and Leeds Metropolitan University. The research for Lucy Kimbell's chapter was developed through 'Designing for Services in Science and Technology-Based Enterprises', a project funded by the Arts and Humanities Research Council and Engineering and Physical Sciences Research Council within the Designing for the Twenty-First Century initiative.

In addition to this book's authors, Sarah Dabbs, Kathryn Grace, Richard Gregory, Peter Higgins, Annabel Jackson, Alistair McKechnie, James Heartfield, David Scothron and Harriet Walsh contributed their expert knowledge and perspectives to these workshops, and we thank them for giving their time to the project. In particular, we thank Mike Rawlinson of City ID, Bristol, who provided the cover images for this book and also invaluable material for one of its chapters. Finally, we thank the many designers who, anonymously or named, have contributed to the researching of this book through giving interviews.

Introduction
Design and Creativity

Liz Moor and Guy Julier

The global rise of design in the past two decades is indisputable. Statistics flow out of national governments, regional administrations, professional institutions and academic centres that testify to its exponential growth in terms of the numbers employed in the design industry, its turnover, its contribution to Gross Domestic Product and its export value. It has become a new object of measurement, placed alongside more traditional indicators of productive well-being such as agricultural output, manufacture and retail.

The enthusiasm with which policy-makers in many countries have embraced and championed this sector – and, by extension, the creative industries as a whole – evidences a more general shift towards the privileging of an entrepreneurial knowledge economy in the developed world. As much of the manufacturing base for making the quotidian objects that permeate our homes, offices, shops and landfills has moved to South-East Asia and Central and South America, so more 'developed' countries turn their attention to the more intangible business of innovation and creativity. Design becomes a leading-edge activity in this move. The characterization of late-modern economies as 'design-intensive' (Lash and Urry 1994) has provoked new interests in the ways in which the aesthetic elaboration of social and cultural themes has become central to economic productivity.

This book is concerned with the processes of design and how creativity is managed within this new economic, political, social and cultural landscape. While 'creativity' remains the intrinsic currency of the design industry, we do not read it in its traditional sense as an essentialistic preserve of individuals. Rather, we take the view that it is contingent within various managed structures, networks of power, economic processes and policy priorities, and we deal with this issue in two ways. First, the influences of systematization are examined *within* specific design fields by reviewing the everyday practices of its actors, and the extent to which their work is shaped by imperatives of accountability, transparency and systematization. Second, such influences are traced to the broader *external* contexts of political economy, urban policy, global markets, and new trends in social and environmental agency. In this way, the book elaborates some of the concrete ways in which the 'values' of design and other creative practices have become imbricated with a range of social and political projects, whilst also addressing wider questions about the causes and effects of such shifts. How, for example, are traditional notions of 'creativity' reworked in the context of new public and commercial imperatives? What are the broader implications of the centrality of creative industries in delivering a range of both civic and commercial goals? How do demands for accountability refocus the priorities of creative practice? Before we explore these issues in more detail, let us first outline the new context for and practice of design in the twenty-first century.

Design in the Twenty-first Century

Globally, the design profession has seen exponential growth over the past two decades. A number of examples bear this out. The European design market grew at around 25 per cent between 1982 and 1989. By 1994, the Netherlands Design Institute was predicting a growth of the European design market from US$9.5 billion to US$14 billion by 2000 (NDI 1994: 9–10). Country by country data appears to lend weight to this prediction. The independent design profession in France is relatively new, with 53 per cent of organizations operating for fewer than ten years. Sweden has seen a rise of 272 per cent in the number of firms between 1993 and 2002 (Bruce and Daly 2006). However, in the twenty-first century, the design profession is set to grow, beyond the preserve of economically advanced countries. China, for example, saw a 23 per cent increase in enrolment on art and design degree courses between 2003 and 2004. A further 1,200 design schools are planned to add to the 400 that have opened in China in the last two decades (Rigby 2007).

The geographic reach of design practices has also extended. Globalization has led to a dispersion of the processes of conception and execution of design artefacts. In 2006, for instance, merchandise trade grew by 21 per cent (WTO 2007). The creative development of objects, images or spaces may be distributed across continents and time zones and they may be assembled from components made in various countries or mediated through multiple communication networks. The location of global design centres for Ford, Sony and Nokia in London since 2000 evidences a presumption that design studios may be physically distanced from both their productive infrastructure and their consumer bases.

At the same time, a variety of 'space-shrinking technologies' (Dicken 2003) speed up and intensify these processes. This is not just in terms of the physical dispersion of design outlined above; it also impacts on the design process itself. For example, until the advent of Computer-aided Design in the last two decades, the typographic designer would mark up a proof for a printer to set up, or a product designer would be reliant on the specialist technical support and working hours of a workshop to make up prototypes. Digitization means that such intermediaries in the process are dropped. Information technologies facilitate a different quality of proximity and the acceleration of interaction between designers, producers and consumers. Designers interchange their proposals with clients more frequently, creating thicker, less linear and less one-directional communications in the development process. A feedback loop between these interests is ever more instantaneous as consumer information and attitudes are more readily and accurately collated.

Historically, design has emerged *from* production. It has been a craft-based activity, born out of the specific requirements of manufacturers. The designer's role was largely to give specific form to the new goods and services of a corporation. The emergence of the consultant designer alongside the more complex aesthetic demands of advanced capitalism reverses this relationship. Designers insert themselves *into* productive activities at various stages. They bring expertise to arenas of commercial competition or governmental policy. Their role and creative outputs therefore become increasingly diverse as new specialist areas for its application are developed. In 2006, British Design Innovation (BDI) – a UK design industry monitoring company – identified twenty-five design sub-disciplines. In addition to activities such as 'branding and graphics' or 'multimedia/ new media', they also specified such approaches as 'design and innovation management', 'social responsibility', 'high-end consumerism', 'internal communications' and 'product testing' (BDI 2006). While the majority of work undertaken by design firms remained in the more traditional disciplines that are medium-based, their survey was designed also to recognize new skill-sets that were emerging in design, particularly in service and proposition creation. The latter, then, is a reflection of a trend in the design practice to move beyond what is usually termed the 'visual translation of client strategy'. BDI classified this typology – which occupies roughly 70 per cent of UK design activity – as the work of the 'design agency'. But it also identified two other typologies. Occupying about 20 per cent of national design activity was the 'design studio': that is, production-led, mostly graphics-related practice that sees projects through to execution. But an expanding third sector, making up about 10 per cent of activity, was that of the 'strategic design consultancy'. Here the emphasis is much more on how design can be used, for example within corporate planning or in policy development to gain competitive advantage or deliver public services more effectively. These days, therefore, the physical output of the design firm may shift from design specifications, for example by way of corporate identity guidelines or technical drawings, to the production of the actual artefacts themselves through to strategic reports and audits, or the orchestration of entire systems that integrate products and services.

The design disciplines covered in this book are not all-encompassing and do not necessarily reflect the respective sizes of the typologies given above. Similarly, it would be impossible in this volume to represent the twenty-five sub-specialisms of design practice that the BDI identifies. Our interest is in those design specialisms – some of which are still emergent – that are of particular significance within this discourse of audit and the systematization of creativity. As design has grown in value and recognition, so it has been encountered in new interfaces in commercial and public sector practices. For example, one of our interviewees in Part III of this book talks of how, as a product designer and strategist, he has had to work with and through many more departments of a corporate client, such is the growing importance accorded and interest shown in design by them. It is in such interfaces with other disciplines and discourses that design gains influence and power (Lupton and Miller 1999). At the same time, within such contexts the work of design has to be more delicately and intelligently negotiated through client interests and priorities, with their attendant codes of conduct, professional norms or *modus operandi*. It is these emergent challenges, where design shifts to a complex process, which interest us in this book.

In both commercial and public sectors, designers mediate between a range of departments, agencies, institutions and other interests. Thus we might not talk so much about 'design management' or 'design leadership' as the 'management of design'. Design management is generally tied to the optimization of design performance within organizations. Design leadership refers more often to the innovation of new strategies of design performance or application. Our interest, by contrast, is in the everyday structuring and coordination of design processes, both internally within the design consultancy and in its alignment with external factors, from client relationships to wider legislative and policy issues of governments. Methodologically speaking, academic concerns in design management and design leadership invariably move from the analysis of scenarios to the modelling of 'best practice' approaches. Our own approach is slightly different. By focusing on case studies that explore the practical ways in which design is managed, and the wider ambitions of commercial or public sector interests in which it is contextualized, we seek a deeper understanding of the processual complexities of design and a more critical perspective on the wider forces shaping its development.

The New Economy and New Public Management

The developments covered in this book – which include the intensification and speeding up of design processes – resonate with a set of wider assumptions regarding the New Economy. At the heart of New Economy practices is the idea of 'faster, better, cheaper'. Within this discourse, creativity and innovation play central roles. In support of this notion, books such as Howkins's *The Creative Economy: How People Make Money From Ideas* (2001) or Ray's *The Cultural Creatives* (2001) set out a business agenda in which creativity and creative people are the frontiersmen of this new economic landscape.

Parallel to such developments in the private sector have been widespread systemic changes in the last twenty years in the way that public sector interests are organized and delivered. The so-called New Public Management has ushered in an emphasis on entrepreneurial approaches to the delivery of public services within an attendant reorientation of their management towards private sector styles, a growth in subcontracting to external commercial agencies and of performance measurement. This new context has resulted in a considerable growth of opportunities for designers. The increase in the outsourcing of public service delivery to private contractors has resulted in a more complex and intense network of parties involved. And as the demand for more efficient and innovative approaches in the public sector has grown, so designers have been used with increasing frequency to aid this process.

The speeding up and intensifications of actions, both in the New Economy and the New Public Management, has meant that creativity and innovation (and, indeed, creative practitioners and innovators such as designers) take on symbolic roles in addition to their functional purposes. Such assumptions about the nature and purpose of creative work have infiltrated the self-image and practices of designers. In her study of London-based fashion designers, for example, Angela McRobbie (1998; 2002) shows how their working patterns were typified by the requirement to network, to be visible and available virtually on a twenty-four-hour basis – patterns of labour that resonate with the emergent entrepreneurialism of the New Economy. Meanwhile business studies academics Scase and Davis (2000: 23) take this notion further to claim that the creative economy is at the 'leading edge of the movement towards the information age [as] their outputs are performances, expressive work, ideas and symbols rather than consumer goods or services'. Arch supporter of New Economy thinking, the American magazine *Fast Company*, supported the claim that business leaders should not only understand design but work creatively as if they were designers (Breen 2005). This championing of the creative industries and of 'creative' methods of thinking and working has effects in quite disparate sectors, both public and private.

In order to fulfil a functional role in the New Economy, the rhetorics of creativity and innovation, however, are de facto contingent upon their management. Hence, for example, writing in the *Harvard Business Review*, Anthony et al. (2006) suggest that, like American football plays, innovation and creativity can be pre-planned, strategized and mapped in order to field and respond to rapidly changing business challenges and scenarios. Similarly, our interest is less on the popular representation of the work of designers as a serially isolated 'one-off' creative acts. Our focus falls more on iterative creative work where designers habitually process projects. As such, creativity in design may be understood to involve the adoption and iterative development of repertoires of action – or what we later term 'scripted improvisations' – that are deployed in response to varying briefs and client demands. In the speeded-up context of the New Economy, this system becomes a kind of 'fast routine' whereby creative processes and solutions can be rolled in a business environment where, as we will shortly see, returns on creative labour time have diminished.

'Creativity' may indeed be the *a priori* currency of designers. However, the coordination of design labour – the management of design – is a necessary action to ensure its successful outcome. In this context, tracking, communicating and evaluating its inputs and outputs becomes more sophisticated and, for the sake of its management and internal and external articulation, more subject to codification. At the same time, the intangible work of designers increases as the 'knowledge' element of their activities grows. Consequently, making explicit exactly what they do involves greater articulation. Repertoires of action may not necessarily be a way of organizing the everyday functioning of a design studio. They may also be translated into schema for helping clients understand the process and value of what they get from different design consultancies.

Within the neo-liberal form of advanced capitalism, design plays a key role in product and service differentiation, and in giving competitive advantage to its clients. This is as evident in its role in helping an urban centre achieve its aims in regeneration as in helping a corporation achieve greater market share. Equally, beyond any aesthetic outcome, designers seek to achieve differentiation in the way they present themselves, in their design processes and in what they bring to their clients. This is partly the result of the design profession's highly varied landscape. Unlike architecture, for example, design is not a profession that is beholden to normative standards. To practise as an architect in Europe, stringent guidelines have been laid down regarding adherence to professional qualifications (Directive 2005/36/EC). By contrast, there are no set qualifications for being a designer. The heterogeneous and nonconformist nature of the design industry may, perhaps, be read as emblematic of many of the diverse and unregulated characteristics of advanced capitalism. Yet this in turn leads to variation in the techniques by which designers represent themselves to clients and other audiences. It also results in a lack of standardization in the ways by which design processes are organized and accounted for. What follows from this is that the respective processes of design firms then invariably become part of the currency by which they differentiate themselves from one another and market themselves, as opposed to the formal outcome of their labour.

There is a compelling dialogue here. On the one hand, the design profession is committed to differentiation and non-normative action. The lack of professional norms and the rhetorics of 'being creative' conspire to continually variegate and fragment the working processes and self-presentation of designers. Partly due to its rapid evolution, design is structurally quite fragmented and heterogeneous. On the other hand, design is subject to increasing levels of audit, measurement, accountability, codification and systematization, both for the purposes of commercial strategy (as individual firms try to distinguish themselves from their competitors) and as the result of external demands (as both private and especially public sector clients expect greater transparency and evidence of how value is created). How creativity is valorized, managed and practised in these circumstances becomes a matter of renewed scrutiny and attention.

Creative Practice

One of our major concerns in what follows is with the ways in which the greater emphasis within government policy and business on 'creativity', the creative industries and the management of innovation has impacted upon the internal organization of design studios and design work. By this, we do not simply mean the ways in which relationships between designers and clients are managed (although these are important too, and are dealt with in a number of chapters here), but also the more 'micro' relations that obtain within specific sites of design production. These might include the layout of work spaces, the technologies employed to assist and monitor production, and the ways in which working processes have been systematized and encoded in company documents or proprietary techniques and models.

In thinking about the management of design in this way, we have been influenced by work in the areas of science and technology studies and economic sociology which draws attention to the new presence and relevance of non-human objects to social life (Knorr Cetina and Bruegger 2002). Work in this field has paid particular attention to the ways in which objects, such as documents, scientific instruments, computer technologies or consumer objects, may be said to have agency (e.g. Muniesa et al. 2007) and may intervene in the construction of particular sites of practice or expertise; whether by 'helping' or 'forcing', the argument here is that 'devices do things ... they articulate actions; they act or make others act' (2007: 2). In this formulation, agency is seen as split or distributed; rather than residing 'in' people or things, it is seen as an outcome of their mutual entanglement, and of the 'compound *agencements*' (ibid.) they make within particular contexts.

Although some of the most important work in this area thus far has been focused on scientific research or relatively 'expert' terrains of economic action such as foreign exchange markets (see Knorr Cetina and Bruegger 2002), we believe that such approaches are also appropriate to the analysis of design practice and research, and perhaps especially in its more systematized and 'managed' forms. This is in part because design seems to share with many other areas of work that have been approached in this way a significant dependence on complex objects and systems. Similarly, its own 'object' (whether a brand, a magazine, a piece of public art or a service system) is likely to exist simultaneously in a variety of forms (e.g. drafts, sketches, prototypes, updates) (Julier 2006) and thus exhibit the distributed, partial or unfinished quality (Knorr Cetina 2001) of other 'objects of knowledge'. At the same time, while design is not subject to normative professional entry requirements or codes of conduct, it shares with other areas of 'expert' work the fact that its practitioners typically need to be familiar not only with particular design instruments and technologies, but also with processes, orientations, forms of 'envisioning' and ways of accounting for their work that they share with a community of other practitioners, but from which client organizations may be relatively excluded (see Soar 2002). Objects and technologies are, we would argue, central to the ways in which this expertise is assembled and deployed.

Another useful contribution of this literature, from our point of view, is its insight into the forms of practice that may exist within certain types of object-centred 'expert' work. Knorr Cetina (2001), for example, notes that existing conceptions of practice (as found in Bourdieu, for example) tend to emphasize its habitual and rule-governed features (2001: 175) and the acquisition of schemes of perception that are then deployed in specific situations. Yet she goes on to note that such a conception may be inadequate in the context of occupations and organizations with a significant knowledge component. Here, she suggests, practice is less likely to be habitual and routine, and more likely to be 'looped through objects' in ways that promote 'moments of interruption and reflection' in the creative process. To follow this argument is to work with a conception of creative practice that is neither about the simple implementation of established routines and processes, nor about a series of pure 'innovations' that punctuate an otherwise stable tradition (Ingold and Hallam 2007). Rather, it is to see creative work as emerging from an ongoing engagement with a material environment that provides both specific problems to be addressed (the 'object' of any given design project) and a material infrastructure through which that process may take place (the various devices that make up the designer's working environment).

While it is beyond the scope of this book to consider the extent to which this in turn may promote new ways of relating to objects and new forms of sociality (but see Knorr Cetina 1997), we would argue that the tension between routine, habitual ways of working and the 'creative and constructive practice ... that obtains when we confront non-routine problems' (Knorr Cetina 2001: 175) is a useful way to think about the organization of contemporary creative work, and the role of objects and technologies within this. On the one hand, many of the technologies now used by designers may hasten, 'routinize' or even auto-mate aspects of practice, significantly reducing opportunities for reflection and critical or creative engagement. This may have tangible consequences for cre-ative industries, not least in terms of the way in which their work is valued by clients. Yet at the same time, such technologies and devices may also 'open up' creative work, providing new volumes of information with which designers must engage creatively, while also making the various iterations of creative work more widely available both within and beyond the organization. The ease and speed with which various iterations of a design project can be shared with clients, for example, can simultaneously create new opportunities for critical and creative practice, while also distributing such opportunities more widely, with interesting implications for notions of creative authorship and autonomy, and for the processes of value attribution (see e.g. Adkins 2005; Lury 1993). Such developments, we suggest, are closely linked to a situation of dropping margins for design agencies and studios, and greater pressures – both internal and external – for rapid turnover of projects. According to the British Design Valuation Survey (British Design Innovation 2006), fee income in the design industry has dropped markedly since 2001, while the actual numbers of designers and design firms practising has not changed significantly. Its conclu-sions are that savings made by designers through, for example, increased tech-nological efficiency or quicker turnaround of projects are being passed on to clients. Designers, in other words, are being more productive for the same money. Designers retain or chase clients by keeping their prices keen or by throwing in added extras. Design consultancies are ever trying to trim their sails to provide more efficient workflows, so their marketing budgets and strategies are increasingly important in the bid to maintain recognition.

Finally, we would follow Knorr Cetina in noting that more object-centred forms of work are not without their elements of power and domination (1997: 11). Indeed, if we turn to the management of creative work within the studio or agency context, one cannot fail to note the ubiquity of technological systems and types of management software (for example Harvest and Oracle Workflow) for monitoring designers' work and accounting for ever-smaller components of their time. These may be thought about in terms of surveillance or control, subjecting workers to new levels of scrutiny and accountability, while also providing new means for connecting workers' efforts to the profitability of the organization. Such systems are also important contributors to the process by which clients and agencies develop new ways of attributing value to different parts of (and actors in) the design process. While there is variation in the extent to which agencies exploit the potential of such systems, they have nonetheless become an accepted part of the creative workplace and one of the major means by which creative work is organized and measured.

Design and Audit

In thinking about the origins and impact of new forms of management on the organization of design work, it is useful also to consider the body of writing that has emerged around the idea of 'audit culture'. This term, most strongly associated with the work of Michael Power, refers broadly to the 'institutionalization of checking mechanisms' and more specifically to the 'control of control', whereby new, higher-level organizations are set up in order to check on already existing lower-level checking processes (Power 1997: xvi). Debates about audit culture are closely linked to debates about New Public Management in so far as one of the key features of an audit culture is deemed to be the extension to the public sector of the more rigorous audit regimes typically associated with the private sector. Yet the wider context is of greater levels of auditing, and associated techniques for checking and accountability, across *all* sectors of economic activity, itself grounded in 'transformations in the conceptions of administration and organization which straddle, or ... dismantle the public–private divide' (Power 1997: 10).

Although few of the design agencies or specialisms discussed in this book are subject to the more extreme levels of external inspection described by Power, there are a number of ways in which the themes of audit are relevant to design work. Firstly, Power himself makes it clear that 'audit is an idea as much as it is a concrete technical practice' (1997: 4), and that the term is not only used *descriptively* to refer to particular practices, but also '*normatively* in the context of demands and aspirations for accountability and control' (1997: 6, emphasis in original). In this respect, any organization that demands high levels of accountability from its workers, or experiences such demands from external agencies, is brought within the orbit of audit culture and its normative claims and demands. Assessing how this new normative environment impacts upon different parts of the design industry is one of the major projects of the book. In fact, almost all of the contexts explored here are characterized by some type of demand for accountability and checking by or on behalf of clients, and in many cases (particularly those involving the public sector) such demands have increased notably in recent years. At the same time, Power suggests that the normative extension of audit means that one may also speak of an 'audit implosion', whereby organizations themselves have become more reflexive, and where company directors, for example, have taken on new responsibilities for internal control systems and risk management (1997: xviii). As Marilyn Strathern (2000) notes, there are many situations in which audit is less about external inspection and checking, and more to do with ensuring that internal controls and monitoring techniques are in place – and that workers within organizations are adapted to audit and are able to monitor themselves. A related development in the creative industries is the fact that many organizations have voluntarily developed new systems for making their work more transparent to clients, and for facilitating the kinds of checking and accountability processes typically associated with the external auditor's role.

How, then, might we think about the ways in which 'audit culture' impacts upon the organization of the design industry? One of the strongest claims made about the negative effects of audit is that it transforms the more substantive practices of organizations to fit the needs of audit itself. This may mean prioritizing those aspects of a practice that can be effectively measured over those which cannot. This is argued to have dysfunctional or unintended consequences, as for example when academic research priorities are re-ordered to take account of new external auditing demands (Power 1997: 100). This 'colonization' of practice by the mechanisms devised to check it may also be seen, according to several authors, in the way in which it creates, over time, 'new mentalities, new incentives and perceptions of significance' (Power 1997: 97), and new interpretive schemes for the conduct of everyday work. Indeed, even when audit is viewed as a kind of 'add-on', adopted only for the purposes of external legitimization, and effectively 'decoupled' from core activities (e.g. Meyer and Rowan, cited in Power 1997: 96), it may still produce new but enduring types of organizational behaviour. Thus practitioners in certain organizations may engage in new types of 'performance' designed to make some (auditable) activities visible while others remain hidden (Strathern 2000: 8) or may adopt aspects of audit as part of a technology of the self directed towards specific types of professional publicity (e.g. Pels 2000).

In terms of the design industry, we would argue that the latter perspective makes most sense; few design agencies and studios are subject to such a degree of external monitoring that core activities are fundamentally altered, but there is nonetheless a widespread acceptance of the demand for new levels of accountability and transparency at the level of both the organization and the individual. Creative workers, for example, generally comply with the demand that their working day is monitored in ever smaller increments and that their work-in-progress is made publicly available for scrutiny (as in AnneMarie Dorland's chapter), while studios and agencies frequently adopt new forms of institutional presentation and promotion designed to showcase particular types of professional accountability to clients (as in Paul Springer's account of a London advertising agency). Indeed, as Dorland suggests in her chapter on graphic design studios in Canada, the institutionalization of such processes and checking mechanisms can directly influence the ways in which designers think about and organize their practice and 'perform' that work for different audiences.

Despite these developments, it is also helpful to retain an awareness of the fact that audit is not a one-way process, and that general shifts towards greater levels of systematization and accountability may also produce new areas for debate, reflection and ethical engagement. Georgina Born (2002), for example, has shown in her study of the BBC in the 1990s that alongside an ongoing debate between the government and the BBC about the introduction of new mechanisms for external accountability, there existed a parallel set of voluntary, informal reflexivities among workers driven by ideas about professional ethos and by ethical, aesthetic and political concerns (2002: 81). In this sense, she notes, the institutional space of the BBC was in fact characterized by great complexity, with new techniques of rationalization and accountability able to co-exist with diverse forms of resistance that supported an 'evolving Reithianism' and new discourses about genre, aesthetics and the conditions for creativity (2002: 68).

In a similar vein, Peter Pels (2000) has argued that the rise of audit may give a new urgency to debates about whom a particular activity is for. Writing in the context of academic auditing and its impact upon the discipline of anthropology, he suggests that the various codes of conduct for research drawn up since the 1960s have reflected a shifting sense of whether the 'client of their expertise' was the group of people studied, the research sponsors or government, or academic colleagues. The constitution of the 'professional self' has therefore demanded different techniques and orientations over time. There are similar dilemmas in design, where work is usually done 'for' a client, whose interests and demands are not, however, always symmetrical with those of the 'end user', citizen or consumer who may purchase, or be subject to, particular products and services. This situation may be further complicated by recent shifts in the organization of creative work. In fields characterized by general insecurity, short-term contracts or persistent freelancing, and in which individuals seek a 'big hit' that will enable them to move into a more secure environment (see McRobbie 2007), an employee's material interests may be even further at odds with those of their employer, as well as those of clients and end users. This is surely an important backdrop to the rise of audit cultures, to the extent that these tend to be characterized by institutional lack of trust, anxiety about the 'moral hazards' of individuals acting against institutional interests (Power 1997: 5), and the development of a set of strategies by those 'interested parties' (such as the state) who imagine that they 'need ... protection from the individual who acts with his or her own ends in mind' (Strathern 2000: 293).

We are not, then, suggesting that design has been 'colonized' by audit culture or by related mechanisms for managing or measuring creative work. Rather, we want to emphasize a more general sense in which the normative dimensions of audit – its broader 'demands and aspirations for accountability and control' (Power 1997: 6) – resonate in the uneven but clearly discernible trend towards greater systematization, routinization, accountability and measurement procedures in creative work. This trend is not 'caused' by audit; it is, as we have suggested, linked more directly to a series of developments – material and social – emerging from the greater economic role for design in advanced capitalist societies. Our point instead has been that debates about the consequences of audit culture have raised important issues about what happens to 'creative' institutions and practices when these are subject to a greater degree of measurement and surveillance. These questions have guided our own thinking and analysis, and shaped the contributions presented here.

Creativity and Scripted Improvisation

Similarly, although creative design work is the focus of this book, is not our intention in what follows to offer a detailed analysis of the concept of 'creativity' itself, nor to propose new accounts and formulations. Indeed, in tracking contemporary formations of the design industry, our interest has been less with the *nature* of creativity than with the ways in which work deemed to be 'creative' has been organized and reorganized within economic systems that see it as a driver of economic growth or as a capacity to be nurtured in order for citizens to compete in the global economy.

Nonetheless, in reading what follows it is useful to have a sense of the ideas and philosophies that underpin particular conceptions of creativity, how these have emerged, and how they have been linked to ways of measuring, managing and valuing creative work. Historically, creativity has been associated with novelty, and in particular with novel 'fusion[s] of disparate cultural configurations' (Liep, cited in Ingold and Hallam 2007: 16). As such, work that follows a template continues a tradition, or operates within a relatively prescribed set of rules or procedures, has tended not to be seen as involving either novelty or creativity. This distinction between novelty and formula, routine and tradition can be seen in part in the various informal status hierarchies that persist between different creative industries and roles, while the way in which 'creativity' functions not as an absolute descriptor but as a relative term with significant discursive power can be seen in the fact that all manner of quite mundane, and in some cases exploitative, forms of labour may be deemed 'creative' to suit both personal and institutional ends (McRobbie 1998, 2007; Nugent 2005).

It is also part of the political and economic history of creativity that it has frequently been seen as a unique capacity that human beings either do or do not 'have'. Sometimes this capacity is seen as something that individuals may acquire (for example through education and training); sometimes – perhaps more often – it is seen as an innate 'gift' or talent that can only be nurtured. In any case, accounts that see creativity as distributed, or that locate creativity in complex social relationships and formations have, in recent history at least, been rather rare. This has begun to change slightly as national and local governments have come to see creative work as more central to economic prosperity. Hence the emergence of accounts of creativity that see it as residing in particular types of urban formation ('creative cities') or relationships between individuals and groups ('creative networks'). Even here, however, there is still an implicit sense that creativity itself is a property of individuals, and that the role of the interested party – whether government or business – is to put in place an infrastructure or set of conditions that will allow them to access, 'unlock' or cultivate individual capacity in order that it may realize itself in the form of a creative outcome or product.

The economic underpinnings of current accounts of creativity can also be seen in the fact that while the 'purest' forms of creativity are, very often, those that appear to be relatively economically disinterested, the idea of creativity as an individual possession or capacity is in fact strongly linked to an economic history in which a high value was assigned to innovation and its role in the production of new commodities (Ingold and Hallam 2007). This was as true for the invention of mechanical devices during the period of industrialization as it is now. Indeed, as Ingold and Hallam (2007) suggest, definitions of creativity and innovation have tended to be made by reading 'backwards' from particular products or outcomes to their purported 'originators', rather than 'forwards' in terms of particular practices or behaviours. This is, of course, also closely linked to the emergence of typically modern (and typically Western) ideas of possession, property rights and authorship (e.g. Leach 2007).

Alternative conceptions of creativity may, therefore, take as their starting point the idea that creativity is less a matter of outcomes than of processes. This is the approach taken by Tim Ingold and Elizabeth Hallam (2007), who suggest that creativity is a forward-moving process of improvisation, best understood in terms of generative, relational and productive movements that are relatively unscripted, and which may involve a good deal of tradition (or 'keeping things going') as well as novelty and rupture. At the heart of their idea of creativity-as-improvisation is the notion that improvisation is a kind of cultural 'bottom line', animating both the 'studied reflections' of art and literature and the conduct of our ordinary activities. Improvisation is generative because even when it is involved in imitating or reproducing an existing model it involves 'a complex and ongoing alignment of observation of the model with action in the world' (2007: 5), in which creative alterations may be made. It is relational because it involves ways of life that are 'entangled and mutually responsive', and because it exists not in the form of an individual agency but in 'the dynamic potential of an entire field of relationships to bring forth the persons situated in it' (2007: 7).

While this account of creativity – as a form of practice that is ordinary, improvisational, relational and generative – is persuasive, what follows from it, as Hallam and Ingold suggest, is that it is most productively analysed in terms of 'the social relations and cultural formations that guide it and in terms of which it has effects' (2007: 20). That is to say, while it may be useful in broad terms to think of creativity (and design) as improvisatory, to understand how this improvisation takes shape in practice one must pay attention to specific instances and see how such improvisatory skills are shaped and guided by particular social and material forces. For as Hallam and Ingold note, 'There is no script for social life ... [but] there are most certainly scripts *within* it' (2007: 12, emphasis in original). While creativity is 'emergent in ongoing social action', it is also 'marked and framed' and 'configured, narrated and reflected upon in discourse' (2007: 20). It is these concrete instances of the organization, narration and framing of a general process of creativity within more specific contemporary design contexts – what we would call its 'scripted improvisation' – that are the focus of what follows.

Structure of the Book

Part I of this book focuses on the relationship between public policy and design. In particular, it highlights the way that design has been instrumentalized to fulfil a number of roles in the context of the New Public Management. Thus its role in reconfiguring the users of public services as 'consumers', its contribution to urban social and economic regeneration targets, and its symbolic value in stimulating creative industries all come into view here. Part II focuses on the management of design and creativity within predominantly commercial contexts. These include not only the emergence of new techniques in design management, but also critical questions about the nature and role of creativity itself. Part III comprises a series of interviews with practitioners, and a concluding chapter summarizing the insights and arguments of the book as a whole.

In the first chapter, Liz Moor examines the ways in which the growing interest in design among governments and policy organizations is linked to changing philosophies of government and new approaches to public service delivery. She shows that a widespread political interest in 'empowering' and educating citizens, and in reshaping their relationships with the state, has tangible outcomes for the design industry in the form of an expansion of certain types of design work and new volumes of public sector clients for particular organizations. At the same time, she also assesses the practical and normative implications of transposing design techniques that have been successful in commercial contexts for the delivery of public services and public goods.

Similarly, Guy Julier follows with a chapter that reviews the role of design in the context of urban regeneration. By focusing on public policy shifts in the past ten years, he shows how urban design has been employed both in the physical and symbolic renovation of cities. Given the complex sets of interests involved in the negotiation, development and implementation of urban design schemes, the emergence of design guidelines and statements and the subsequent the 'codification' of design, Julier's focus here is on the newly important processes of *mediation* between urban designers and non-design specialists.

Katie Hill and Guy Julier's co-authored chapter looks at the way that creativity and innovation is handled in the context of New Public Management. It uses a case study of how central government directives on the creative development children's play policies comes into conflict with the complexities and contradictions within local government bureaucracies. Due largely to a lack of capacity to carry out ambitious national programmes, local authorities may employ creative consultancies – which include the skills and techniques of trained designers – to help develop strategies and their implementation.

In the following chapter, Doug Sandle critically examines the processes of evaluation that have come into play with respect to public art in design-led urban regeneration. He shows how art in the public realm has been expected to move beyond its mere aesthetic elevation and to contribute to social and economic objectives in the transformation of towns and cities. The way its impact is measured, Sandle argues, becomes an increasingly complex and contested issue.

This section on design and policy is concluded with a chapter by Jane Pavitt. This takes the exhibition and other initiatives of London's Victoria & Albert Museum as a case study to show how public museums and galleries policies have become oriented towards supporting government notions of 'creative industries'. Thus the museum becomes not just an exponent, collector or creator of the *outcomes* of creativity, but also the patron and client of leading-edge design. In so doing, she shows how the museum is recruited to help to broadcast certain values of creativity to the wider public, while its presence and impact within the creative industries is at the same time carefully monitored and evaluated.

The second part of the book deals with the management of design in specific contexts. It begins with AnneMarie Dorland's study of graphic design studios in Canada. She shows that while stereotypical notions of the playful, unstructured 'creative workplace' continue to have considerable purchase, and indeed are widely exploited for promotional purposes, this contrasts with what are in fact highly regulated and systematized forms of working practice. Basing her analysis on interviews with both studio and freelance designers, she shows that designers typically respond to the ubiquity of formal review processes and tracking systems by orienting their work towards different audiences at different stages, whilst also employing various shortcuts and 'routines of production' to hasten workflow within organizations characterized by tight deadlines and careful monitoring of individual productivity and efficiency.

Paul Springer's chapter focuses on the ways in which tracking and review processes have developed within advertising and communications design agencies in London. He shows that growing client demands for transparency and accountability have led many agencies to develop their own tracking procedures and measurement techniques, both for the purposes of promotion and to ensure client 'buy-in' at an early stage in the process. He goes on to show how greater client involvement in the creative process, combined with new possibilities to incorporate information from the digital profiling of consumers, has had the effect of shifting both the scope and nature of 'creative' work, creating new opportunities in some areas while dramatically reducing them in others.

Nitzan Waisberg discusses the role of researchers within innovation, design and market research consultancies based in the United States. Her chapter examines how these specialists contribute to 'design thinking' in their engagement in a systematic path to innovative breakthrough solutions for their clients. She identifies three roles for the design researcher in this process. The first is in developing and managing a routinized and structured approach to user research that is of use to designers. Second, then, their work involves finding ways of communicating back and forth between research data or end-users and design action. Finally, there is a performative element to their work, in which the work of researchers plays a symbolic role in so far as it communicates a certain status of the design and innovation consultancy as the undertaker of systematic, informed, risk-reduced innovation.

Lucy Kimbell's chapter focuses on the relatively new area of service design. In contrast to other chapters in this section, she is concerned less with the internal processes of service design organizations, and more with the broader factors influencing the consolidation and formalization of this area of practice into a distinct discipline. In this regard she identifies three factors as of particular importance: first, the growing attention paid to design and design management in organizational theory; second, the continuation or otherwise of the trend towards greater employment of service designers in the development of public services; and third, the implications of service designers' involvement in 'capacity building' for other organizations. In this way, Kimbell's chapter resonates with perspectives developed in the first part of the book, which suggest that the growing interest in the values and processes of design work from government and the public sector are a critical force in the development both of particular specialisms and the degree of formalization in their practice.

By treating cinema as a design object and process, Damian Sutton's chapter reveals the way that mainstream Hollywood movies are tightly orchestrated around many more aesthetic markers than merely narrative and cinematography. His discussion leads us through the complex world of networked firms, revealing that creative ownership of film studios in the post-Fordist era of film production resides in their access to, and the coordination of, these. In turn, he argues that movies are carefully fashioned to stimulate the 'add-on' franchising market for related merchandise. Design plays a crucial role in fixing the intellectual property that lies at the heart of this system.

The final chapter of this section, by Sarah Owens, deals with the area of editorial design, and takes as its focus the question of where creativity is located, and how it is to be understood, within contexts characterized by clearly prescribed rules and templates and tight deadlines for production. While her chapter illuminates one of the general themes of the book – namely the practical organization and management of design in situations where it is critical to economic success and organizational reputation – its further contribution is to remind us (as in Hallam and Ingold's work) that creativity often resides less in 'big' projects and interventions, and more in the smaller day-to-day ways in which people work within structures and constraints towards the continuation of a project and its evolution over time.

The final part of the book is a collection of short interviews with designers and others currently employed in design firms. As with the other chapters, these do not represent a clear cross-section of the design industry as a whole, but they do reflect organizational and disciplinary specialisms that we believe are of particular interest within a context of greater systematization, formalization and codification of working practices, and greater attention to predicted outcomes or values. We have included these more mundane perspectives in an explicit attempt to complement – or counterpoint – the perspectives offered in the main chapters of the book. Our aim is to offer readers the opportunity to make connections between, on the one hand, the broad trends and issues outlined in the more systematic reflections of specific chapters and, on the other, the kinds of preoccupations and reflections that emerge in a more direct and unmediated way from those involved in design work. Interviewees were chosen who broadly represent the design sectors covered in the main chapters of the book. Three of these provide experience from Finland, California and New Zealand, and it is interesting to note that their responses in many areas are similar to those found in the UK, thereby underlining, perhaps, the globalizing of design action and thinking.

Ultimately, our motivations in editing and co-authoring this volume are threefold. Firstly, we believe it is important to understand the agency of design in reinforcing particular ideological priorities that are made within neo-liberal economies and governance. In so doing – and secondly – we hope to show the links and disjunctures between these latter notions and the everyday actions and dispositions of designers. We have a concern to show the dignity (and indignities) of the particular. Thirdly, our hope is that by providing this investigation into design and creativity in their relationships and multiple contexts, the reader will emerge equipped with further understandings. And it is through understanding that new markers for practical steps or experimentation might arise.

References

Adkins, L. (2005), 'The New Economy, Property and Personhood', *Theory, Culture and Society*, 22 (1): 111–30.

Anthony, S. D., Eyring, M. and Gibson, L. (2006), 'Mapping Your Innovation Strategy, *Harvard Business Review*, 84 (5): 104–13.

Born, G. (2002), 'Reflexivity and Ambivalence: Culture, Creativity and Government in the BBC', *Cultural Values*, 6 (1–2): 65–90.

Breen, B. (2005), 'The Business of Design', *Fast Company*, 93: 68.

British Design Innovation (2006), 'The British Design Industry Valuation Survey – 2006 to 2007' (report), Brighton: BDI.

Bruce, M. and Daly, L. (2006), 'International Evidence on Design: Near Final Report for the Department of Trade and Industry' (report), Manchester: University of Manchester.

Dicken, P. (2003), *Global Shift: Reshaping the Global Economic Map in the Twenty-First Century*, London: Sage.

European Union (2005), 'EU Directive 2005/36/EC of the European Parliament and of the Council of 7 September 2005 on the Recognition of Professional Qualifications', *Official Journal of the European Union* 30 September 2005, L255/22–140.

Howkins, J. (2001), *The Creative Economy: How People Make Money From Ideas*, London: Allen Lane.

Ingold, T. and Hallam, E. (2007), 'Creativity and Cultural Improvisation: An Introduction', in E. Hallam and T. Ingold (eds.) *Creativity and Cultural Improvisation*, Oxford: Berg.

Julier, G. (2006), 'From Visual Culture to Design Culture', *Design Issues*, 22 (1): 64–76.

Knorr Cetina, K. (1997), 'Sociality with Objects: Social Relations in Postsocial Knowledge Societies', *Theory, Culture and Society*, 14 (4): 1–30.

Knorr Cetina, K. (2001), 'Objectual Practice', in T. R. Schatzki, K. Knorr Cetina and E. von Savigny (eds.), *The Practice Turn in Contemporary Theory*, London and New York: Routledge.

Knorr Cetina, K. and Bruegger, U. (2002), 'Traders' Engagement with Markets: A Postsocial Relationship', *Theory, Culture and Society*, 19 (5–6): 161–85.

Lash, S. and Urry, J. (1994), *Economies of Signs and Spaces*, London: Sage.

Leach, J. (2007), 'Creativity, Subjectivity and the Dynamic of Possessive Individualism', in E. Hallam and T. Ingold (eds.), *Creativity and Cultural Improvisation*, Oxford: Berg.

Lupton, E. and Miller, J. A. (1999), *Design Writing Research: Writing on Graphic Design*, London: Phaidon.

Lury, C. (1993), *Cultural Rights: Technology, Legality and Personality*, London: Routledge.

McRobbie, A. (1998), *British Fashion Design: Rag Trade or Image Industry*, London: Routledge.

McRobbie, A. (2002), 'Clubs to Companies: Notes on the Decline of Political Culture in Speeded-Up Creative Worlds', *Cultural Studies*, 16 (4): 516–31.

McRobbie, A. (2007), 'The Los Angelisation of London: Three Short-Waves of Young People's Micro-Economies of Culture and Creativity in the UK', *Transversal*. Available at http://eipcp.net/transversal/0207/mcrobbie/en [last accessed 9 January 2008].

Muniesa, F., Millo, Y. and Callon, M. (2007), 'An Introduction to Market Devices', in M. Callon, Y. Millo and F. Muniesa (eds.), *Market Devices*, Oxford: Blackwell.

Netherlands Design Institute (1994), *Design Across Europe: Patterns of Supply and Demand in the European Design Market*, Amsterdam: Vormgevingsinstitut.

Nugent, E. (2005), 'Building a Creative Persona', Ph.D. thesis, Goldsmiths College, University of London.

Pels, P. (2000), 'The Trickster's Dilemma: Ethics and the Technologies of the Anthropological Self', in M. Strathern (ed.), *Audit Cultures: Anthropological Studies in Accountability, Ethics and the Academy*, London and New York: Routledge.

Power, M. (1997), *The Audit Society: Rituals of Verification*, Oxford: Oxford University Press.

Ray, P. (2001), *The Cultural Creatives: How 50 Million People Are Changing the World*, New York: Random House.

Rigby, R. (2007), 'Can Design Inject Some Creativity into China's Karaoke Economy?', *Design Council Magazine*, 3: 22–9.

Scase, R. and Davis, H. (2000), *Managing Creativity: The Dynamics of Work and Organization*, Milton Keynes: Open University Press.

Soar, M. (2002), 'An Insular Profession: Graphic Design and Consumer Culture', *Journal of Consumer Culture*, 2 (2): 271–5.

Strathern, M., (ed.) (2000), *Audit Cultures: Anthropological Studies in Accountability, Ethics and the Academy*, London and New York: Routledge.

WTO (World Trade Organization) (2007), *International Trade Statistics 2008*, Geneva: World Trade Organization.

Part I

DESIGN AND POLICY

CHAPTER 1

Designing the State

Liz Moor

When we think of the relationship between design and the state we tend to think of big, dramatic building projects or high-profile pieces of public art and architecture. We think of historic buildings and we may know a little about the contexts in which these were commissioned – often for explicitly political ends, perhaps for symbolizing national success, for the purposes of social and economic regeneration, or for reinvigorating a sense of national or regional identity. The public debate surrounding projects like the Millennium Dome in Britain, or François Mitterand's *grands projets* in France suggests most people are aware that national governments or regional authorities tend, from time to time, to commission pieces of design work with such goals in mind, and this in turn can lead to controversy about the use of public funds. Indeed, as other parts of this book suggest, the perception that such projects are funded directly by citizens is one of the reasons why creative design work in the public sector is subject to such complex accounting and legitimization processes.

We are less inclined to notice the imprint of the state in smaller or more mundane aspects of our material culture and environment, such as the design of tax forms, the posters in doctors' waiting rooms or the leaflets that come through our doors. Indeed, in some cases it may be that the point of such objects is to be relatively unobtrusive or to slip by unnoticed. Yet such objects make up a significant part of our material world, and as Michael Billig (1995) has pointed out in his analysis of 'banal nationalism', even small objects such as emblems and coins can be part of the construction of a 'national habitus', part of the way in which the state is folded into our everyday activities. More recently, the literature on place branding has drawn attention to the ways in which such projects have included as one of their aims the effort to shift the habitus of local citizens, not only through large 'statement' pieces of art or architecture, but also through smaller interventions (such as new street furnishings, for example) that aim to provide designed 'cues' to alter perceptions of the built environment and the identity of a town, city or region (see e.g.

Julier 2000; 2005). Designed *objects*, in other words, are very often part of the making up of national *subjects* (Moor 2007).

In this chapter I want to focus on a further example of the relationship between design and the state, to do with the ways in which designers have been used by the state and government agencies in Britain in the delivery of public services and policy initiatives. The British state's interest in design, so I want to argue, has not been limited to its role in creating potent national symbols, nor simply to encouraging the development of creative industries because of their potential contribution to national economic competitiveness or local regeneration, but has in recent years expanded to include the possibility that designers may have a significant role to play in redesigning public services, communicating government policy and – indirectly – shaping political subjectivities and forms of citizenship. As we shall see, these policy developments underpin many of the issues addressed in this volume – about the pressures on designers to *account for* their practices, to explain and measure the value of their work, and to review their own processes in the light of such concerns – but they also, in this instance, raise normative questions about who should be involved in the design and delivery of public services and under what kinds of terms, and how the use of design fits in with particular philosophies of government. In this chapter, therefore, I seek to describe two areas of government activity – awareness-raising campaigns and public service delivery – in which designers are newly prominent, and, drawing on a wider social science literature on neo-liberal governance, to sketch out a preliminary account of the *political* role of designers in neo-liberal societies. My aim, however, is neither to focus on specific policies nor to provide a detailed account of how these efforts work out in practice (both of which are addressed elsewhere in the chapters that follow) but rather to examine the broader political context driving new uses of design and designers by the state.[1]

The Political Context: Marketization

To put the social and public role of design into context, it is necessary to understand the transformations that have occurred within British public sector organization and management from the 1980s onwards. Public service reforms during this period have been driven by a number of themes, including the presumed superiority of the market over bureaucratic and state mechanisms of coordination, and a new centrality of managerialist language and practice to conceptions of governance (Clarke and Newman 2007). There has been a much greater emphasis on the creation of markets and 'choice' in the provision of public services, with public, private and voluntary organizations all being invited to compete for contracts to provide particular services. At the same time, the figure of 'the consumer' or 'user' has become more central to government discourse, indeed the figure in whose name such market reforms are undertaken. As Tony Blair put it in 2001: 'We are proposing to put an entirely different dynamic in place to drive our public services; one where the service will be driven not by the government or by the manager but by the user – the patient, the parent, the pupil and the law-abiding citizen' (cited in Clarke and Newman 2007: 740). This 'user' is imagined in terms that mirror the image of consumers in commercial transactions; in place of the supposedly 'passive' and 'dependent' consumers of the past (and previous models of public services), the new consumers are 'self-directing and self-possessing individuals ... exercising choice in pursuit of self-realizing lift projects' (Clarke 2007: 160–61). Yet at the same time – as some commentators have pointed out – such consumers are not simply pre-existing; they are to be 'remade' through new types of state-led initiatives. Through education and information they are to be 'empowered' to make decisions; through the exercise of choice they are to be made responsible for their own direction and life chances, a process which, according to the market logic of many such initiatives, should in turn force service providers to become more sensitized and responsive to their needs (Malpass et al. 2006).

Although such developments may seem removed from the practices of commercial design agencies, they have influenced their work in several ways. Firstly, there is simply more work available to be undertaken for public sector clients. A survey in 2008 estimated that the amount of work being outsourced to private and voluntary organizations had doubled over the previous decade (Timmins 2008). This includes 'everything from National Health Service treatments to bin emptying, IT, back-office functions and RAF pilot training' (Timmins 2008), but also, of course, various types of design work. The Design Council's (2005) *Business of Design* survey showed that 'public administration, health and education' make up 22 per cent of the total clients for design businesses, while the *British Design Industry Valuation Survey* shows a steady rise in the number of design businesses doing work for public sector or non-profit clients over the past few years: in 2000–01 (the first year of the survey), 25 per cent of agencies did this kind of work; by 2004–05 it was 49 per cent. (BDI 2003; BDI 2006).

Secondly, these developments have led to growth in particular *types* of design work. The emphasis on user-centred approaches in the delivery of public services has benefited design agencies specializing in service design, particularly where they are able to demonstrate strengths in the area of 'user insight'. Indeed, as we noted in the introduction, areas such as 'service and proposition creation' and strategic design consultancy have grown in recent years (BDI

2006), and while this is not solely attributable to public sector demand, it has played a significant role. Similarly, the emphasis on information, education and 'empowerment' has created new volumes of work in communications design and graphics. Statistics on the design industry do not break down type of work by type of client, but it is worth noting that communications design (including 'graphics, brand, print, information design, corporate identity') is the largest single category of all design work done in Britain, and that the number of agencies doing such work has risen from 48 per cent in 2000–01 to 65 per cent in 2003–04 (British Design Innovation 2003; 2004). These figures can, of course, be set alongside the statistics above showing a greater volume of work done by *all* design agencies for public sector and non-profit clients.

Finally, as developments within the public sector have created more work for private design companies, they have also been an important influence in the use of new techniques of measurement and accounting within those organizations. Although sophisticated measurement and auditing techniques are usually associated with private sector institutions seeking reassurance about return on investment and 'value added', the spending of public money on design solutions increasingly demands even greater levels of accountability and proof of 'effectiveness', and design agencies have had to respond to this. Indeed the shift to a more pervasive 'audit society' (Power 1997) is typified by the widespread adoption of such techniques by non-commercial public sector institutions; Michael Power, the arch theorist of this shift, notes that 'The audit explosion has its conditions of emergence in transformations in conceptions of administration and organization which ... dismantle the public–private divide' (1997: 10). As we shall see, public sector demands for accountability have forced some (private) design consultancies to improve their methods for demonstrating 'effectiveness' and, in some cases, to develop new techniques for measuring non-financial aspects of such effectiveness.

In looking at the relationship between design and the state in Britain, then, we can see that a particular form of governance characterized by marketization, 'choice', outsourcing and the promotion of active citizenship has reconfigured government's relationship to the design industry, with greater volumes of work being made available in the first place, a particular emphasis on design work that involves the transformation of services or the promotion of particular ways of thinking and acting by citizens, and a new incentive for design agencies to find ways of measuring the 'value' of their work and its effects. In the remainder of this chapter, I want to concentrate on the last two of these: the role of design in trying to forge a political subjectivity among citizens that is consonant with broadly neo-liberal philosophies of government, and the forms of measurement and accounting that have been developed to support this kind of work.

Design for Governance: Awareness-raising Campaigns

Changes in the organization of governance in Britain have not only altered the volume of work available to independent design agencies, but also what design is called upon to do. I have already noted that more work is available for designers specializing in strategy, services and 'user insights', but there has also been a growing role for communications design. Of course governments have always used designers to produce printed materials (booklets, posters and so on) advertising their services and initiatives, but there has, so I want to argue, been a shift in the 'tone', as well as the volume, of such materials, which are now expected to work on citizens in new kinds of ways. Increasingly, design for government is expected to promote not just the availability of a given service or facility, but also particular types of relationships between government and its citizens, as part of 'a determined effort to recast the balance of responsibility between the state and its citizens' (Malpass et al. 2006: 3).

The effort to 'responsibilize' citizens is, in turn, part of what Nikolas Rose (cited in Malpass et al. 2006: 6) describes as a trend to 'de-socialize' modes of governance, where the goal is to act on individuals and their self-regulating behaviour as consumers, rather than to institute broader-based policy measures or incentives. This is linked to the idea of 'stakeholder citizenship', in which 'everyone is responsible' and in which citizens are seen as the bearers of responsibilities as well as rights (Rose 1999; Harvey 2005). Such 'de-socialization' can be seen in a number of areas. These include, for example, what Hajer and Versteeg (cited in Malpass et al. 2006) describe as the individualization of food risks that has developed through the move towards product labelling and web-based information services. Here, rather than prohibiting certain potentially dangerous or unhealthy ingredients – a move that would involve direct state intervention in public choice, and potentially bring the government into conflict with powerful business interests – the government increasingly sees its role as one of encouraging citizens to educate themselves and become personally responsible.

Given this emphasis on individual responsibility through education and 'empowerment', there has, unsurprisingly, been a corresponding emphasis on the role of communications design in informing and encouraging would-be consumers and users. Many policy statements and think-tank reports have drawn attention to the importance of 'positive and inspirational messages' and 'high-profile national communications' in 'developing a new inspirational goal and a branded statement' to harness the activities of diverse groups of stakeholders (Defra 2005: 32). Malpass et al. (2006) have argued that such documents and reports typically emphasize a renewed place for the 'art of influencing' and see a role for government in 'influencing behaviour ... through the classical arts of *rhetoric*' (Malpass et al. 2006: 7, emphasis in original). Yet such documents are often highly contemporary in their approach to communications. A 2003 Demos/Green Alliance report for Defra, for example, paid explicit attention to 'the growing focus on "brand", and the need to create an identity that resonates with the consumer' (Collins et al. 2003: 7), noting that 'Straightforward advertising as information provision ... is long gone, and has been replaced with more sophisticated campaigns' (2003). There is, in other words, a heightened emphasis on the work of communications design in educating and informing 'citizen-consumers' (Clarke and Newman 2007), and a particular emphasis on forms or models of communication borrowed from the more commercial sides of graphic design, such as branding.

This new emphasis has led to a higher volume of work being available to such institutions, in part because government does not have sufficient staff or expertise – either numerically or in terms of skills – to do this work itself, but also because of an ideological commitment to efficiency, markets and choice in the provision of services. The introduction of 'Best Value' legislation and guidance since 1997 has imposed on local authorities a legal duty to secure 'continuous improvement' in service delivery, prohibiting them from delivering services directly where 'other more efficient ... means are available' (Martin 2002: 131) and insisting that they promote a 'mixed economy of provision' and cultivate interest from private and voluntary sector providers. As we shall see in the following section, getting good value for money may now include the requirement that design agencies provide 'capacity building' for government employees, but one of the more fundamental concerns in awarding contracts in this area is that they must include ways of measuring effectiveness and outcomes. The outsourcing of public services to non-state actors has, as I have noted in the previous section, led to concerns about accountability and the mechanisms through which this might be achieved (Bevir and Trentmann 2007: 2), and the need for public sector institutions to be seen as responsible in their use of public money has been one of the principal drivers of various kinds of auditing and measurement practice within the creative industries.

Design projects undertaken within this new system are many and varied. While the *Design of the Times* (Dott 07) programme, led by the UK Design Council and focused primarily on services, is considered to be a model of best practice (see Hill and Julier, in this volume), others include promotional campaigns aimed at encouraging children to walk to school, various health websites, recycling campaigns, campaigns against knife crime and information packs about healthy eating. The extent to which designers are required to demonstrate the 'effectiveness' of such projects may vary according to a number of factors. These may include clients' own demands for accountability, but relate more often to the cost or scale of the project. It is also the case that some types of design intervention lend themselves to measurement more easily than others, at least on the surface. So for example a campaign to improve rates of recycling in a particular area can be measured against actual increases in recycling rates over time – even if those increases are not in fact directly linked to the promotional campaign. In any case, while the specific demands placed on agencies may vary according to context, the general trajectory is towards a greater level of accountability, even in areas where the aim of the project is to shift attitudes or perceptions – and where 'effectiveness' is therefore hard to assess. This has led, in some cases, to the development of techniques for capturing moments of contact between consumers and information, so that these can be measured. One way of doing this has been to include more *interactive* opportunities in awareness-raising campaigns; these may now encourage people to send a text message, call a helpline or visit a website in order to request further information. Such interactive opportunities are useful because they can be recorded and measured, creating new types of information and 'facts' that can be used to indicate 'effectiveness' in terms of reaching an audience, as well as helping to break down cost per user. Furthermore, to the extent that such interactive features require *action* by citizens, they make it possible to claim that citizens have become 'engaged', motivated and 'empowered' through information and action – precisely the kinds of outcome that many policy-makers want to see. Yet of course such measures cannot measure more complex qualities such as attitudes and intentions, and they should therefore be seen as proxies whose use and value lies in their legitimacy – that is, their shared acceptance by other actors in a field – rather than their accuracy (see Arvidsson 2006: 134).

The emphasis on awareness-raising and information dissemination arises from the policy context described in the previous section, and has both normative and practical implications. As Andrew Barry has suggested, 'the extraordinary range and quantity of information that citizens and institutions are expected to process' is a characteristic feature of contemporary government (Barry 2001: 153). Such information, he claims, is more than simply 'raw data' because it implies an audience who *should* be informed. It also, he goes on to note, generally has regulatory effects; its existence 'is thought to imply a transformation in the conduct of those who are, or who should be, informed'. This is very clear in the kinds of awareness-raising campaigns undertaken by designers for government; these are not simply alerting citizens to particular facts, risks or dangers. Rather, they carry the implication that since the citizen is now – in the very moment of reading – 'informed', responsibility for such risks and dangers is henceforth his or her own. Similarly, for Barry, interactivity is more than 'a particular possibility inherent in the development of media', but something seen as having the capacity to transform the person (Barry 2001: 129). Interactive technologies and devices have been seen as 'a key resource in the making up of citizens' (127) through their presumed ability to 'foster agency ... thus enhancing the self-governing capacities of the citizen' (135). Technologies that appear to be about 'empowering' citizens, in other words, are more accurately seen as technologies to *create* particular models of citizenship and to endow citizens – whether they like it or not – with particular types of responsibility.

There are a number of problems with this effort to 'empower' and 'responsibilize' citizens. Perhaps the biggest concern is that such campaigns, like the commercial advertising campaigns on which they are frequently modelled, tend to be aimed at changing individual attitudes and behaviour, rather than addressing the broader economic, cultural or systemic factors that may determine matters such as responsiveness to healthcare messages, propensity to carry knives, and so on. At the most basic level, this means that such campaigns may not 'work', in the sense of promoting any substantial or durable shift in behaviour. There is a big difference between the kind of tasks that design and marketing communications are called upon to perform in a commercial context (e.g. persuading a consumer to switch from one brand of baked beans to another) and the kind of work they are asked to do in a public or social context (e.g. persuading an entire population to overhaul its diet). While it may be expedient, if not strictly accurate, for commercial interests to conceive of the society or group that makes up their 'market' as an aggregate of individual decision-makers, the same cannot be said of the social groups targeted by public awareness-raising campaigns. Indeed campaigns aimed at shifting behaviour often fail to recognize that moving from the level to the individual to that of the group, community or population is precisely *not* simply a matter of aggregating individual choices, but in fact touches upon more complex extended social networks, where the 'consumers' they address are enmeshed in relationships – to other people, but also to institutions – that implicate them in circuits of influence and obligation, and constrain them in numerous ways. On the other hand, even when a more complex social basis for attitudes and behaviours is acknowledged, there remains a reliance on forms of communication aimed primarily at individuals presumed to be relatively free and autonomous.

This transfer of techniques from the commercial to the public sector has normative dimensions too. While 'information' appears to be neutral and universal, and the individualist logic of these campaigns implies that responsibility for action falls equally upon all actors (Barnett et al. 2004), there are also entrenched inequalities in people's ability to respond. Just as the ideology of the free market – in which consumers are free to choose from a range of goods – conceals the fact that social and economic inequalities place significant practical constraints on that freedom, so too does the ideology of 'neutral' information and equal responsibility conceal the fact that some people are in a better (economic, social, structural) position to respond to government injunctions than others. This, as Nikolas Rose points out, can produce new categories of 'problem' citizens and consumers, and 'anti-communities of the depraved or the poor' (Rose 1999: 189), who are then subject to renewed observation and measurement, so that their 'pathologies' can be charted and their values and behaviour further worked upon (ibid.).

Design for Governance II: Services, Experiences and Encounters

If the presentation of information to 'educate' and 'empower' citizens through various types of communication and awareness-raising campaign is one of the ways in which designers have been implicated in the shaping of political subjectivities, another is through the effort to work on people's *experiences* with the state and its services. Such work has taken a variety of forms, from involvement in redesigning healthcare services to the design of environments (such as schools and hospitals) so that they create positive feelings and sentiments. As we shall see, some work in this area has been important in generating new metrics by which the 'value' of design can be understood. In other cases, however, it shares with the communications design work outlined above some problems associated with the over-reliance on values from commercial marketing. This, I want to argue, may undercut the usefulness of some aspects of design's contribution to government and public service.

Service design, although still not especially well established in Britain (see Kimbell, in this volume), has grown considerably in recent years. Although many of its clients are from 'traditional' service industries such as banking and personal finance, a significant proportion come from the public sector, and in some cases these make up the majority of the client list.[2] To understand why service design is appealing to government, it is useful to recap some of the points from the previous section. The emphasis on the 'user' in recent public service reforms – as someone to be empowered, and someone to drive efficiency within organizations – is an obvious outgrowth of the emphasis on markets and competition; in some contexts the term is used interchangeably with the term 'consumer'. But it also chimes with the emphasis in contemporary design literature on the idea that design should serve to enable particular

types of experiences (see e.g. Press and Cooper 2003), and that it should do
this by focusing on the needs of the user. What dedicated service design consultancies bring to the traditional design process is a greater than usual
emphasis on user needs and experiences,[3] and on those aspects of a service –
often called 'touchpoints' – through which services are encountered in tangible
form by users. This is because services are understood primarily as a type of
interaction between customers and providers (Sisodia 1996; Parker and Heapy
2006) rather than a product or commodity. Agencies offering service and
experience design have therefore emphasized user research, prototyping and
testing with target markets, all of which makes them appealing to government
agencies that may lack the means to do this themselves, but which have an ideological commitment to 'empowering' the user or consumer, and to reforming
services along these lines.

So what do service designers do for the state? As I have suggested, one key
area has been in the development and redesign of public services such as
healthcare. As Lucy Kimbell outlines in her chapter in this volume, the
agency live|work was involved in reviewing and redesigning an NHS smoking-
cessation service. Its work involved interviews with managers, observation of
the service operating in pharmacies, projects to map the 'customer journey'
and a review of the service's 'touchpoints' – that is, those points where the
service took a concrete form that was visible and tangible to customers, and
with which customers had some element of interaction. The same agency has
also done work with jobless people on behalf of a local council in the north
of England, and in London for getting homeless people into accommodation.
In all cases, the contribution of service designers has been to advise not only
on usability, functionality and aesthetics, but also to assess the viability of an
entire product-service system, and to suggest new models and blueprints for
service delivery.

As I noted at the beginning of the chapter, the involvement of private design
companies in the shaping and delivery of public services has demanded higher
levels of accountability and in some cases driven the development of new techniques for measuring outcomes and effectiveness. In their project with jobless
people in Sunderland, live|work needed to find ways of demonstrating the
value of its work to the local council in order to justify investment. This meant
assessing the current cost of jobless people to the state, and calculating how
far their work could reduce these costs. They did this by prototyping a service
and testing it on a small group of users, in order to devise a metric for measuring design intervention. When the 'uplift' to clients (getting them back into
work) reached a level where it overtook the cost of the design work, the
company could claim a positive return on investment. They point out, 'By
showing ROI at a project level, we could also demonstrate that the project

would add to GVA [gross value added] and that, if scaled up, the benefits would be massive' (Løvlie et al. 2008: 76). In other areas, however, live|work have moved beyond purely financial measures of return on investment, and used techniques based on the concept of the 'triple bottom line' (Elkington 1999) to develop new ways of measuring value. Their work with Streetcar, a (private) car-sharing service, used this strategy to measure the impact of the company (and their own contribution to it) in terms of its environmental and social, as well as economic, contributions. This involved generating estimates about the reduction in levels of private car ownership and use, and the likely reductions in carbon dioxide emissions. It also involved generating 'soft' indicators of social impact, assessing the likely extent to which the existence of the service could 'rethink a behavioural norm' or expand people's sense of their travel options (see Løvlie et al. 2008).

Clearly there are reasons to be cautious about the adoption of social and environmental auditing techniques by private clients such as Streetcar, for whom they may serve as a type of marketing or promotional material aimed at building brand identity and reputation among a target market. Any measure that demonstrates even marginal positive social and environmental benefits would reflect well on their company, and they therefore have an indirect financial incentive for adopting them. It is less clear that such measures would be adopted by companies competing in other sectors – particularly when doing so is entirely optional. Yet the development of such techniques by live|work and other agencies may have a significance beyond its importance to specific clients. If design firms can be seen as agents with interests, projects and values that sometimes extend beyond simple profit maximization (Swedberg 2003), their role in developing techniques for measuring non-financial value may be viewed in a more positive light. Furthermore, since such agencies operate within networks, and are increasingly involved in 'knowledge transfer' or 'capacity building' projects with public sector clients, they may have the capacity to disseminate their techniques across a range of institutions, providing a method for making those institutions' social and environmental impact knowable and visible. This may turn out to be especially important for the public sector, where market competition and economic efficiency have recently dominated debates about the delivery of public goods.

Yet there are other examples of non-financial measures of value being adopted or proposed by policy professionals, where a clear link to substantive social values is harder to discern. In these cases, promotional concerns sometimes appear to take on a life of their own and become abstracted from social dimensions of value, or enduring ideals of public service or public goods, and connected instead to a set of narrow technical or instrumental aims. One recent example of this can be seen in a joint project between the left-wing think-tank, Demos, and the service design consultancy, Engine (Parker and Heapy 2006). Explicitly aimed at bringing insights from commercial service design consultancies into debates about public service reform, its authors criticize the early Blairite emphasis on markets, managerialism and efficiency measures in public services, and argue instead that reform should put 'people and places, not targets and key performance indicators (KPIs) at its heart' (2006: 9). Yet their suggestions for doing this involve, in essence, simply borrowing customer service techniques and auditing strategies from commercial organizations, with little rationale for how or why these would represent an improvement on 'the detached measurements of customer satisfaction and proxy measures of performance such as waiting times' (2006: 67–71). In fact, while the authors place great emphasis on the need to build 'relationships' with public service users, or find 'new ways of connecting intimately' with them (2006: 8), their reasons for suggesting this move between the instrumental – that it provides a framework in which users can be 'mobilized, coached and encouraged' (13) – and the more obviously promotional – that it can build legitimacy for public services (16) or contribute to a 'sense that the service is supporting you' (10). What this suggests is that, far from representing a break with earlier political impulses, such accounts are more appropriately located at the point where neo-liberal social philosophies intersect with new brand management techniques based on relationship marketing and 'experiential' communication.

One of the areas where this promotional influence is most visible is in Parker and Heapy's discussion of measurement. Arguing that public services could usefully learn from the 'experience metrics' of the commercial sector to assess the 'customer experience' of public service users, the authors mention the 'propensity to recommend' measure used by Orange, the 'customer journey' maps used by BUPA, the 'customer value metrics' used by Tesco, and the 'mystery shopper' techniques used by Pret a Manger.[4] In the latter case, interactions between customers and staff are assessed through metrics such as 'Did the barista look you in the eye and smile? Did they tell you how much change you were receiving?' (Parker and Heapy 2006: 67). As in the previous section, borrowing techniques from retail and consumer-oriented service organizations means that public service users are imagined as relatively atomized individual consumers who are, nonetheless, free to choose, rather than as more fully social beings who may be constrained in various ways. While Parker and Heapy acknowledge that many of their ideas 'originally grew out of organizations seeking to reinforce their brand in ways that went well beyond marketing and mass advertising campaigns' (Parker and Heapy 2006: 26), they fail to note the extent to which service *design* in these organizations is therefore very tightly bound up with service *marketing*, and the attempt to use service delivery as an additional site for the building of brand loyalty (see Witz et al. 2003). There is, in other words, no sense of how public and private organizations might differ in substance or purpose, nor any discussion of whether, or how far, a promotional mode of address – that seeks to reinforce brand values through carefully designed 'customer experiences' – is appropriate in public sector institutions.[5]

This example is not intended to dispute the potential value of service design to public and non-profit institutions. Rather, the point is to demonstrate that such applications may be over-determined by quite narrow political concerns, which in turn may inhibit effectiveness in the delivery of social or public goods. The use of design by governments has, historically, very often been bound up with the search for a 'technical fix' to problems that are more fully social or structural in nature; typically associated with liberalism (Otter 2007), its more recent manifestations have included the 'nudge' philosophies and 'libertarian paternalism' adopted by some elements of the British Conservative party (Thaler and Sunstein 2008; *The Economist* 2008), and the neo-liberal emphasis on individual 'empowerment' and responsibility adopted by the Labour party and outlined here. While both rely on the attempt to 'design in' particular outcomes, they are distinguished from their predecessors by the way in which design is now married to promotion. The technical solutions that designers appear to offer are thereby supplemented with a tone or mode of address taken from commercial marketing and branding, which implicitly or explicitly addresses citizens as sovereign consumers pursuing individual wants. Yet this is very often not how service users see themselves; a recent survey of health service users conducted by Clarke and Newman (2007) found very limited public identification with the terms 'customer' or 'consumer'; these terms, according to the authors, 'are not the primary categories through which they live, and think about, their connections to public services. The consumerist model does not describe who they [are] – or who they want to be' (2007: 753). Rather, interviewees described themselves in terms that relied more heavily on collective imaginaries and a sense of belonging ('member of the public', 'patient', 'member of the local community'). While some designers may be highly sensitized to such insights from service users, the broader policy context often has rather different goals. How far this actually matters at the level of individual design projects may depend upon the extent to which design firms are able to pursue their own interests and how far they are constrained by the need to account for their practices along the lines I have set out above.

Conclusion

In this chapter I have argued that the state's use of design has, in recent years, involved a change of emphasis and tone; rather than simply informing people that a service exists and encouraging them to make use of it, designers are increasingly employed to provide communication materials to inform, 'educate' and 'empower' citizens, and to encourage them to take responsibility for their own behaviour – to see matters ranging from their health and education, to the levels of recycling in their borough or the degree of antisocial behaviour on their streets, as matters of individual responsibility. As governments have developed these kinds of approaches, they have looked for communications techniques that actively engage their target audience, and which can be proven to do so. Hence more 'interactive' techniques such as websites, sending text messages and so on, are useful because they provide a proxy measure for 'effectiveness' (by proving that someone has taken an action in response to a message), whilst also fostering some kind of agency – even if that agency is *only* sending a text message. This is one of the ways in which a compulsion to measure effectiveness now gets built in to the design process and the choices made about techniques and materials.

In following this line of argument, my aim has been to show how a changing vision of the value of design among government agencies has been an important driver of change in design agencies themselves, most notably in relation to the greater volume of work for design agencies and consultancies, the shift towards particular *types* of work, the increased amounts of time spent on measuring outcomes and effectiveness, and the effort to devise new techniques for measuring value. Designers routinely note that work with public sector clients may be more laborious than with private clients because of the greater number of people needed to 'sign off' on a project. While policy shifts that see a new role for design have led to greater volumes of public sector work available for agencies, they have also meant that designers may spend more of their time liaising with various 'stakeholders' on the client side, getting 'buy-in' from these stakeholders, and devising accounting and measurement techniques that demonstrate outcomes and effectiveness.

Although it has not been a focus of this chapter, the increase in the amount of time spent with 'stakeholders' and in devising measurement techniques that can establish the agency's legitimacy in the eyes of the client may also impact upon the creative process itself. On the one hand, there is now some evidence (see for example Ennis and Julier, in this volume) of a 'cut and paste' approach to design for public sector clients, particularly where turnaround time is tight, where designers are balancing a number of projects or where the vast number of stakeholders who must give permission drives designers to follow schemas that have previously been successful with other public sector clients. There may also be a tendency towards 'design by committee', where the large number of stakeholders not only have the potential to veto a project, but also feel able to request changes and influence the final form that the design project will take. The need to 'get a project past the client', in design as in other creative industries, may ultimately militate against the more ambitious, uninhibited and innovative projects that are typically associated with traditional notions of 'creativity'.

Yet nor has my aim been to defend traditional definitions of creativity or the creative process – certainly there is plenty in those formulations that can be criticized, and there may in any case be plenty of 'creativity' in the ways that designers conduct and implement user research or find novel ways to measure the value of their inputs. The point rather has been to show how a broader political context and set of policy preoccupations may channel the work of design industry down particular paths, create new opportunities for some types of design work rather than others, and provide the impetus for new forms of reflection within the design firm, including new modes of self-assessment, accounting and valuation. In doing this, I have sought to show that the relationship between design and the state is characterized not only by practical issues of industry organization, structure and accountability, but also by larger normative questions of social responsibility, fairness and the nature and purpose of public goods and services. If we look behind the contemporary drive to measurement and accountability in the design world – and the ways in which this is propagated, reworked or resisted by particular design firms – we may trace a more fundamental debate going on, about competing definitions of the design user, the nature of his or her social ties, and about who and what, ultimately, design is for.

Notes

1. While neo-liberal philosophies of government take different forms in different places, my aim here is to draw attention to some of their broader impulses and general manifestations in the British context.
2. The service design consultancy Participle, for example, was set up explicitly to work with public sector clients.
3. While most design agencies emphasize user research and insight generation as a key stage in their creative process, there is growing evidence that such stages are often treated rather briefly and informally within specific sectors of commercial design, primarily because of time or budgetary constraints (see e.g. Dorland, in this volume), or because it is believed that employees can 'stand in' for the target audience or user. By contrast, the nature of service design work is such that agencies and consultancies are more frequently called upon to provide proof of user research, testing and insight generation.

4. Orange, BUPA, Tesco and Pret a Manger are all private retail and/ or service companies operating in Britain.
5. Parker and Heapy's recommendations would clearly have consequences for public sector workers as well as users, potentially subjecting their interactions with users to higher degrees of scrutiny and surveillance. In this regard, it is interesting to note that in 2008 the UK government announced the launch of a 'compassion index' in the National Health Service, to measure levels of compassion and care among nurses, and to include reference to how frequently they smiled at patients (Carvel 2008).

References

Arvidsson, A. (2006), *Brands: Meaning and Value in Media Culture*, London and New York: Routledge.
Barnett, C. et al. (2004), 'Articulating Ethics and Consumption', *Cultures of Consumption Working Paper Series*, No. 17. Available at www.consume.bbk.ac.uk/publications.html.
Barry, A. (2001), *Political Machines: Governing a Technological Society*, London and New York: Athlone Press.
Bevir, M. and Trentmann, F. (2007), *Governance, Consumers and Citizens: Agency and Resistance in Contemporary Politics*, Basingstoke and New York: Palgrave Macmillan.
Billig, M. (1995), *Banal Nationalism*, London: Sage.
British Design Innovation (2003), *BDI Design Industry Valuation Survey 2002–03*. Available at www.britishdesigninnovation.org [last accessed 5 April 2006].
British Design Innovation (2004), *BDI Design Industry Valuation Survey 2003–04*. Available at www.britishdesigninnovation.org [last accessed 20 July 2007].
British Design Innovation (2006), *BDI Design Industry Valuation Survey 2005–06*. Available at www.britishdesigninnovation.org [last accessed 22 January 2009].
Carvel, J. (2008), 'Nurses To Be Rated on How Compassionate and Smiley They Are', *The Guardian*, 18 June.
Clarke, J. (2007), 'Unsettled Connections: Citizens, Consumers and the Reform of Public Services', *Journal of Consumer Culture*, 7(2): 159–78.
Clarke and Newman (2007), 'What's In A Name? New Labour's Citizen-Consumers and the Remaking of Public Services', *Cultural Studies*, 21(4–5): 738–57.
Collins, J. et al. (2003), 'Carrots, Sticks and Sermons: Influencing Public Behaviour for Environmental Goals', Demos/Green Alliance for Defra.
Defra (2005), 'Securing the Future – UK Government Sustainable Development Strategy'. Available at http://www.sustainable-development.gov.uk/publications/uk-strategy/index.htm.
Design Council (2005), *The Business of Design: Design Industry Research 2005*, London: Design Council.
The Economist (2008), 26 July, p.40.
Elkington, J. (1999), *Cannibals With Forks: The Triple Bottom Line of 21st-Century Business*, London: Capstone Publishing.
Harvey, D. (2005), *A Brief History of Neoliberalism*, Oxford and New York: Oxford University Press.
Julier, G. (2000), *The Culture of Design*, London: Sage.
Julier, G. (2005),'Urban Designscapes and the Production of Aesthetic Consent', *Urban Studies*, 42: 689–888.
Løvlie et al. (2008), 'Bottom-Line Experiences: Measuring the Value of Design in

Service', *Design Management Review*, Winter: 73–9.

Malpass, A., Barnett, C., Clarke, N. and Cloke, P. (2006), 'Problematizing Choice: Responsible Subjects and Citizenly Consumers', paper presented to conference on 'Citizenship and Consumption: Agency, Norms, Mediation and Spaces', Cambridge, March.

Martin, C. (2002), 'Best Value: New Public Management or New Direction?', in K. McLaughlin, S. P. Osborne and E. Ferlie (eds.), *New Public Management: Current Trends and Future Prospects*, London and New York: Routledge.

Moor, L. (2007), *The Rise of Brands*, Oxford: Berg.

Otter, C. (2007), 'Making Liberal Objects: British Techno-Social Relations 1800–1900', *Cultural Studies*, 21(4–5): 570–90.

Parker, S. and Heapy, J. (2006), *The Journey to the Interface: How Public Service Design Can Connect Users to Reform*, London: Demos.

Power, M. (1997), *The Audit Society*, Oxford: Oxford University Press.

Press, M. and Cooper, R. (2003), *The Design Experience: The Role of Design and Designers in the Twenty-First Century*, Aldershot: Ashgate.

Rose, N. (1999), *Powers of Freedom: Reframing Political Thought*, Cambridge and New York: Cambridge University Press.

Sisodia, R. J. (1996), 'Designing Quality into Services', *Design Management Journal*, 3(1): 33–9.

Swedberg, R. (2003), *Principles of Economic Sociology*, Princeton, NJ: Princeton University Press.

Thaler, R. and Sunstein, C. (2008), *Nudge: Improving Decisions About Health, Wealth and Happiness*, New Haven and London: Yale University Press.

Timmins, N. (2008), 'UK Outsourcing to Private Sector Doubles', *Financial Times*, 9 July.

Witz, A., Warhurst, C. and Nickson, D. (2003), 'The Labour of Aesthetics and the Aesthetics of Organization', *Organization* 10(1): 33–54.

CHAPTER 2

Designing the City

Guy Julier

Designing the city may be read in terms of a range of actions, from the design of information leaflets or signage to its municipal transport infrastructure and the strategic design of 'iconic' buildings. In addition, urban design provides the physical hardware that ties many of the components of a city together. It also re-presents the public realm, marking out the heritage, civic pride and modernity of a location. It therefore folds the functional and symbolic together.

In the civic context, design is deeply embedded into bureaucratic processes. These may involve coordination between several local authority departments. They may also require the co-option and buy-in of various other stakeholders. Decisions are not just the preserve of designers, but usually have to be made in conjunction with property developers, urban planners, politicians and citizens. Thus, often, the challenge is not with the bureaucracy of such different interests themselves but with the alignment of their different forms, expressions and types of codification and systematization. In its turn, this has a strong framing effect on the nature of creativity and, indeed, the professional status of designers concerned with the public realm.

All manifestations of design have undergone growing intensity in terms of their instrumentalization in urban policy and planning in the past decade. However, by focusing on urban design, this chapter tracks the journey from the emergence of a particular policy shift with regards to the material aspect of the public realm to its practical, on-the-ground implementation. In the UK the rise of the use of urban design, and an attendant bureaucracy of practice, has been increasingly evident in the past decade. It is also found in North America, Europe and parts of Australasia. National government agencies, regional authorities, city, town and even some village councils as well as institutions that represent the interests of architecture, town planning and urban design professionals, have produced a plethora of best-practice guidelines, design guides or statements. This has been supplemented by further advice on how to formulate these. Thus a criss-crossing, and often self-replicating, professional sub-specialism has emerged in the authorship of such resources. These guides are driven by a number of concerns: an ambition to achieve high standards of design in the urban realm and therefore to promote and safeguard the professional status of urban design specialists; and a way of localizing and making appropriate national guidelines to focused areas, ensuring that wider policy issues, such as sustainability and access, are incorporated into schemes. Importantly, though, given the variety of interests involved in urban design issues, such documents also help to achieve a workable level of shared criteria and understandings between these.

The following text begins with a review of the shifts in policy towards urban centres in recent years. The emergence of urban design as a distinct professional specialism is then analysed, bringing into view its distinctly *in-between* nature: between design and other disciplines; between commercial and civic interests; and between policy demands such as sustainability and social inclusion and the pragmatic world of economic viability. The next section looks at how a plethora of urban design policies has been shaped in order to mediate such varying interests. Then, drawing on primary research, the chapter concludes with a review of the relationship of the everyday world of undertaking urban design to the wider policy demands, and the role of creative practice therein. Just as wider policy aspirations express a desire for greater social connectivity, so this rhetoric of connectivity finds its way into the actual role of the urban designers as mediators between disparate interests.

Urban Renaissances

While the physical size and political stature of cities throughout the world has grown in the past thirty years, so the cultural resonance of 'being urban' has strengthened. Up until the 1970s, cities had come to be seen as the repository of problems – hangovers of their frenzied growth since the Industrial Revolution. Instead, more recently, they have been conceived of as resources (Parkinson 2001). They contain and express all kinds of capital. They are viewed as seats of innovation, creativity and conviviality (Landry 2000; Florida 2002). The combination of this increased concentration of political power and cultural value leads to their intensification as nodes of economic activity (Castells 1996; Sassen 2002). Their competitiveness is viewed in relation to each other and is exhibited often through similar signifiers of their financial and material infrastructures. This process of promoting cities is done through the hardware of buildings, transportation, public spaces, leisure facilities and housing. But it also engages the software of components such as reputation, aspiration, outlooks and knowledge. Design has been employed both to put value into cities, contributing to their use-value through facilitating improved infrastructures in all their manifestations. Furthermore, these add to their value *in potentia*. They catalyse further investment by their symbolic power. A new design for a public square and a city marketing campaign signal a direction and velocity towards future realities. They reveal the vectors of development of a city, both in terms of its aspirant modernity and difference from other urban centres (Evans 2003).

The leveraging of urban design and city branding into policies of regeneration ranges far and wide. This has given rise to the use of the term 'design-led regeneration' (Bell and Jayne 2003), which signals the embedding of design into economic planning. But it also assumes design's role in affecting more deeply the productive and consumer processes of an urban centre, to produce a particular designerly and aspirant disposition (Julier 2005).

Historically, four overall trends are discernible within this process. First – originating in Baltimore and Boston in 1970s America – was the use of waterfront development, combining public and private funding to regenerate post-industrial areas of cities through a mix of new housing development and high-end cultural infrastructure such as theatres, museums and new restaurants. By 1989, there were some 221 such waterfront development schemes under way in the UK (Smith 2003: 165). Second, alongside this trend has been a move towards city 'boosterism' through high-profile public relations campaigns. The development of city slogans and logotypes has become a key and highly visible component. Within this, the assumption is that a distinctive identity for a city can be identified and communicated (Olins 1999). Third, the creative capital of a city – its resources in terms of the skills and knowledge of the people who live and work there – has taken an increasingly orthodox position in regeneration. Spurred on, not least by policy-formers such as Florida (2002) and Landry (2000), the concentration of both cultural consumption and production into 'creative quarters' became a key part of many urban regeneration initiatives. Finally, urban design has been given an increased role in design-led regeneration. Its chief concern is with the spaces between buildings – street layout, urban squares, public realm furnishing and the like. But it invariably encompasses broader remits concerned with the character, identity, distinction, connectivity and sustainability of a place. In so doing, it overlaps with architecture, town planning and landscape architecture.

As urban agglomerations have de-industrialized, so new strategies for the enrichment of their public spaces have emerged. The contemporary approach differs from earlier, more spectacular practices of urbanism such as the grand modernist planning of the period after the Second World War, which envisaged wholly new architecture and urban layouts that both involved centralized, uniform and 'top-down' approaches. The retreat of the state in these matters to a more regulatory role has meant that urban design is sandwiched between private sector interests of property development and house-building and the public sector challenges of strategic planning that embrace economic, social and environmental issues. Thus, contemporary urban design involves the orchestration of the public realm in partnership with a variety of interests. Its scope now engages masterplanning, housing market renewal and growth, city centre development, as well as sustainability and quality of life issues. As such, urban designers interact with a variety of stakeholders (Carmona et al. 2002). Ultimately, urban design thus fills a professional gap, working in the space between single sites (the chief concern of the property developer) while specifying more concrete form and guidelines than the broader view of the urban or regional planner would.

The Urban Design Profession

While training in urban design exists at postgraduate level in many countries, it lacks the status of professional accreditation that the former disciplines carry. By contrast, in the USA, Canada, New Zealand, Australia and the UK, as in many other countries, the architecture profession is standardized by registration or licensing requirements from a recognized institution.[1] Urban design, meanwhile, may be seen as a way of working that is undertaken by architects, building conservationists, engineers, landscape architects, planners or surveyors as much as by people who label themselves as urban designers (Cowan 2008). As such there is no 'typical' context, skill-set or career structure to being an urban designer. Instead, they are to be found in city authority urban design or planning offices, specialist commercial practices as well as appended into a range of other professions such as architectural practices or civil engineering firms that are concerned with the built environment.

It is noteworthy that urban design training rarely exists at undergraduate level and is more often to be found at graduate level. This suggests that it is often seen as an 'add-on' discipline to other specialisms such as town planning or landscape architecture. The departmental location of this graduate training frequently and understandably creates biases in its approach to the subject. According to Kesner et al. (2003: 9), where it is located within architectural departments, it tends to foreground issues of built form ('building character, typologies, style, materials, signage, and street amenities such as canopies and arcades'). Where it is found alongside landscape architecture, spatial considerations are more prevalent ('streetscape, planting ... spaces between the buildings, and signage'). When attached to planning departments, land use policy ('development scenarios and processes, view corridors, setbacks, building bulks and heights, and street amenities') dominates the teaching of urban design.

This educational distribution reflects the wider, fragmented reality of urban design in professional practice. It is therefore hardly surprising to find a plethora of good practice guidelines relating to urban design that can be found across its professional interests and locations. Of all design disciplines that are not professionally accredited, urban design may be the sector that is most redolent of codes, guidelines, policy documents, models and other forms of published advice. It has become densely codified. Each professional sector that engages with urban design has its own publications. These are orientated inwardly as a way of setting and justifying standards for its own respective professional development. But it is also a means by which each profession establishes a language and procedure for communicating with its audience, be this property developers, politicians, the general public or, even, others engaged in urban design in other professional sectors. Added to this, as we shall see, such codifications are rolled out across different locations. They are formulated and mediated not just within separate professions but at various policy levels of national governments through to local civic authorities. Firstly, though, it is necessary to understand how this codification of urban design has come about through a review of its rise in the UK.

Urban Design Policy

In the UK, a watershed to this codification of urban design came in 1997. The election of Tony Blair's New Labour government, after seventeen years of Conservative mandate, brought with it a reassessment of approaches to urban planning and design. Under the chairmanship of architect Lord Richard Rogers, the Urban Task Force (UTF) was set up a year later. According to its mission statement, this body was charged with the challenge of identifying the causes of urban decline, developing solutions that would reinvigorate urban living, and establishing a vision for urban regeneration based on principles of design excellence, social well-being and environmental responsibility within a viable economic and legislative framework (UTF 1999).

The key resulting publication of this body was *Towards an Urban Renaissance* (1999). Its first few pages identified three key challenges for the design of towns and cities. The first was the shift from an industrial era to the information age, resulting in the reconfiguration of key drivers that shape the raison d'être and form of cities. Secondly, the ecological imperative of climate change demands a reconceptualization of the city, not as a vast consumer of resources, but as a self-supporting organism. Finally, changing lifestyles brought about by, for instance, the ageing population and a turn away from the nuclear family as the dominant form of household, means that housing and public space uses are also changing. Overall, then, the UTF report ambitiously proposed a 'new vision for urban living' that championed a move 'back to the city' (Lees 2003). Buoyed by precedential examples of the regeneration of major cities such as Barcelona and Amsterdam through the 1980s and 1990s, so the UTF posited that the strategic use of design was key to an 'urban renaissance'.

The UTF report was followed, in 2000, by the UK government's Urban White Paper (UWP), the first urban policy paper to be published for over twenty years. This expanded on the sentiments and recommendations of the UTF report, ensuring that they were carried into practice at national, regional and local levels. Three key differences distinguish this Urban White Paper from its 1976 predecessor. Firstly, the earlier UWP had viewed the problems of cities as being spatially concentrated: this being normally on their inner city zones. The 2000 UWP took a wider view of the city, emphasizing the need to strengthen functional linkages between housing, leisure, workplaces and welfare services. Secondly, the 1976 UWP saw urban regeneration as an issue that involved just public, community and voluntary sectors. The 2000 UWP included a strengthened role for the private sector in this process. Thirdly, while the 1976 UWP was authored in the straitened context of economic recession, the 2000 UWP was established with a view to increased public spending in buoyant financial circumstances. Thus, the importance of urban design, planning and architecture was matched alongside the delivery of main-stream welfare services such as education, social services and crime reduction – in a more holistic package for regeneration (Parkinson 2001).

Through the Urban Task Force and subsequent Urban White Paper, and the latter's roll out to national, regional and local government policies and practice, a new environment for urban design has been instigated. This has been through linking design more explicitly to a range of other measures required for urban regeneration. 'Design-led urban regeneration' is defined for the first time through these reports, while it is also seen as insufficient on its own to reverse decline (Regan 2000). Regeneration therefore involves multi-agency collaboration. Within this, and in particular in relation to inter-ests in the built environment, design may become the glue that binds them together. This became increasingly explicit in governmental policy. For example, by 2005 the UK government's Office of the Deputy Prime Minister (ODPM) produced its Planning Policy Statement (PPS) – guidance notes, effectively, on national planning policies. Here, design is seen to undertake a more pervasive role in urban planning, going beyond the visual to embed social and environmental qualities into its processes. Thus, the first 'key principle' of the PPS is that 'Development plans promote outcomes in which environmental, economic and social objectives are achieved together over time' (ODPM 2005: 6). Within this it is explicit about planners' responsibility to ensure improvement through design:

> Design which is inappropriate in its context, or which fails to take the opportunities available for improving the character and quality of an area and the way it functions, should not be accepted. (ODPM 2005: 13)

The UTF report set out clear design principles for compact, mixed and integrated neighbourhoods wherein connectedness was deemed important (an issue also raised in the PPS and the UWP). Design is therefore at the managerial hub of regeneration that involves connecting different professional interests but, more literally, is the way by which barriers to urban social integration can be physically reduced. Likewise, the PPS stated:

> High-quality and inclusive design should create well-mixed and integrated developments which avoid segregation and have well-planned public spaces that bring people together and provide opportunities for physical activity and recreation. (ODPM 2005: 14)

While design may be accorded a pervasive status in the conceptualization and management of regeneration processes, at the same time, in the context of urban design practice, it has been subjected to detailed and often repetitious codification. A consequence of central UK government policy formation on urban design in the late 1990s has been its trickle-down into more localized contexts and a range of associated professions. Alongside the work of the Urban Task Force, the UK's Commission for Architecture and the Built Environment (CABE) was founded in 1999. As a chief advisory group on public building projects, this government-funded body developed a range of guidelines that interpret government planning policies (e.g. CABE 2005; CABE 2006) as well as give advice on carrying through urban design projects in line with the approaches that were enshrined within the UTF report (e.g. CABE Space 2007a; CABE Space 2007b). Beyond CABE, coursing through a range of agencies and interests we find a proliferation of 'How to ...' guidelines that overlap with each other. These include material from English Partnerships (2000), the Urban Design Group (2002), the Countryside Agency (2003), and the Royal Town Planning Institute (2007). At more local levels, these are adopted by way of urban design compendia (e.g. Sheffield City Council 2004), design statements (e.g. Warmington Parish Council

2002) or design manuals (e.g. Edinburgh 2007) that are specific to a location. Finally, if this density of publications relating to urban design guidance may be read as specifically and peculiarly British, then it is worth noting that the commissioning of research reports on the value of urban design has reached pan-European level (e.g. European Union 2004) and Australasia (e.g. Ministry for the Environment 2005).

Policy in Practice

The rest of this essay reviews the relationship between this codification and the everyday practice of urban designers. It draws from a set of interviews and conversations conducted with urban designers working in both commercial and civic sectors, as well as planning professionals who engage with urban design.[2] It shows how, despite the ambitions of national government policy to connect design thinking into a wider remit of urban imperatives, *in practice* the codification of design leads to a more reductive and less questioning and integrated processing of design briefs.

At base level, urban designers give form to or specify the features that make up the space between buildings – paving, lighting, seating, signage, plantings and so on. These respond to a range of demands. Accessibility and ergonomics

Figure 2.1 A selection of urban design guidelines, statements and compendia used by the Design Team, Sustainable Development, Leeds City Council. © Joe Julier.

are practical considerations that are required, often by legal standards. Cognitive factors such as the 'legibility' of the space – how it is read and understood in itself and in relation to its surroundings – must be taken into account. Then there are strategic decisions to be made that revolve around space usage and to which practical considerations relate. For example, is the space to be designed around leisure usage, pedestrian throughflow, retail demands or a combination of demands? Other design decisions relate fixed, externally controlled aesthetic requirements. Locations may be subject to design guidance that sets parameters around the visual nature and character of the place. In turn these may relate to planning controls with regard to the heritage of the area.

Beyond giving form to public spaces, the work of urban designers also involves advisory capacities to other interests. Indeed, the Urban Design Group (2008) lists 'Site and Area Design' as just one of seven areas in which the urban designer might work. The other six they list are:

• writing policy such as design policies for a development plan;
• carrying out appraisals such as a development feasibility report;
• giving design advice, for instance to prospective planning applicants or to politicians and local government officers;
• preparing guidance and statements such as a design code or planning principles for an area;
• managing the implementation of urban design, such as organizing public and stakeholder involvement in the process; and
• design awareness and promotion, such as setting up a local design awards schemes.

As such, the urban designer's clients may be multiple. While the public is an end-user, it may also be a client within a consultation or participation process. The urban designer may be brokering between property developer and local authority planning departments. The local authority itself might be the client, where the urban designer is employed to help develop planning policy. Within a local government office, the urban designer may work in conjunction with planners to help monitor planning application approvals or manage the implementation of projects in collaboration with developers. Urban design thus nearly always involves the interfacing of public and private bureaucracies. The urban designer is called upon to broker such relationships.

Urban designers may therefore draw on published design guidelines as a common framework and language between parties. In turn, this can make the design and negotiation process more efficient for urban designers. Reflecting on the use of the Urban Design Compendium (a widely used and thorough design guide produced by English Partnerships) for this purpose, an informant commented:

> I think it's ... about efficiency ... because they're good methods – they produce results that are quite easy to understand. You do end up making the same design choices, the same analytical choices as well; what you actually look at [is] based on that. The environments we work with are so complex and when you try to sit down and analyse spaces like that you have to have a methodology that is quite quick and efficient. (Interview, Urban Designer A)

Meanwhile, the limitations of this approach are recognized by this urban designer:

> But it does mean that you do leave some things out – some things that are site-specific. For example, as a standard you always look at pedestrian movement and obviously that's most relevant to most sites. But how we look at it ... that might not always be the most obvious way you should look at. I mean I believe that it's important to have walkable cites. But does that mean that every single project should be approached like that? (Interview, Urban Designer A)

In preparing reports such as site guidelines for a property development, these documents sometimes provide a framework to follow. Reflecting on this in terms of making the process more efficient an urban designer opined that, 'There is a danger, especially when time is tight, that you just cut and paste between documents,' adding, 'that's why you need really good people – such as CABE Space enablers – monitoring it' (Interview, Urban Designer B).[3] If operating within a regeneration context, there may be checks and balances of other experts involved in a project that might temper this 'cut and paste' approach. The 2000 Urban White Paper put particular emphasis on the need to improve the skills of planners, designers and developers in the context of the urban renaissance agenda. However, the alignment and efficiency of procedures appears often to override a critical discussion of the process that may emanate from well-informed professionals in the 'production chain' of urban design.

The alignment of procedures and aspirations between designers and clients may be achieved through understanding or even adopting the latter's processes. In carrying through urban design projects, councils invariably employ dedicated project managers whose approaches are drawn from construction. These may be internal project managers, or this role may be contracted out. In interfacing with project managers, one head of an urban design consultancy noted how their procedures were much more linear than a 'bunch of designers', involving the need to sign off pre-set stages in the design and implementation process. He noted that all his team had learnt Prince2, the standard construction project management software. This was so that they could understand the project manager's processes and needs, and then be able to adapt to these in creative ways (Interview, Urban Designer D).

The alignment of the commercial urban design studio with the external auditing demands of the clients has impacts even before the design process begins. Local authority and property development bureaucracies often require demonstration of the urban designer's adherence to official measures such as the British ISO standards on Occupational Health and Safety, Environmental Management or Service Management. In addition, they invariably have to demonstrate alignment with European Union directives on procurement that are mediated through the Office of Government Commerce (OGC). In 2008, the OGC had some sixty 'Best-Practice Guidance' publications available (OGC 2008) to contractors working with local government, to ensure adherence to such policy issues as sustainability, social issues and competitive tendering. This therefore involves a complex set of requirements that the urban designer may have to demonstrate knowledge of and adherence to, even in the pre-qualification process prior to arriving at the design brief or the pitch. This changes the way that the urban design studio has to present itself to clients, shifting the emphasis away from its professional status as creative worker to a more bureaucratically encoded form of self-presentation. It also costs the studio additional money and time that might otherwise be dedicated to the creative process. Furthermore, such pre-qualifications are issues that the local authority client will be making calculations over. The design brief may be tightly controlled by pre-delivery cost calculations of relative value, made according to the parameters of procurement and other directives. In its turn, this means that the client is unlikely to be willing to negotiate with the urban designer 'on the nature or details of the brief' (Interview, Urban Designer D).

If, in the commercial context, this leads to the urban designer's aspirations for creative solutions being dampened, then similar effects take place in the city authority context. It is rare for a UK local authority to maintain an urban design unit that actually undertakes design work. More often, their role would be in assisting the planning processes through advising, for example, property developers on their schemes. This often involves creating design guidelines and helping in their interpretation, ensuring their adherence to the wider planning and design aims of that local authority. At the thin end of this wedge, the role of the designated local authority officer may not even be in the creative direction of the project but in merely managing the overall spend. Thus the creative input of the local authority may be seriously reduced while its outsourcing may lead to its curtailment as external agents look to turn projects around quickly, in turn using a 'cut and paste' approach drawn from previous projects and processed through the structures of various urban design guides and compendia (Interviews, Urban Designers A, B, C, F).

Historically, the creative 'envisioning' of the urbanscape – taking the more strategic view of the location, interrelationship and form of urban functions – more often took place in planning departments. One interviewee observed that in the twenty-first century, planning departments were too heavily wrapped up in the mere promulgation of procedural elements. Their need to ensure adherence to ever more complex national and local government regulations meant that little time was left over for the more creative strategic thinking that, previously, had typified the role of the planner (Interview, Urban Designer E).

Arguably, the vacuum left by the absence of this 'envisioning' undertaken within local authority planning departments has led to the rise of 'masterplanning' as an extended exercise. This not only embraces a land use plan, but includes a 'strategic decision-making tool based on economic, market and social appraisals' (Ardron et al. 2008), where the scale of regeneration is significant. As such it is not finite in that it will create a broad outline and strategy for an area, the details of which get filled in through the development process. However, it should be supported by delivery mechanisms including social, economic and financial documentation. It is a 'joined-up' approach that had already been advocated by the Urban Task Force (1999).

Given the way that masterplans set the strategic context for further stages of delivery, the urban designer's job is invariably to take part in the filling in of detail. Again, this points to the designer's intermediary role. This may involve such things as undertaking consultation processes with stakeholders, ensuring that landscaping proposals made by property developers adhere to masterplan objectives, or liaising with representatives of national frameworks such as CABE Space enablers or offices within Regional Development Agencies charged with the overall orchestration of regeneration processes (Interview, Urban Designer E).

Within the public sector in the UK, there has been a rise of so-called 'Design Champions'. Their role is to provide leadership in ensuring the insertion of high-quality design thinking at all levels of their respective organizations, be it housing or hospital design, landscape design, visual communication or the uniforms of employees. By 2006 there were Design Champions in more than two-thirds of local authorities, healthcare trusts, local education authorities and police authorities (CABE 2008). In short, their role is that of a 'knowing proxy client'. While they might not be the end-client to projects, they act as expert intermediary or gatekeeper between designers, developers, planning departments and the commissioners. This role is largely played out by 'enlightened amateurs'. There is no formal qualification required. CABE recommends that the individual should be a councillor who is a 'good communicator' and 'consensus builder' able to help 'develop a vision' (CABE 2004).

The Design Champions' role may be bound up in the details of brief-writing or procurement, but their more general activity in advocating the use of good design resonates with the wider instrumentalization of design towards the promotional culture of urban centres. Their input, in conjunction with that of councillors, local authority officers or external agencies such as urban design consultancies, may involve taking strategic decisions on the sequencing of projects. This may be done for pragmatic planning reasons, but invariably the sequencing is closely bound up with political and policy issues regarding funding streams. Thus it is common for the more 'spectacular' piece of urban design – such as an architect-designed footbridge or a city centre square, feature high-profile public artists – to be programmed early on in a design-led regeneration process. This ensures media, general public and policy-maker attention that will, hopefully, draw in subsequent funding from central government or other sources. The temporal structures in which urban designers work and thus effect their creative input may thus be driven by sequence as well as speed. Summing this up, an urban designer observed:

> Either for [the Regional Development Agency] to show it was delivering or [the city] … I'd say that there was an element of the project needing to be delivered for the sake of delivering a project within a timescale and to prove that something had been happening in terms of setting out a like-new public realm: re-paving the streets with quality items, [installing] new furniture [and] lighting that was meant to lift the area. This was on the waterfront, so quite lot of people go there … you'd want something to last, but it's only been down a year and it's starting to look shabby … [the Regional Development Agency] wanted to say to all sorts of other people, 'Look at what we've done' … it was handled through the regeneration team and maybe there was a problem there as well because it was run by project managers who … maybe weren't familiar with all the issues that urban designers and engineers would know to be conscious about. (Interview, Urban Designer F)

In this example, the management of the design process was clearly bound up with pressure to instrumentalize the renewal of the urban realm as part of wider campaign of public relations and city 'boosterism'. The loss of design and build quality may be played off against the pragmatic incentive of this leading to further funding opportunities.

Conclusion

The election of the New Labour government in 1997 clearly instigated a turn to the embedding of design into regeneration processes in the UK. But this must also be seen as part of a global movement towards reconfiguring the importance and function of cities. Many of the effects described above have been experienced elsewhere in the world. More specifically, this trend has seen the rise of city 'boosterism' – using urban planning, urban design and visual communication in more strategic ways to encourage inward investment and flow of human capital. At the same time, design has been more closely bound into related issues of economy, social inclusion, citizenship and environmental concerns of urban centres than ever before.

This emboldened policy of using design in cities as a leading edge of regeneration has brought with it a bureaucratization and codification of its operations. In the first instance, a plethora of design principles, guidelines and codes have been produced to help both educate and enable the successful commissioning and processing of projects. Often the users of these are not design specialists. Thus these give clients and commissioners a language and procedure for employing designers and other creative practitioners. At the same time, urban designers adopt these as a way of easing communication with clients and speeding the design process through.

Dealing as it does with the public realm, urban design has always been involved in bureaucratic processes. Policy on space usage has always been embedded into city authority systems and its design involves a toing and froing between several parties – between different departments of a council as well as developers, planners and architects. However, in its zeal to promote good design as part of regeneration processes, urban designers are also interfacing with other gatekeepers such as CABE Space enablers or Design Champions. Additionally, the rise of increasingly detailed exigencies with regard to council conduct, procurement, health and safety law and so on has added to this. The requirement for demonstrating 'best practice' and, on the part of the city authority, 'best value' (Martin 2002), equally adds to a weight of considerations that invariably act as a brake on the exploration and implementation of creative solutions to a context.

In its inclusion into regeneration processes, urban design cannot be uncoupled from an attitudinal shift that brings together genuine concerns for social connectivity, economic success and environmental sustainability with a perceived need to situate the city in a discourse of promotional culture. Urban design performs functional as well as symbolic requirements. However, the temporal, management and bureaucratic pressures that are placed on its processes may often result, for pragmatic reasons, in the domination of codes and procedures. In their defence, design guidelines are an attempt to ensure good quality and appropriate design in various contexts. While no doubt created with the good intentions of ensuring best practice within complex and often competing demands, the fundamentally ideological question of why you design something in the first place may be left out.

In 2005, the Urban Task Force was reconvened to review the progress made since their first report of 1999. Their resulting report noted a measurable recommitment to urban living as having emerged. However, particularly in terms of design, it was more critical. It identified the lack of design expertise, skills and understanding (or, at least, good advice) within procurement and commissioning of regeneration projects (UTF 2005: 6–7). Design standards were also compromised by ambitions for short-term commercial value over long-term economic gain, it noted, with an emphasis on quantity over quality. Most notably in the context of this essay, 'Design quality is threatened by an excessive reliance on design codes rather than design professionals' (UTF 2005: 7).

Here lies an essential quandary for urban design and creativity. Design codes are produced to ensure good-quality design and generally raise standards of the urban public realm. But they also act as mediatory structures and information between different interests within the urban design process. These interests may have varying understandings and knowledge of design and so codification at least facilitates the promulgation of design action. But it also contains it into preconceived notions of 'quality'. The need for design understanding amongst a wide and varied client base means that these measures of quality have to be highly explicit and, therefore, potentially restrictive. The urban designer's creativity resides not just in the formal shaping of public realm environments, but in the management of the design process between various stakeholders. The multiple roles that urban design is expected to undertake – incorporating environmental, social and promotional functions – within designing the city means that its management and creative value are finely balanced.

Notes

1. In 2007 the Landscape Institute began to discuss undertaking professional accreditation of urban design courses in the UK. In 2008, the Urban Design Alliance undertook a consultation on the capacities required of professionals who either work in or with urban design.
2. In addition to formal interviews and informal conversations, as a tutor on the Master's degree courses in Urban Environmental Design (renamed as MA Urban Design in 2008) and Landscape Architecture at Leeds Metropolitan University since 2001, I have had frequent access to many professional urban designers and planners. I have also had professional engagement with urban processes as a company director of LeedsLoveItShareIt, a Community Interest Company founded to explore new approaches to urban regeneration and sustainability.
3. CABE Space enablers belong to a panel appointed by CABE. They are allocated to projects for between five and fifteen days to provide advice on good practice on the planning, management, design and maintenance of the public realm.

References

Ardron, Rose, Batty, Elaine and Cole, Ian (2008), *Devising and Delivering Masterplanning at Neighbourhood Level: Some Lessons from the New Deal for Communities Programme*, London: Department for Communities and Local Government.

Bell, D. and Jayne, M. (2003), '"Design-led" Urban Regeneration: A Critical Perspective', *Local Economy*, 18(2): 121–34.

CABE (Commission for Architecture and the Built Environment) (2004), *Local Authority Design Champions: An Introduction*, London: CABE.

CABE (Commission for Architecture and the Built Environment) (2005), *Making Design Policy Work: How to Deliver Good Design Through Your Local Development Framework*, London: CABE.

CABE (Commission for Architecture and the Built Environment) (2006), *Design and Access Statements: How to Write, Read and Use Them*, London: CABE.

CABE (Commission for Architecture and the Built Environment) (2008), http://www.cabe.org.uk/default.aspx?contentitemid=1667.

CABE Space (2007a), *It's Our Space: A Guide for Community Groups Working to Improve Public Space*, London: CABE.

CABE Space (2007b), *Spaceshaper: A User's Guide*, London: CABE.

Carmona, M., de Magalhae, C. and Edwards, M. (2002), 'Stakeholder Views on Value and Urban Design', *Journal of Urban Design*, 7(2): 145–69.

Castells, M. (1996), *The Rise of the Network Society*, Oxford: Blackwell.

City of Edinburgh Council (2007), 'Edinburgh Tram Design Manual' (report).

Countryside Agency (2003), *Town Design Statements: Why and How to Produce Them: Good Practice Advice*, Cheltenham: Countryside Agency.

Cowan, R. (2008), 'Capacitycheck: The Urban Design Capacity Framework', consultation document of the Urban Design Alliance published at www.udal.org.uk [last accessed 13 August 2008].

'Edinburgh Tram Design Manual' (2007), report, Edinburgh: City of Edinburgh Council.

English Partnerships (2000), *Urban Design Compendium*, London: English Partnerships.

European Union (2004), 'Urban Design for Sustainability: Final Report of the Working Group on Urban Design for Sustainability to the European Union Expert Group on the Urban Environment' (report).

Evans, G. (2003), 'Hard-Branding the Cultural City – from Prado to Prada', *International Journal of Urban and Regional Research*, 27(2): 417–41.

Florida, R. (2002), *The Rise of the Creative Class: And How It's Transforming Work, Leisure, Community and Everyday*, New York: Basic Books.

Julier, Guy (2005), 'Urban Designscapes and the Production of Aesthetic Consent', *Urban Studies* 42(5–6): 869–88.

Kesner, B. et al. (2002), 'A Model for Undergraduate Study in Urban Design', *Association of Collegiate Schools of Planning Annual Conference Proceedings*, Baltimore, MD. Available at http://works.bepress.com/vdelrion/3 [last accessed 25 August 2008].

Landry, C. (2000), *The Creative City*, Demos: London.

Lees, L. (2003), 'Visions of "Urban Renaissance": The Urban Task Force and the Urban White Paper', in Imrie, Rob and Raco, Mike (eds.), *Urban Renaissance? New Labour, Community and Urban Policy*, Bristol: Policy Press.

Lopez, E. and Warah, R. (2006–7), 'Urban and Slum Trends in the Twenty-First

Century', *UN Chronicle*.

Martin, S. (2002), 'Best Value: New Public Management or New Direction?', in McLaughlin, K., Osborne, S. and Ferlie, E. (eds.), *New Public Management: Current Trends and Future Prospects*, London: Routledge.

Ministry for the Environment (2005), *The Value of Urban Design: The Economic, Environmental and Social Benefits of Urban Design*, Wellington: Ministry for the Environment.

ODPM (2005), *Planning Policy Statement 1: Delivering Sustainable Development*, London: ODPM.

OECD (Organization for Economic Cooperation and Development) (2006), *Competitive Cities in the Global Economy*, Luxembourg: OECD Publishing.

OGC (Office of Government Commerce) (2008), 'Best-Practice Guidance'. Available at www.ogc.gov.uk/procurement_documents_best_practice_guidance_.asp [last accessed 31 October 2008].

Olds, K. (2001), *Globalization and Urban Change*, Oxford: Oxford University Press.

Olins, W. (1999), *Trading Identities: Why Countries and Companies Are Taking On Each Other's Roles*, London: The Foreign Policy Centre.

Parkinson, M. (2001), 'The Urban White Paper: Halfway to Paradise?', *New Economy*, 8(1): 47–51.

Regan, Sue (2000), 'Towards an Urban Renaissance: The Final Report of the Urban Task Force', *Political Quarterly*, 71(1): 115–18.

Royal Town Planning Institute (2007), *Shaping and Delivering Tomorrow's Places: Effective Practice in Spatial Planning*, London: RTPI.

Sassen, S. (ed.) (2002), *Global Networks, Linked Cities*, London: Routledge.

Sheffield City Council (2004), *Sheffield City Centre: Urban Design Compendium*, Sheffield: SCC.

Smith, M. (2003), *Issues in Cultural Tourism Studies*, London: Routledge.

Urban Design Group (2002), *Urban Design Guidance: Urban Design Frameworks, Development Briefs and Masterplans*, London: Thomas Telford.

Urban Design Group (2008), 'Employing an Urban Designer'. Available at http://www.udg.org.uk/?document_id=332 [last accessed 25 August 2008].

UTF – Urban Task Force (1999), *Towards an Urban Renaissance*, London: Spon.

UTF – Urban Task Force (2005), 'Towards a Strong Urban Renaissance' (report). Available at www.urbantaskforce.org [last accessed 31 October 2008].

Warmington Parish Council (2002), 'Warmington Village Design Statement' (report).

WGUDS – Working Group on Urban Design for Sustainability (2004), *Urban Design for Sustainability: Final Report of the Working Group on Urban Design for Sustainability to the European Union Expert Group on the Urban Environment*, Wien: Bundesministerium für Land- und Forstwirtschaft, Umwelt und Wasserwirtschaft.

Interviews

Urban Designers A, B, C – junior designers in landscape architecture and urban design consultancies. Interviewed 21 May 2008 (A) and 10 June 2008 (B and C).

Urban Designer D – principal designer and head of urban design consultancy. Interviewed 31 July 2008.

Urban Designer E – head, urban design unit, city authority. Interviewed 6 June 2008.

Urban Designer F – urban planner and designer, planning department, city authority. Interviewed 20 August 2008.

CHAPTER 3

Design, Innovation and Policy at Local Level

Katie Hill and Guy Julier

Introduction

During the past two past decades, local government across much of Europe, the USA and Australasia has engaged with the so-called New Public Management. In brief, this form of public sector organization includes a shift towards more entrepreneurial management, explicit standards and measurement of performance, an emphasis on output controls, decentralization of services, the promotion of competition, a stress on private sector styles of management and the disciplining of resource allocation (Osborne and McLaughlin 2002; Du Gay 2004).

The stereotypical era of large-scale, monolithic and mostly unchanging bureaucracies of local government – the public administration approach – may have ended in the 1980s. This does not, however, mean that it has been replaced by wholly light-touch, decentralized and flexible systems. In fact, according to Hoggett (1996), the New Public Management displays three interlocking layers of strategy that are, perhaps necessarily, in conflict. First, operational output may be decentralized from national to local levels but also outwards from local authority level to subcontracted companies or groups – what Whitfield (2001, 2006) calls 'agentification' – while policy and strategy are increasingly centralized to the national government. Second, the introduction of competition running through this quasi-decentralization process becomes the dominant model for coordinating it. Third, performance management and audit have emerged as ways to measure and give accountability to the first two strategies.

At the heart of much thinking behind this 'shake-up' of local authorities is the demand for a move towards greater innovation on the part of local government (and, indeed, all other aspects of state, including policing, healthcare and education). In Australia and the UK, this was clearly embedded into government thinking from the late 1990s (Considine and Lewis 2007). The UK

Government's White Paper, 'Innovation Nation' (Dept. for Innovation, Skills and Universities 2008), lists climate change, the ageing population, globalization and higher expectations of public sector users as drivers of the need for innovatory approaches to service delivery. Within this paper, the UK Design Council's 'Design of the Times' (henceforward referred to as Dott 07) programme of eight design and social innovation projects is cited as a best-practice case. Dott 07 prototyped, among many themes, new forms of welfare service delivery and energy consumption reduction strategies in north-east England. This is a typical example of a central government's supporting 'best practice' examples of modernization ahead of legislation (Newman et al. 2001) – an entrepreneurial initiative is championed as a 'beacon of excellence' for other localities to follow, regardless of whether the infrastructural support for this exists elsewhere or not. More generally, the role of design and its contribution to a new culture of innovation in both private and public sectors is mentioned on just about every page of the 'Innovation Nation' document. It would seem that designers might be well poised to play a central role in this new culture of public sector innovation.

This chapter therefore reviews the tensions that exist between central government concerns to embed design and innovation into local authority and the de facto management context of their implementation. In particular, it takes the case study of a national programme to develop local government policies for children's play in England, in which a clear requirement for innovation was made, as a way of tracking the process of trickle-down of centrally generated policies to their local implementation. In this way, it draws attention to the way that, despite a rhetoric of the need for the localization of decision-making in order to derive sustainable benefits and local ownership of innovation, New Public Management conspires to ensure a recurrent centralization of expertise. At the same time, the complexities of working in multi-agency environments of local authority governance, and the roles of creative consultancies therein, are revealed.

The agentification process certainly leads to the production of more design artefacts as the move from centralized delivery of services and infrastructure by local authorities becomes outsourced to external companies. Independent firms delivering such things as school meals, hospital cleaning or traffic monitoring all require promotional literature, uniforms or Internet platforms to be designed. Furthermore, the demand for 'best value' (Martin 2002) and for pursuing continuous improvement in the way functions are exercised, provides opportunities for design consultancies to create money-saving systems. An example of this is the UK graphics company Corporate Document Services, which provides print management services that help local authorities reduce their costs and the efficiency of their publication processes (CDS 2008). Local authorities have increasingly engaged consultancies, including service design specialists, discussed in the chapters by Moor and Kimbell in this book. In addition to service design consultancies, a heterogeneous range of firms – such as Erskine, Heads Together, UsCreates or Participle – do not necessarily place design at the centre of their identity but engage the expertise of creative practitioners, including designers, in innovating public sector service delivery. It is this latter category of consultants that this chapter addresses.

This chapter's co-author, Katie Hill, is a design graduate who has worked in this specialism. Based in Leeds, UK, she built up a portfolio of work in design for communities, working directly for grass roots organizations doing graphic and theatre set design, and for housing associations facilitating workshops for services users, designing creative evaluation systems, and engaging users in designing facilities. In 2006 she began working for the regeneration consultancy, Erskine Corporation LLP. Erskine describes itself as a firm that 'thinks differently', specializing in creative research and policy development for regeneration, the built environment and children and young people. At Erskine she worked directly with several local authorities across England on policy development and community engagement for new facilities, play provision and childcare. She was at the front end of policy development, seeing at first hand the application of national policy at local level, and became involved in aiding the implementation of the Children's Play initiative. Much of the empirical data for this chapter is drawn from her experience of working with Erskine in developing programmes within this and other public sector initiatives.

Innovating Children's Services

The Children's Play initiative began in 2006 with a commitment from the UK's Big Lottery Fund to invest £155 million in play provision and infrastructure as a response to the UK government's 2004 report, *Getting Serious About Play* (Department for Culture, Media and Sport, 2004). This report cited 'activities for young people' as the most requested improvement for local authorities, and a range of concerns about the state of children's play as being the reasons for proposing action in relation to improving children's play opportunities. As well as concern about children not playing outdoors as much as they used to, the report argued that parents were increasingly concerned with children's safety and less likely to let children go out and play independently. Equally, play providers, including local government, were afraid of litigation and blame culture and therefore more reluctant to provide play opportunities. Consequently, play facilities had become a low priority when it came to local policy and allocation of funding. According to its aims and objectives, the Children's Play initiative in England (2006–7) was developed with creativity and innovation at its heart. Its second published aim was to 'support innovation and new ways of providing for children's play' (Big Lottery Fund 2006a).

A large proportion of its £155 million fund – £124 million – was dedicated to the generation of new children's play facilities to be provided by local authorities. In order to be able to apply for this funding, each interested local authority had to go through a prescribed process to produce a five-year play strategy for the area, which would set out how it would be supported through various council activities, including the projects that the Big Lottery Children's Play fund would pay for. The process was set out in a book of guidelines called *Planning for Play* (National Children's Bureau/ Big Lottery Fund 2006). After producing the strategy, they also had to complete a Big Lottery Fund application form and submit both documents to them in a bidding process.

A sum of £15 million was allocated for the setting up of Play England, a network of regional play experts with a remit of supporting and developing the infrastructure within which the projects would be created. The remaining £16 million was intended for an 'innovation programme' entitled 'Playful Ideas' (Big Lottery Fund 2006b), which town and parish councils and the community and voluntary sector (but not local authorities) could apply for. Across the whole of the Children's Play initiative, there were no explicit guidelines around engaging creative industries in developing the policy documents and project proposals that would shape these services. It was expected that the creative industries, including designers, were to be brought into the latter stages of this project once briefs had been formed for specific projects.

The scheme is an example of how the public sector struggles with the concept of innovation. There were demands for innovation in funding calls for local authorities, town and parish councils, and the voluntary and community sector. The responses to the calls for funding showed that rather than a multitude of novel approaches to play, which would be expected from a call for creative and innovative projects, most applications were for a limited range of projects. Throughout the duration of their appointment as consultants to local authorities, Erskine undertook regular analysis of play projects that had been funded through the scheme in order to be able to advise authorities on what projects had been successful. It became clear from an early stage that funded projects fell into a few recognizable categories. For example, mobile play projects, skate and BMX parks and play rangers were the most common types of play projects proposed.

Examining the type of projects that have already been funded through a particular scheme is common practice amongst funding advisers. It improves the likelihood of a funding application being successful if the applicants know that they are proposing the type of project that funders have already been prepared to support. This creates a tension between the applicants' desire for innovation, and therefore the submitting of novel proposals to funders, and the anxiety felt by applicants (and their supporting consultants) around applying for funding for an idea or project for which there is no precedent. There would be no evidence to show that either the funding application or the project is likely to be successful.

Ultimately, the 'Planning for Play' guidelines provided a default position for local authorities lacking the capacity or ambition to develop their own innovations. Redolent with 'checklists', bullet-pointed 'essential elements' lists, a suggested play audit typology and a pre-prepared implementation structure, it is hardly surprising that local authorities would largely stick to the prescribed script within the bidding process. Thus the enthusiasm for innovation in this programme may, in fact, be tempered by centrally produced guidelines, as well as anxiety around meeting the requirements of funding bodies.

'Playful Ideas' was a fund within the scheme, directly targeted at developing innovation in play. However, throughout the duration of the project the definition of innovation was softened as organizations struggled to generate innovative ideas about play. The guidance stated that, 'Projects seeking funding from this programme must display a creative and novel approach to addressing an identified problem within the field of children's play' (Big Lottery Fund 2006b: 8). This statement did not change throughout the duration of the call; however, its interpretation, as mediated to applicants by the Play England regional advisors, did. While local authorities themselves could not apply to this fund, many were keen to support their local town and parish councils and their community and voluntary sectors. As part of their contract with Erskine, they commissioned support for applicants to this fund. Over the course of several months, Erskine delivered support for 'Playful Ideas' applicants and were in conversation with Play England on how applicants could successfully apply to the fund. It was through these conversations that the changing definition of innovation was conveyed, and in turn Erskine passed that on to the local authorities and potential 'Playful Ideas' applicants.

The early implication was that design propositions within funding applications for play should be unique and original. However, within a year of its launch, as town and parish councils and the voluntary and community sector grappled with this challenge, often lacking the internal expertise to deliver a meaningful response, so applications for this funding dropped off. In response, the parameters of 'innovation' were changed. Successful proposals subsequently could promise 'uniqueness' to the respective locality rather than on the basis of 'never having been done before, anywhere', allowing for best-practice models from elsewhere to be adopted and reproduced.

The Bureaucratic Context of Local Authorities

In order to develop a critical understanding of the 'fit' between national government aspirations, local authority implementation and the role of creative consultants such as Erskine who sit between these, it is first useful to understand the roles and structures of local government within which demands for innovation reside. Local government in England, as in most of the developed world, assumes responsibility for the delivery of the majority of the infrastructure and services that we use in our daily lives, although admittedly not as much today as fifty or so years ago. While decisions about broad political directions are made centrally by national government, most of the day-to-day provision of services and running of our towns, cities, villages and rural landscapes is done by local government.

According to the National Association of Local Councils (NALC), local authorities in England employ 2.1 million people, making them one of the largest employers, and are one of the largest purchasers of goods and services in the country. Local authorities undertake an estimated 700 different functions, but primarily they are responsible for the local implementation of national government initiatives as well as the running of some local services which include education, waste management, transport, social services, planning, housing and cultural provision.

In recent years, many traditional services have found their remit strategically widened. Many schools have opened their facilities and services to the wider community through Extended Schools Services, and libraries have incorporated community halls, cafés, sports and recreation facilities into their services. Erskine has seen this shift at first hand through working with both Extended Schools Services as part of their work on play and childcare, and through working with library services to develop new facilities. In 2006 Erskine began working with a small community library in Leicester on the development of proposals for a new library building. Erskine provided support for funding applications and designed and carried out community engagement processes. Katie Hill designed the second phase of community engagement, the consultation on the plans for the new library and community centre. The proposal included a café, community training kitchen, community rooms and music studios as well as the library. Working with the city architects, central library services as well as local librarians and other local service providers, the process brought to light the increasingly interdisciplinary context within which local authority officers work.

This diversification of services means that the roles and responsibilities of the officers working in local authorities are shifting. The larger authorities are better equipped to deal with this, having a larger pool of staff and therefore greater expertise to draw upon, but for smaller authorities this can mean that individual roles can change dramatically according to shifts in policy.

This raises issues around the capacity of authorities' human resources to respond to the changing demands of national policy. For example, when developing play policies across different authorities, Erskine worked with several different departments in different authorities including those of parks, regeneration, sports and leisure, youth service, and of course children's services and play departments where they existed. Some authorities had full teams dedicated to play services, while for others it was just one part of a council officer's role to oversee the development of the play policy. However, central government placed the same demands on all authorities, regardless of size or capacity (although, admittedly, the larger authorities had larger amounts of money to bid for and therefore more projects to set up). The differing background and expertise of the departments that led the projects influenced the types of projects proposed.

The capabilities of authorities are therefore by no means standardized. This is one reason why the government provides such strict guidelines along with its directives and demands for policy development. No matter what the capacity of the local authority, there are guidelines to follow that make policy development foolproof. Such centralization may help the smaller or weaker authorities where capacity is lacking. The challenge is that such guidelines discourage authorities from making their own local policies or innovating their own approaches.

Gyford, Leach and Game (1989) discuss the challenges to professionalism amongst council officers who once had enjoyed a position of being relatively unchallenged and seen as the experts who should be listened to. Officers no longer have the influence on decisions that they used to. In a climate where the demands made upon officers are constantly changed and diversified, it is almost understandable that the government resorts to over-regulation to make sure that its directives are carried out. The notion of valued expertise has shifted from being that held by local officers with local knowledge, to that held by national subject experts who can advise more strategically across the whole country. Furthermore, Newman et al. (2001) suggest that some see the demand for innovation as an opportunity to embrace new practices (typically those more closely aligned with central government's political agenda), whilst others undertake innovations more through 'compliance' – a need to be seen to be doing *something* as a way of gaining recognition and influence. A corollary to this is that this search for legitimacy leads to 'innovations' that are largely symbolic. Thus public consultation becomes, in their words, 'fashion following' rather than a desire to use it to drive innovations.

Within the enormous body of work that local authorities undertake across the country, it would be impossible to say which is the dominant response to adoption of innovation. One illustration of a situation where genuine adoption of innovation seemed to be embraced was again in library services, where within a particular authority the push for the merging of services was implemented both by widening the remit of what the libraries themselves do (the approach suggested by central government), but also by enabling other services to act as libraries. In this case the Children's Centres (where services for children under the age of five years old and their families are located) were equipped to operate as libraries themselves. It is not unique for Children's Centres to provide books for children; however, this is not normally integrated into the formal library service. In this instance, the Children's Centre computers were fitted with the software to work on the local library system, and staff were trained to operate the system so that users of the centre could register and borrow books as they would at a regular library. This seems to be a local innovation driven mainly by the commitment and inspiration of local library service staff rather than any national precedent. This was a recognition by local officers that the government approach to broadening the appeal of libraries and making them more approachable would still not meet the needs of some of the most vulnerable targeted library users – that is, families with young children – and that an innovative solution would be to take the services out of the library all together and put them where those people will use them.

'Designing' National Policy into Local Government Implementation

Government in the UK comprises of between two and four tiers of separate organizations, depending on the location. The development of authorities has been largely due to evolution rather than design, resulting in a complex system across the country. As well as the issues of capacity raised by standardized directives trickling through a tiered system that is not standard, the complexity of structure also raises the issue of multiple agendas. As policies move from central to local government levels, they pick up agendas and priorities from each tier of government. For those local authorities that have two or three levels of policy above them, the scope within which they can address local needs becomes more restricted. Because the passing on of agendas from one level to another carries resources with it, particularly money, the local authorities at the bottom of the chain have little choice but to adhere to the agendas of those tiers of government that sit above them, and the agendas of the partners with whom they work. The actual delivery of local services is, therefore, a result of a combination of different factors, agendas, hierarchies and commercial, political and practical pressures. This complexity means that service delivery is often the result of a highly negotiated and contested process, where there is little room for creativity. The following section follows the trickle-down of political agendas through the tiers of government that impact on one of Erskine's clients, a London borough.

Policy and strategy documents are the thread that connects the different tiers of government to one another, and enables the transfer of ideas and resources down the hierarchy of government from national to local level. At the same time, policy at all levels has to be based on identified need within the community. Policy development usually involves public consultation processes where the relevant communities are asked what their needs are in relation to the specific policy areas. This means that, at least in theory, as policy directions flow down through the tiers of government, rather than simply repeating through the layers of policy, each tier introduces an element of local knowledge and consultation to draw out and refine the policy to suit local needs.

As with the organizations themselves, policies fall into a tiered system, and are often referred to according to their position in the hierarchy; for example, you might hear that 'This policy falls under that policy', or 'This policy sits above that policy'. The policies at the top of the tier system are the national policies, and in the case of the Children's Play initiative it would be 'Every Child Matters: Change for Children' (HM Government 2004). This level of policy outlines the aims of the government for the whole country for every issue relating to children, and all policies that come under the national policies have to relate directly to their aims and deliver their objectives. Already, at national level, regulations are beginning to form, and much of the guidelines and stipulations that come with national policies are aimed at ensuring that local policies deliver national objectives, without leaving room for error.

Erskine worked for several London boroughs on the implementation of the Children's Play initiative. For London boroughs, the next tier of policies below the national level are the mayor of London's policies – in the case of policies concerning children such as play policy, the 'Making London Better for All Children and Young People' strategy (Greater London Authority 2004). These carry forward the national policy aims and expand on them as appropriate for the specific context of the London boroughs. Most of the 'action points' in 'Making London Better for All Children and Young People' relate to the mayor's office placing requirements upon the boroughs concerning the way that they carry out the work that they are responsible for; for example in relation to planning guidance and play, 'The mayor will encourage the London boroughs to involve young Londoners in planning, developing and designing their play, recreational and leisure services' (Greater London Authority 2004: 82). This downloads responsibility for delivering on national policy aims through the mayor's office to the borough authority.

The tier of policies that follows is the borough policies themselves, and in most cases these policies are the ones that contain the most specific information about what will actually be done in that borough, and what services the general public will see delivered in their own neighbourhoods. Within the borough policies there are still a number of different levels and types of policy that all work together.

The top tier of borough policy would normally be a general policy such as a Community Plan. This will be a long-term strategy (ten or fifteen years) produced by a local partnership including all of the organizations that are responsible for delivering public services in that borough, including the borough council, other public service organizations such as the police force and healthcare trust, and local businesses. These plans tend to divide areas of responsibility into different sections, or strategic priorities, and create separate (but interdependent) plans for things such as children and young people, community safety, health, the environment, transport and employment. Below the community plan is the Local Area Agreement (LAA), which draws together funding from partnership organizations in an agreement of how the Community Plan will be implemented. The LAA provides the basis on which subsequent evaluation and measurement is undertaken and it is therefore subject to frequent progress reports on its implementation.

The next tier of policy is that of the business plans for the organizations in the partnership, each organization having a separate business plan that focuses on their area of responsibility. This is usually a shorter-term plan, for around three years, and it outlines in detail the aims, budgets and targets for all of the council's tasks in delivering the broader Community Plan.

Funding for policy delivery is again complex, coming from a range of partner organizations as well as grant funding and private finance. For the Children's Play initiative, the involvement of the funding organization was paramount. The initiative was led by the Big Lottery Fund and was a direct response to the government's *Getting Serious About Play* (Department for Culture, Media and Sport 2004). It required the production of a local authority policy on play in order for authorities to apply for funding, and it also funded Play England, the successor to The Children's Play Council as the national advisory organization for children's play. This merging of policy development and non-public grant funding brought together two highly regulated areas.

Once areas of responsibility and sources of funding have been defined in the LAA and the council's business plan, there is a final layer of policies which are specific to areas of work and contain detailed action plans that will be implemented 'on the ground'. For example, this is where the play policies generated as part of the Children's Play initiative would normally sit. Other related strategies on this level might also include policies concerning sport and leisure, health, youth justice, obesity and community safety, all of which might refer to the play strategy (and vice versa). The connection between policies is often articulated within policy documents and is referred to as 'strategic fit'. The better the fit, the more likely a policy is to have resources allocated to it. For example, within a play policy, a proposed project that can also address objectives in health or community safety policies will be more likely to be prioritized for funding allocation within the authority: play provision targeted at teenagers might be prioritized if it is placed in an area with an established antisocial behaviour problem.

We can see, in the above example, how policies are increasingly specific as they move down the hierarchy. The most local level of policy can come down to neighbourhood level, where neighbourhood plans set policy priorities for very small, specific areas.

Within the Children's Play initiative, the impact of the levels of policy not only existed on paper, but through the involvement of members of higher tiers of government, as well as partner organizations, in the Play Partnerships. Play Partnerships were part of the infrastructure required for the development of the play policy and projects stipulated by central government in *Planning for Play*. One of Erskine's key roles was to recruit and manage the Play Partnerships for authorities, including inviting members, drafting terms of reference, and organizing and chairing initial meetings. The organizations involved in the Partnerships had political influence on the local authority policy, both through their involvement on the committee that made decisions about the writing of the policy and design of projects, and through the influence of their policies and related resource allocation and priorities.

It is also apparent, in this example, that in order to differentiate themselves, councils often adopt individual titles for their policy documents. Rather unhelpfully, the terms 'policy', 'strategy' and 'plan' seem to be used interchangeably. Policy documents are also often given catchy titles or strap lines, so a whole language of strap lines, abbreviations and acronyms develops around policies in different authorities, making discussing policy a linguistic minefield.

This in itself raises questions of accessibility and transparency (glossaries are rare, and officers often have accepted shorthand names with which they refer to their own policies). If these strap lines are about differentiation, then this also raises the question of how truly local the local authority policies are. Subtleties of language are used to create local ownership of policies that are in effect a repetition of centralized policy. At times, the processes which local authorities go through to create policy are more about generating 'buy in' and ownership of national policy directives than truly investigating what an effective local strategy

might be. At a strategic level, all share similar needs that are chiefly characterized by being a rural coastal area, resulting in similar policy aims. Yet to create
local ownership and support for the policy, authorities try to embed particular
local characteristics in the language used to articulate their policies.

As a consultant working within this environment, the need to participate in
this local differentiation of policies through the seemingly superficial means of
language and style was embedded into working practices in several ways.
Firstly, the ability to quickly assimilate the relevant titles and abbreviations of
local policies, and to use them in conversation with the officers, was a crucial
part of being accepted as someone who understood the local situation and was
qualified to produce policy for that authority. It was also necessary to participate in the generation of the individual strap lines and concepts for policies. It
could be compared to developing a brand for each policy, and on final presentation the local 'brand' would be articulated through the presentation, the
title, the colour and font of the final document. Some authorities required
Erskine to develop this for them, and others required policies to be produced
by in-house graphics departments within the authorities, according to an in-
house style guide. A common preoccupation voiced by clients was that Erskine
was working on multiple policies for different authorities (as were most other
consultants working on the scheme). They were concerned that their policy
would be too similar to other policies in other areas. Meanwhile, the questions
asked of the community through consultation processes are often so generic
that the same priorities appear across different authorities. Even after comprehensive consultation has been carried out and embedded in policies, the differences are subtle and the policies reflect more of national guidelines and the
accepted wisdom of national experts than local differences.

Expertise

With regards to the Children's Play initiative, its policy guidelines for local
authorities were authored by the country's leading experts on the subject of
play, for example Tim Gill, Issy Cole-Hamilton and Adrian Voce, all dominant national voices on play. The guidelines were highly prescriptive, outlining
the process through which local authorities should produce their strategy and
the key issues that those policies should address. The level of detail included
suggested a table of contents for policies, and suggestions for components of
the action plan. At the same time, as we have already identified, a competing
demand for creativity and innovation was embedded into this centralized
policy. Creativity becomes an auditable demand that nonetheless sits within a
highly structured and prescribed set of values. The question of expertise, who

has it and how knowledge of the policy area is distributed or supported, goes back to the issue of capacity.

Local authorities frequently bridge the capacity gap by bringing in consultants to work on specific projects. The consultancy was often brought in very late in a process, close to deadlines. Often, authorities had tried to do the work in house, but were not able to meet central government deadlines (and, importantly, would miss out on funding) without a consultancy's support. Nonetheless, there was frequent political resistance to the use of consultants, who were seen as parasites on traditional domains of public service. Erskine worked for one authority which, during its appointment, had issued an election promise to ban consultants. This was a relatively small authority where the workloads of the officers were already enormous and diverse, and the resources were low. The prospect of them not completing planned work without additional capacity made the services in that area look precarious. Ironically, it would seem that whilst being unpopular amongst the public and to some extent amongst authorities, the capacity that the consultancy sector provides is necessary for local authorities to deliver on targets set by the national government.

Designers and Public Sector Innovation

The centralized demand for creativity and innovation could be the obvious opportunity for designers to lend consultancy support to local authorities. Erskine was predominantly a research organization, but had a strong emphasis on design. Designers were engaged, particularly for community engagement and for the presentation of policies. Erskine also had a sister company, which has become the larger part of the business, called Erskine Design – a 'socially responsible' web design company. The policy development team was able to incorporate the work of Erskine Design by using blogging as a consultation medium, developing specialized databases for data storage and analysis, and for supporting online collaboration between client and consultant. Erskine understood the potential connections between design and policy research, and the application of designer's skills to this area of work. Furthermore, the presence of designers within the team served to orientate Erskine's research towards more in-depth qualitative and creative processes. Research methodologies therefore incorporated those developed from user-centred design, such as 'cultural probes' (see Gaver et al. 1999), narratives and diaries that sought out more personal and emotional issues of human experience in relation to local authority service users. In turn, this data helped support strategy development while working for a number of local authorities.

At the same time, consultancies such as Erskine were reliant on finding obvious alignments between their recommendations and local authority action plans such as the Local Area Agreement. By identifying specific points of coincidence, so the consultancy could then make a stronger case to be employed in order to undertake further follow-up work in terms, for instance, of developing strategy implementation. Resources will only follow up action points – it is, after all, delivery on action points that provides the evidence for accountability.

The experience of Erskine demonstrates the resistances that are embedded into the complex scenario of local authority governance. Put most briefly, they attempt to bridge the conflicting demands of central government's enthusiasm for innovation and entrepreneurialism, enshrined in the New Public Management, and the reality of the normative systems of the bureaucratic order of local authorities and the culture of audit that this entails. By contrast, the Design Council's Dott 07 project represents a much more unbounded, carte blanche attempt to show how a networked approach to public sector interests in a location produces innovative solutions and processes within public sector concerns. By bringing together designers, a range of agencies, community organizations and local authorities, the programme demonstrated how effective solutions to social, economic and environmental challenges could be derived. Its core funding was modest for its scale. However, its £610,000 budget drew a further £7m from its mostly local partners, making it a strong example of multi-agency, cross-sector collaboration. Importantly, the programme was directed by John Thackara, a stalwart champion of the engaging of social innovation through co-creation methods of design (see Thackara 2005), where stakeholders and developers work collaboratively in problem-solving.

Dott 07 may therefore be interpreted as an example of so-called 'network governance'. Here, 'The role of the state is to steer action within complex social systems rather than control solely through hierarchy or market mechanisms' (Hartley 2005: 30). In the public sector, this has been identified as a third phase of local authority management. Evolving from the New Public Management, it is expected to resolve the tensions between centralization and decentralization. It is also a classic case where central government releases resources for experimentation and collaboration to orchestrate the interests of different stakeholders. Policy creation and its implementation are not necessarily undertaken either through stratified bureaucratic systems of 'public administration' or within the entrepreneurially driven and consumer-responsive context of the New Public Management. Instead, programmes are coordinated rather than managed; their outcomes are safeguarded through reputation rather than legal recourse.

In this context for network governance, project delivery involves mutually dependent, individual firms or agencies operating together as a single entity. This system may lend itself well to projects that engage creative industries. After all, labour in this sector has been typified as being highly engaged in so-called 'network sociality' (McRobbie 2002). Designers, it is claimed, are adept at working in teams that bring together various sectors and interests, and the role of social connections between these is paramount to their success.

Erskine's involvement in the Children's Play initiative tells a different story, however. The call for 'compulsory' creativity and innovation as part of its bidding and funding process clearly laid pressure on local authorities and the consultants involved in its delivery. The inclusion of designers in Erskine's processes may have helped in the development of substantive responses within this programme. Their skills in using user-centred approaches and in their interpretation into creative proposals may well have helped local authorities develop design led innovation processes and outcomes as well as funding bids to support these. However, the complex bureaucratic structures of local government, the variation of organization and enthusiasm for innovation amongst them, and the need to justify resource allocation in the context of frequent and rigorous auditing often mitigated against this.

Conclusion

We have already noted the tendency of central governments to produce 'best practice' examples ahead of legislation. Programmes such as Dott 07 are both laboratories for new design practices as well as markers of innovation that it is expected that local government should adopt. However, this sequencing means that where calls for innovatory approaches are made elsewhere, the necessary infrastructure of governance to support their successful implementation may be absent. Local authorities combine modes of governance. 'Public administration', 'New Public Management' and 'networked governance' often overlap (Hartley 2005). Thus designers involved in strategy development for the implementation of nationally prescribed policy are often working in three-speed situations. Furthermore, the heterogeneous nature of local government means that some may be well equipped to deal with centrally generated calls for the innovation of service delivery, while others may suffer expertise shortages. In either case, innovations are still required to address pre-prescribed local authority action points in order to be worthy of resourcing. To add to this complexity, the motivations for the adoption of innovation in local authorities may be varied. Some may embrace it wholeheartedly. Others may be going through the motions. This does create opportunities for consultancies that can navigate this complex environment to deliver on calls for innovation, however the experiences of Erskine show that even where the capacity and motivation for innovation are there, the structures within which local authorities operate still restrict the creativity of output. As central government policy measures trickle through to local authority level, so its language may be given a 'local dialect' in order to generate buy-in amongst its participants. However, the content remains largely the same. At other times, the prescriptive nature of national guidelines that are authored to help the development of strategies at local level leave little room for manoeuvre in determining new approaches to problems. This is exacerbated in local authority contexts that, again, do not carry sufficient capacity to develop their own approaches. In this climate, it is small wonder that expertise, including that of designers, continues to be concentrated at the national level while opportunities for grass roots innovations remain more of an aspiration than a reality.

References

Big Lottery Fund, (2006a), *Planning for Play*, London: National Children's Bureau/Big Lottery Fund.
Big Lottery Fund (2006b), 'Children's Play Programme: Guidance Notes' (report).
CDS (2008), 'CDS Wins Essex Local Authorities' Print Framework Contract'. Available at http://www.cds.co.uk/news.asp#essex [last accessed 22 December 2008].
Considine, M. and Lewis, U. (2007), 'Innovation and Innovators Inside Government: From Institutions to Networks', *Governance: An International Journal of Policy, Administration, and Institutions*, 20(4): 581–607.
Department for Culture, Media and Sport (2004), *Getting Serious About Play*, London: Department for Culture, Media and Sport.
Dept. for Innovation, Skills and Universities (2008), *Innovation Nation*, London: HMSO.
du Gay, P. (2004), 'Against "Enterprise" (But Not Against "Enterprise", For That Would Make No Sense)', *Organization*, 11(1): 37–57.
Flynn, N. (2002), *Public Sector Management*, Harlow: Pearson Education.
Gaver, W., Dunne, A. and Pacenti, E. (1999), 'Design: Cultural Probes', *Interactions: New Visions of Human-Computer Interaction*, Jan–Feb.
Gibson, G. (2006, updated 2008), *Careers in Design: Doing the Business*, London: Design Council.
Greater London Authority (2004), 'Making London Better for All Children and Young People' (report), London: Greater London Authority.
Gyford, J., Leach, S. and Game, C. (1989), *The Changing Politics of Local Government*, London: Unwin Hyman.
Hartley, J. (2005), 'Innovation in Governance and Public Services: Past and Present', *Public Money and Management*, 25(1): 27–34.
HM Government (2004), 'Every Child Matters: Change for Children' (report). Available at http://www.everychildmatters.gov.uk/publications [last accessed 25 January 2009].

Hoggett, P. (1996), 'New Modes of Control in the Public Service', *Public Administration*, 74 (1): 9–32.

Horton, S. and Farnham, D. (1999), 'New Labour: Legacies, Impact and Prospects' in S. Horton and D. Farnham (eds.), *Public Management in Britain*, London: Macmillan, pp.247–58.

Macauley, C. (2003), *Job Mobility and Job Tenure in the UK*, London: Office for National Statistics.

Martin, Steve (2002), 'Best Value: New Public Management or New Direction?', in K. McLaughlin, S. Osborne and E. Ferlie (eds.), *New Public Management: Current Trends and Future Prospects*, London: Routledge, chapter 8.

McRobbie, Angela (2002), 'Clubs to Companies: Notes on the Decline of Political Culture in Speeded-Up Creative Worlds', *Cultural Studies,* 16(4): 516–31.

Newman, J., Raine, J., and Skelcher, C. (2001), 'Transforming Local Government: Innovation and Modernization', *Public Money and Management*, 21(2): 61–8.

Noble, M., McLennan, D., Wilkinson, K., Whitworth, A., Barnes, H., and Dibben, C. (2008), *The English Indices of Deprivation 2007*, London: Communities and Local Government.

Osborne, Stephen P. and McLaughlin, Kate (2002), 'The New Public Management in Context', in McLaughlin, Kate, Osborne, Stephen P. and Ferlie, Ewan (eds.), *New Public Management: Current Trends and Future Prospects*, London: Routledge, chapter 1.

Sanderson, I. (2001), 'Performance Management, Evaluation and Learning in "Modern" Local Government', *Public Administration*, 79(2): 297–313.

Stewart, J. (2000), *The Nature of British Local Government*, New York: St Martin's Press.

Thackara, J. (2005), *In the Bubble: Designing in a Complex World*, Cambridge, MA: MIT Press.

Whitfield, D. (2001), *Public Services or Corporate Welfare: Rethinking the Nation State in the Global Economy*, London: Pluto Press.

Whitfield, D. (2006), *New Labour's Attack on Public Services*, Nottingham: Spokesman.

CHAPTER 4

Public Art, Design-led Urban Regeneration and its Evaluation

Doug Sandle

Notwithstanding its problematic sub-texts, the term 'the lipstick on the gorilla', which suggests a superficial glamorization or makeover, has often been cited as criticism of public art and design, especially when such is used as add-on attempts to improve the quality of the built environment. Contributing to a debate in the pages of the magazine of the Australian Architectural Association, Newton (2001) suggests that the use of regional design review panels to improve the environment, particularly if reduced to a policing role, is potentially limited 'to putting lipstick on the gorilla'. More concretely, John Dales (2008) of the UK's Commission for Architecture and the Built Environment (CABE), states that:

> I've had numerous schemes featuring fancy paving materials, shiny stainless steel and exquisitely manicured landscaping presented to me as examples of good urban design practice when, to be honest, they're no more than 'lipstick on a gorilla'.

The phrase – as do its companions 'plop art', 'plonk art', 'the turd on the plaza' and 'corporate baubles' – has a particular specificity and legitimacy in referring to those sculptures and street ornaments of the middle and following decades of the twentieth century that adorned shopping malls, corporate entrances and civic spaces without too much consideration for their aesthetic, semiotic or sustainable relationship to either their surroundings or users. Moreover, they did little for the creative integrity of their artists. This was not confined to the UK or the developing urban environments of Europe. Hughes (1990), for example, summarizes the impact of modernist examples of public art in American cities

> as abstract ironmongery and sculpture that means nothing but is part of the perfunctory etiquette of urban development, most of it larger than it needs to be.

Locked in a losing battle with the big-city environment, it manages to look both arrogant and depleted.

While Brecknock (2002: 2) suggests that historically the momentum for modern public art was a response by artists to Herbert Read's 1948 clarion call for sculpture to come 'out in the open, into the church and the marketplace, the town hall and the public park' and for their work 'to rise majestically above the agora, the assembled people', the working practices, objectives and the short-term attitudes of developers, planners and civic councils must bear much of the responsibility for the more mundane, dispiriting and intrusive examples. However, it also fair to state that much of contemporary public art has tried to be more diversified, engaging and innovative, and part of a more challenging intervention by artists and designers into public space. Accordingly, what is now often referred to as 'art in the public realm', a term used to reflect its broad range of activities, purposes, scope and methodologies, requires more than an overused metaphor for its assessment, particularly given the rapid growth of public art in Britain during the last ten years or so.

This chapter discusses the roles of public art within wider strategies of design-led urban regeneration. As such, it sees public art as part of a set of material and visual interventions into the public realm that include urban design, architecture, landscape architecture and visual communication, and their instrumental deployment towards economic, cultural and social improvement. Hence, 'design-led urban regeneration' also refers to the specific objects that are developed for this process as much as to their role as signifiers for internal and external audiences of urban centres. With this instrumentalization of public art towards a number of regeneration objectives comes issues of the evaluation of its impact, policy, management and commissioning. The roles of public art and the way these are evaluated are issues that strike at the heart of debates concerning the ownership and use of creativity.

Public Art, the Creative Industries and Urban Regeneration

The impetus for the recent development of public art has been driven by a number of factors, including the expansion of artist-in-residence schemes, the utilization of art in the growing heritage sector and the notion of 'Per Cent for Art', where it is argued that a percentage of capital expenditure on new buildings and environmental construction, usually between 0.5 and 2 per cent, should be devoted to new art and craft design. The advent of European funding for social and environmental regeneration, the National Lottery, and the professionalization of public art through the emergence of consultants, agencies and specialist local authority public art officers, have also significantly contributed to the growth of public art. No longer confined to statues or abstract structures, public art embraces temporary as well as permanent work, uses new media such as digital sound and light, incorporates film and performance, and is often as much concerned with process as with the end product. Public art is a growth industry, with many cities and regional councils adopting strategic policies, employing public art officers and hiring consultants to devise, implement and evaluate their programmes.

While some public artworks continue to be 'plonked' into place, there is nonetheless a growing recognition of the need for artists to work intrinsically with architects, planners and construction engineers from the initial stages of a project, as exemplified by Bridlington's award-winning South Promenade, where the artist Bruce MacLean contributed from the early conceptual stage in a partnership with the architects, Bauman Lyons. Such a working process has since been encouraged by the initial art and architecture scheme of the Royal Society for Arts and, more recently, its successor, PROJECT, which was conceived 'to widen the artist's remit and involvement, not just to working with architects and architecture, but to include planning and urban design, working directly on masterplanning with developers' (Minton 2008: 3).

The most powerful driver for the recent expansion of public art has been its use in environmental and social regeneration and also its often-presumed consequential role in the branding, promotion and the signification of cities, towns and regions. With the increasing role of public art in physical regeneration, there has also been a contingent emphasis on its potential social value, particularly when it engages with community needs (Sharpe et al. 2005). Accordingly, claims for the social efficacy of public art are found in an increasing number of policies, planning guidance strategies and mission statements throughout the country. However, while it is 'perhaps the perceived potential of contemporary public art to work on multiple levels and its adaptability that gives it such cultural viability' (Sharpe et al. 2005: 1004), such can be problematic. A study by the University of Westminster (Roberts et al. 1993) draws attention to a comment by an American critic, Plagens (1986), who argued that public art was being asked to carry an impossible burden by being required to be popular, inoffensive to minorities, profit-inducing, civically enhancing and aesthetically pleasing. The end result, it was suggested, was too often one of mediocrity. A review and survey of public art in Wales noted that:

> Public art has often been required to serve a range of cultural and social needs as well as satisfy different stakeholders and conflicting interests. Whether it be regeneration, social welfare, community health or heritage and tourism it is frequently the case that the artist is required to play different roles and meet a

diverse range of expectations, often at the expense of his or her own creativity and aesthetic integrity. (Roberts et al. 2003: 1)

As Belfiore and Bennett (2008) demonstrate in their intellectual history of the social impact of the arts, a belief in the social instrumental usage of the arts, and the opposing belief in their intrinsic aesthetic value, has a complex historical and philosophical provenance. However, in more recent decades, the former has been both a contributor to, and an expression of, an increasingly political and policy-driven agenda. Bell, O'Connor et al. (2007), Hall and Robertson (2001), Heartfield (2005), Holden (2004) and Selwood (2002, 2006), for example, highlight the political shift from a view of culture as having intrinsic values to an increasingly instrumental agenda, particularly with regard to the use of the arts to address environmental regeneration and social exclusion. Selwood (2002) documents various policy initiatives – from 1979 with the new Conservative government's concern for 'value for money', to the cultural interventionist policies of New Labour. Regarding the latter, Holden (2004) notes that although 'New Labour was committed to supporting culture for its own sake, it sought various ways in which to justify this commitment, assume managerial control over cultural spending, and to audit the results' (2004: 15). In 1999, a report on arts and sport to the Cabinet Office Social Exclusion Unit by the Policy Action Team 10 (PAT10), highlighted the contribution of both to neighbourhood renewal, improving health, employment, crime prevention and individual pride. In turn, the Arts Council of England (1999: 1), perhaps mindful of the source of its funding and the increasing impetus for accountability, responded with a framework document entitled *Addressing Social Exclusion: A Framework for Action*, in which it stated, 'The arts have a vital role in community development – delivering tangible social and economic benefits such as jobs, improved skills, and learning opportunities.' If this agenda was operationalized through the Arts Council and its grant-awarding powers, the political impetus came from a complex positioning of culture and the arts, which on the one hand economically were reformulated as part of the cultural industries, on the other as a social service. With regard to the latter, as Heartfield states, New Labour's Department for Culture, Media and Sport (DCMS) 'promised to make cultural provision accessible to "the many not just the few" and cast cultural institutions in the role of "centres for social change"' (Heartfield 2005: 12).

A number of key studies and publications that purported to demonstrate, highlight or advocate the instrumental contribution of the arts to economic, environmental and social development were also influential in both contributing to and expressing this political agenda. With regard to the arts generally, Reeves (2002), among several, draws attention to the importance of

Myerscough's (1988) often cited work, *The Economic Importance of the Arts in Great Britain*, which she states, 'had a far-reaching impact on the cultural sector and strengthened its argument for the economic impact of the arts as a powerful justification for continued public funding'. Reeves highlights later key work on the economic status and contribution of the arts and the cultural sector generally, such as O'Brien and Feist (1995), Casey, Dunlop and Selwood (1996), Pratt (1997) and the DCMS (2001).

While the cultural industries sector is much broader and diverse than just the arts, such reports on its purported economic contribution added to the growth of the instrumentalist agenda for art, as did those publications that set out to demonstrate the contribution of culture to social, community and personal development, particularly as located within the policy framework of social inclusion. In this respect, Reeves highlights the work of the consultancy organization Comedia – which, supported by the Arts Council, resulted in the discussion document *The Social Impact of the Arts* (Landry, Bianchini et al. 1993), and also work by Galloway (1995), and Landry et al. (1996). As do many other commentators, Reeves draws particular attention to the influential work of Matarasso (1997), whose *Use or Ornament? The Social Impact of Participation in the Arts* was particularly influential with the Labour government and the DCMS. Heartfield (2005: 12) summarizes Matarasso's influence on the social inclusion agenda, as follows:

> Matarasso invested the arts with extraordinary qualities ... The real purpose of the arts, he wrote, was to contribute to a stable, confident and creative society. Participation in the arts could promote tolerance and contribute to conflict resolution, provide a route of rehabilitation and integration for offenders, help people feel a sense of belonging and involvement, be an effective means of health education, and extend involvement in social activity.

With particular regard to public art and environmental design, Hall and Robertson (2001) cite the influence of the Arts Council's *Art into Landscape* initiatives of the 1970s (Arts Council of Great Britain, 1974, 1977), Petherbridge's *Art for Architecture* (1987) and the 1988 Action for Cities Programme, in which 'the significance of the arts as a route to urban regeneration was first enshrined' (Hall and Robertson, 2001: 6). Stakeholders within the public art constituency thus found themselves literally placed and grounded within the social and community arena, and accordingly endeavoured to fulfil such purposes. While enthusiasm for such may well have been driven by a genuine sense of altruism, the instrumentalist agenda and its application to environmental and social problems also provided a means for the advocacy of public art, the promotion of professional interests and for the financial benefits of 'policy attachment', a concept identified by Gray (2002) as a process used by the cultural sector generally as a 'strategy that allows a "weak" sector with limited political clout to attract enough resources to achieve its policy objectives'.

Evaluating Public Art

However, with the instrumental use of the arts there was a price to pay, as there was also a concomitant political and pragmatic imperative to demonstrate their efficiency and effectiveness in fulfilling that role and to justify the advocacy that developed around it. While this was largely in response to the best value and economic efficiency politics of accountability of both the Conservative and Labour governments (Selwood 2002), such an imperative was also reinforced by those eager to demonstrate the validity of their advocacy. In particular, if through a strategy of 'policy attachment' the arts gained more public funding, this nonetheless had to be justified and shown to be efficiently deployed as for any other government-funded sector. As Selwood (2006) notes, with the Labour government's establishment, in 1997, of the DCMS, there was an imperative that increases in funding 'would be linked to recipient organizations meeting its expectations' as part of the DCMS's closer control over its political agenda.

On a more local level, whether funded by the public or private sector, if a commissioned work of public art is 'required' to contribute to tourism, to regenerate a particular environment, or to bring some socially fragmented community together, it might seem reasonable for such to be demonstrated as being achieved or otherwise. For example the brief for an evaluation of the 'Welcome to the North' public art programme requires evaluations of both the particular constituent projects, and an overview evaluation of the pan-regional programme. Despite the methodological complexity, such evaluation is required to demonstrate whether as a result of the programme and its projects there has been improved quality of place(s), increased positive perception of the North of England nationally and internationally, growth in the number of visitors to the North of England, and increased economic impact.

It is not surprising, therefore, that a culture of individual project and programme evaluations is accompanied by a growing body of overviews, reviews, evaluations of evaluation itself and a consideration of whether they justify, demonstrate and argue for the efficacy of instrumental interventions by art (and the arts generally) into the physical and social environment. Government agencies, consultancies, researchers and academics, and commissioning bodies have initiated such endeavours, which are variously characterized by a literature review, a summary of policy context, the identification of good and/ or bad practice, a closer look at particular case studies, a consideration of methodological and practical issues, a call for more research and sometimes the production of a tool kit for evaluation. For example, the Arts Council of England and the Scottish Arts Council commissioned reviews of the arts and social exclusion (Jermyn 2001; Goodland, Hamilton, and Taylor 2002), the DCMS itself commissioned a review of the contribution of culture to regeneration by researchers at London Metropolitan University (Evans and Shaw 2004) and also a research study by Leeds Metropolitan University on the dimensions of social inclusion through culture and sport (Long, Welch, Bramham et al. 2002).

Generally, attempts to produce hard empirical and quantifiable evidence to evaluate the success or otherwise of arts instrumental interventions, except for some notable exceptions, have been found to lack validity and reliability through flawed methodology. Reeves (2002) identifies such methodological weaknesses as including a lack of conceptual clarity and narrow conceptualizations of social and economic impact, the use of small samples, the reliance on self-reports with little corroborating evidence of impacts, over-reliance on official statistics, lack of methodological transparency, especially with regard to sampling frames and methods, simplistic and naive explanations for attributing positive outcomes to arts projects, a lack of baseline data and the need for longitudinal research and also additionality. The latter refers to the extent that arts interventions might achieve outcomes that are more efficient or economic than other kinds of intervention. Another often cited issue is that of attribution, where it cannot always be assumed that where an outcome has been demonstrated, it has been achieved by the project under evaluation rather than by another unrelated cause.

In public art this is particularly problematic where particular works are an integral part of an overall design intervention. It may be difficult to de-segregate and attribute any found outcomes to the artwork alone, or identify its particular contribution to this. Some particular assumed outcomes of public art and its economic impact are also oversimplified – tourism being an example (Allnott 2000). Apart from the requirements of surveys to clarify whether 'tourists' or 'visits' are being counted, distinctions between chance encounters and those sought out for the tourist gaze need to be differentiated.

There are other practical concerns with regard to the evaluation of instrumental interventions by cultural initiatives and the arts in general, which also apply to public art. For example, the process of evaluation has a tendency not only to be cumbersome and time-consuming, but often neither budgeted nor timetabled into projects by sponsors or commissioners. Evaluation guides for public art projects still remain time-consuming and, for example, the evaluation toolbox provided by the public art thinktank Ixia, while rationalizing and standardizing, still requires either a facilitator or some training. Conversely, attempts to systematize evaluation can also result in a tick box mentality, which can lead to a superficial involvement by project workers. Long et al. (2002: 81) from their review of the projects they examined, comment that:

> Projects are more concerned to demonstrate that they are delivering the services that they committed themselves to than to engage in the complexities of evaluation. Indeed, evaluation of outcomes capable of 'proving' the case may be beyond the resources/capacity of projects like these. They have to address competing priorities on limited resources and keep funding agents happy with a view to extending the life of the project (and in some cases their own employment).

Problematizing the Instrumental Roles of Public Art

However, apart from the pressures of delivery there is also, among the arts constituency, some resistance to the very notion that art projects can be measured or evaluated to produce evidence-based policy, a view also reflected by some researchers and academics. Among Reeves's list of reasons for the lack of robust research and evaluation there is 'lack of interest by the arts world (outside the context of funding relationships) in developing evaluative systems through which to prove its value', and 'negative perceptions of evaluation by those involved in arts projects, who often regard it as intrusive' (Reeves 2002: 34). Such resistance can reflect deeper philosophical and critical differences regarding the nature of aesthetic values and art practice, particularly where aesthetic experience is regarded as having intrinsic qualities that are not regarded as accessible to evidence-based justifications. Belfiore and Bennett assert that:

> The production of measurable evidence that might throw light on the claims made for the transformative power of the arts is particularly problematic. For a start, the idea of transformation is so complex that it is impossible to imagine how it might be reduced to a set of measurable attributes ... The aesthetic encounter, above all, is an individual subjective experience and, although it can be shown that certain elements of this are historically and socially determined, there are very real limitations to the extent to which further meaningful generalizations can be made ... Whatever economic contribution the arts might make, and however much they might promote social cohesion and community empowerment, these are not the primary characteristics of the aesthetic experience. (Belfiore and Bennett 2008: 6–7)

Moreover, there are a set of other issues that also have implications for the instrumental role of the arts, and public art in particular, which challenge the very rationale for such practice and consequently the status of its evaluation. Hall and Robertson (2001), for example, remind us of the assumed essentialism of much of the language and concepts of urban design and public art, particularly with regard to notions of space, place, public and identity (issues that have also been identified from multidisciplinary discourses such as cultural geography and the interrogation of modernist notions of the city and urban space). They question public art's claim to turn 'space into place' and 'invest the abstract with social meaning', whereby such meaning is assumed to be consensual, unique, and trans-historical.

For some, however, the very association of art with urban and environmental regeneration, and its instrumental application as a 'sticking plaster' for the problems of social exclusion and deprivation, is itself flawed. Merli (2002: 5), in her criticism of Matarasso's *Use or Ornament?*, asserts that his methodology only allows him to gather ideas and information from his respondents and not 'to evaluate real modifications in their daily conditions of existence in relation to specific social issues'. Moreover, she likens his and other policymakers' interest in participatory arts to the behaviour 'of "new missionaries" who play guitar with marginalized youth, the disabled and the unemployed, aiming at mitigating the perception which they have of their own exclusion' (Merli 2002: 7–8). With reference to the kind of outcomes his research sought to establish, she argued that:

> It does not seem that, feeling differently ... about the place where one lives will transform slums into wonderful places, nor that just helping 'transform the image of public bodies' ... will transform the reality of public bodies, nor that having 'a positive impact on how people feel' ... will change people's daily conditions of existence – it will only 'help' people to accept them. However, making deprivation more acceptable is a tool to endlessly reproduce it (Merli 2002: 8).

Malcolm Miles (1998, 2000) is also critical of public art's collusion with some of the problematic outcomes of regeneration, such as the anti-democratic nature of its gentrification and commodification. For example, he writes of 'the phoney facades of London's Gabriel Wharf' as representing 'the city as a space for the tourist gaze and mini shopping mall, both setting up relations of consumption rather than sociation', and accuses public art as a means of 'legitimizing public enclaves', and that 'the importation of art or heritage to 'humanize' developments such as Docklands contradicts the erasure of the real histories of work and dwelling of such sites' (Miles 1998: 20). Miles is also critical of the hegemonic professionalization and mystification of urban design and architectural practice in imagining and designing the city. Cities, he argues, are a product of planning and design professions, which 'serve a dominant ideology' and whose methodologies are also 'ideologically constructed around particular attitudes to society'.

However, the very notion that environmental regeneration programmes and the cultural interventions that increasingly accompany them are always necessarily divisive, exploitative and socially dysfunctional, has been questioned. In particular, it might be argued that in some cases the use of culture can have a more fundamentally positive contribution in enabling such programmes to be both rooted within the needs of places and their communities, and to be effective in addressing them. Steven Miles (2005) sees a dynamic and positive relationship between the cultural and historical roots of the Newcastle Gateshead Quays area of the North-East and its regeneration programme. He suggests that Broudehoux's assertion that 'the imposed ready-made identities of regeneration can often reduce several different visions of local culture into a single vision that reflects the aspirations of a powerful elite and the values, lifestyles, and expectations of potential investors and tourists' (Broudehoux 2004: 26) reflects a rather static image of city life and the meanings people attach to it. Conversely, the iconic redevelopment of the Newcastle Gateshead Quays, he suggests, connects with a particular history and culture that is located within the experience and identity of its local inhabitants, and which both shapes and is embodied by the particular redevelopment. He argues that to describe such a process as depoliticizing, underestimates the degree to which the meanings that people invest in such developments are 'individualized and place-specific'.

Similarly Bailey, Miles and Stark set out 'to take issue with Zukin's suggestion that culture-led regeneration actively undermines urban distinctiveness' (2004: 49). They accordingly suggest that culture-led regeneration may be most successful 'in those circumstances in which it, intentionally or unintentionally, teases out that distinctiveness'. Bailey et al. reach their conclusions, as does Miles, from a consideration of the early results from a ten-year review and evaluation programme of the Newcastle Gateshead Quays regeneration, undertaken by the Cultural Investment and Strategy Impacts Research (CISIR) at Northumbria University. From their analysis of the CISIR's early findings they suggest that:

Perhaps successful urban regeneration is not about a trickle-down effect at all, but in fact almost the reverse: it is about revitalizing cultural identities in a way which represents a counter-balance to broader processes of cultural globalization. In other words, culture-led regeneration perhaps provides a framework within which, given the right conditions, local people can re-establish ownership

of their own sense of place and space and, perhaps more importantly, of their
own sense of history. (Bailey et al. 2004: 49)

Significantly, Bailey et al. regard the contribution of the *Angel of the North* as
the key that allowed the potential of the Quays to be to be unlocked, and
accordingly public art is an integral element in their regeneration.

The work of the CSIR addresses some of the failure of evaluation to take
account of longitudinal impacts, and provides an opportunity for a comprehensive investigation into the cultural, environmental and social interventions of a
major regeneration programme involving public art. Consequently, it provides
an opportunity to addresses some of the weaknesses and methodological flaws
of evaluation as previously highlighted. While reviews and meta-analysis of the
evaluation of instrumental art interventions have clearly highlighted such weaknesses, there continues to be refinements and developments that seek to improve
the effectiveness and validity of evaluation through the development of more
appropriate qualitative methodologies, the use of Scientific Realism (Jackson
2007) and logic models. Holden (2004), for example, with reference to what he
has termed 'Cultural Value' (a concept he develops in part as an attempt to
avoid the assumptive language of essentialist notions of art), claims that:

> The type of measurement that may be used in the calculus of Cultural Value will
> display wider and more holistic characteristics than current measurement
> systems. They will tend to include a greater emphasis on qualitative measures
> and pay more attention to public perceptions. They will also tend to be more
> open-ended and future-focused rather than being engaged in tracking outcomes
> against predetermined expectations.

Equally, Merli (2002) also suggests modifications in evaluation, such as less
reliance on questionnaires and more on the use of in-depth interview, which
she regards as more appropriate for assessing the impact of participatory art
programmes on social deprivation in that they enable the 'interviewer to
understand and not simply measure' (2002: 13). Merli's critique explicitly
highlights the relevance and importance of theory in contextualizing the sociological nature of deprivation, its impact and consequences and the role of the
arts and their evaluation. The lack of theoretical grounding in such is regarded
by Merli as a major problem and she acknowledges the importance of a
theoretical underpinning from sociology and other disciplines, such as theories
of creativity and art perception and empirical studies in cognitive psychology
on the effect of the arts on behaviour.

While such underpinnings are rare, Lister (2007) draws upon the ethnographic theories and research of Prus and Simmel to identify, produce and

monitor processes and mechanisms that both govern and indicate stages of both social exclusion and social engagement. Such an approach acknowledges the importance of societal, cognitive and phenomenological responses to both the work and processes of art and its interventions into the social and physical environment, and accords with an increasing recognition of the importance of interdisciplinary approaches to their critique and evaluation. Along with a recognition of the dynamics and complexities of concepts such as 'space', 'place' and 'public', this takes us back to a consideration of reception of, and responses to, public art and also environmental design in general. This may be understood in respect to the observation by environmental psychologists Proshansky, Fabian and Kaminoff (1983), who argue that the processes by which a person defines him/ herself in a society are not restricted to making distinctions between oneself and significant others, but also include objects and things, and the spaces and places in which they are found.

Conclusion

Just as the policy and professional grounds of urban regeneration have widened, so art in the public realm has become a more diverse discipline. Regeneration involves the interlocking of a number of concerns, which may include pressure to provide an urban scenario that attracts inward investment, an ambition to lay down 'attitudinal markers' that communicate place identity, and to engage citizens in a collective re-imagination of their locality. Public art has increasingly become absorbed into a government instrumentalist agenda that sees such aspects of the creative industries as necessary to achieving regeneration aims. It has become part of wider remit of 'design-led regeneration' alongside other creative practices in the built environment. As an instrumentalist process, contributing to wider environmental and social regeneration aims, public art has become increasingly subject to audit and measurement, while the multi-layered demands of regeneration and the diversity of art practices it involves make this process potentially problematic. Concurrently, the practices of public art have also become more complex, moving beyond the simple 'dressing' of public space to a wider range of engagements and uses of media, which might conform to or challenge such agendas. At the heart of these developments, it seems, is the question of ownership over creativity and, indeed, its evaluation.

Public art and the problems of its evaluation highlight the complexity of space and place, its public perception and the sociocultural processes involved in public reception and ownership. Art and design, and their interventions into the environment and their evaluation (including critical discourse of their aesthetic value), need to be framed and contextualized within an understanding of the wider cultural, social and psychological processes that characterize and determine the interrelationships of practice, public response and ownership. Ultimately, and in common with many chapters in this book, this ownership, however, may be distributed across actors and 'actants', across structures and networks of people and things. It is the alignment and orchestration of these and, indeed, the struggle to wrest power over this process, where the tensions between policy and its management are revealed.

References

Allnutt, D. (2004), 'Review of Tourism Statistics', *National Statistics Quality Review Series, Report No. 33*, London: Department of Culture, Media and Sport.

Arts Council of England (1999), *Addressing Social Exclusion: A Framework for Action*, London: Arts Council of England.

Arts Council of Great Britain (1974), *Art into Landscape*, London: Arts Council of Great Britain.

Arts Council of Great Britain (1977), *Art into Landscape*, London: Arts Council of Great Britain.

Bailey, C., Miles, S. and Stark P. (2004), 'Culture-Led Urban Regeneration and the Revitalization of Identities in Newcastle, Gateshead and the North-East of England', *International Journal of Cultural Policy*, 10(1): 47–65.

Belfiore, E. (2006), 'The Social Impacts of the Arts – Myth or Reality', in Mirza, M. (2006) (ed.), *Culture Vultures: Is UK Arts Policy Damaging the Arts?*, London: Policy Exchange. Available at www.policyexchange.org.uk/Publications.aspx?id=164 [last accessed October 2008].

Belfiore, E. and Bennett O. (2008), *The Social Impact of the Arts: An Intellectual History*, Basingstoke: Palgrave Macmillan.

Bell, D., O'Connor, J., Taylor, C. and Gonzalez, S. (2007), 'Yorkshire Cities and Culture. A Review of Current Thinking' (report commissioned by the Yorkshire Cultural Observatory and the Yorkshire and Humber Key Cities group), Leeds: University of Leeds.

Brecknock, R. (2002), 'This Place – This Time – This Culture' (report), Brecknock Consulting, Darwin. Available at: http://www.brecknockconsulting.com.au/07_downloads/AILA-Darwin-Brecknock.PDF [last accessed August 2008].

Broudehoux, A. (2004), *The Making and Selling of Post-Mao Beijing*, London: Routledge.

Casey, B., Dunlop R. and Selwood, S. (1996), *Culture as Commodity? The Economics of the Arts and Built Heritage in the UK*, London: Policy Studies Institute.

Dales, J. (2008), 'The Best Schemes Are Not Necessarily the Biggest or the Most Beautiful', *Resource for Urban Design Information*. Available at RUDI, http://www.rudi.net/node/19641 [last accessed September 2008].

DCMS (2001), *Creative Industries Mapping Document 2001* (2nd ed.), London: Department of Culture, Media and Sport.

Evans, G. and Shaw, P. (2004), *The Contribution of Culture to Regeneration in the UK: A Review Of Evidence*, London: DCMS.

Galloway, S. (1995), *Changing Lives: The Social Impact of the Arts*, Edinburgh: Scottish Arts Council.

Goodland, R, Hamilton, C. and Taylor P. D. (2002), 'Not Just a Treat: Arts and Social Inclusion' (report to the Scottish Arts Council, Scottish Centre for Cultural Policy Research and Department of Urban Studies), Glasgow: University of Glasgow.

Gray, C. (2002), 'Local Government and the Arts', *Local Government Studies*, 28(1): 77–90.

Hall, T. and Robertson, I. (2001), 'Public Art and Urban Regeneration: Advocacy, Claims and Critical Debates', *Landscape Research*, 26(1): 5–26.

Heartfield, J. (2005), 'The Creativity Gap', *Blueprint Broadside*, May. Available at http://www.design4design.com/broadsides/creative.pdf [last accessed July 2008].

Holden, J. (2004), *Capturing Cultural Value: How Culture Has Become a Tool of Government Policy*, London: Demos.

Hughes, R. (1990), *Nothing if Not Critical: Selected Essays on Art and Artists*, London: Collins-Harvill.

Jackson, A. (2007), *Evaluation of Public Art: A Literature Review and Proposed Methodology* (evaluation report for Yorkshire Culture), Bath: Annabel Jackson Associates.

Jermyn, H. (2001), *The Arts and Social Exclusion: A Review Prepared for the Arts Council of England*, London: The Arts Council of England.

Landry, C., Bianchini, F., Maguire, M., and Worpole, K. (1993), *The Social Impact of the Arts: A Discussion Document*, Stroud: Comedia.

Landry, C., Green, L., Matarasso, F. and Bianchini, F. (1996), *The Art of Regeneration: Urban Renewal Through Cultural Activity*, Stroud: Comedia.

Lister, R. (2007), 'The Arts of Survival: Defining the Participatory Arts as a Tool of Social Change', unpublished thesis in part requirement of the award of M.Phil., University of Lincoln.

Long, J., Welch, M., Bramham, P., Butterfield, J., Hylton, K. and Lloyd, E. (2002), 'Count Me In: The Dimensions of Social Inclusion through Culture and Sport' (report for the Department for Culture, Media and Sport), Leeds: Centre for Leisure and Sport Research, Leeds Metropolitan University. Available at http://www.leedsmet.ac.uk/carnegie/countmein.pdf [last accessed November 2008].

Matarasso, F. (1997), *Use or Ornament? The Social Impact of Participation in the Arts*, Stroud: Comedia.

Merli, P. (2002), 'Evaluating the Social Impact of Participation in Arts Activities. A Critical Review of François Matarasso's *Use or Ornament?*', *International Journal of Cultural Policy*, 8(1). Available at http://www.culturaldemocracy.net/paperview.php/1 [last accessed September 2008].

Miles, M. (1998), 'Strategies for the Convivial City: A New Agenda for Education for the Built Environment', *Journal of Art and Design Education*, 17(1): 17–25.

Miles, M. (2000), 'After the Public Realm: Spaces of Representation, Transition and Plurality', *Journal of Art and Design Education*, 19(3): 253–61.

Miles, S. (2005), '"Our Tyne": Iconic Regeneration and the Revitalization of Identity in Newcastle Gateshead', *Urban Studies*, 42(5/6): 913–26.

Minton, A. (2008), 'The Project Initiative', in *Artists and Places: Engaging Creative Minds in Regeneration*, London: CABE (Commission for Architecture and the Built Environment).

Myerscough, J. (1988), *The Economic Importance of the Arts in Great Britain*, London: Policy Studies Institute.

Newton, C. (2001), 'Putting Lipstick on the Gorilla?' *Architecture Australia*, May/June. Available at: http://www.architectureaustralia.com/aa/aaissue.php?article=16&issueid=200105 &typeon=3 [last accessed September 2008].

O'Brien, J. and Feist, A. (1995), *Employment in the Arts and Cultural Industries: An Analysis of the 1991 Census, ACE Research Report No. 2*, London: Arts Council of England.

Petherbridge, D. (1987), *Art for Architecture: A Handbook of Commissioning*, London: Department of Environment.

Plagens, P. (1986), 'The New Patronage and the New Public Art', *Art Criticism*, 5(1): 19–33.

Pratt, A. C. (1997), *The Cultural Industries Sector: Its Definition and Character from Secondary Sources on Employment and Trade, Britain 1984–91*, London: London School of Economics, cited by Reeves (2002).

Proshansky, H., Fabian, A. and Kaminoff, R. (1983), 'Place-Identity: Physical World Socialization of the Self', *Journal of Environmental Psychology*, 3(1): 57–83.

Reeves, M. (2002), *Measuring the Economic and Social Impact of the Arts: A Review*, London: Arts Council England.

Roberts, G., Ball, S., Entwistle, T., Sandle, D. and Strange, I. (2003), *A Review of Public Art in Wales 1998–2003*, Cardiff and Leeds: RKL/The Arts Council of Wales.

Roberts, M., Marsh, C. and Salter, M. (1993), *Public Art in Private Places: Commercial Benefits and Public Policy*, London: University of Westminster Press.

Selwood, S. (2002), 'The Politics of Data Collection: Gathering, Analysing and Using Data About the Subsidised Cultural Sector in England', *Cultural Trends*, 12(47): 15–54.

Selwood, S. (2006), 'Unreliable Evidence. The Rhetorics of Data Collection in the Cultural Sector', in Mirza, M. (ed.), *Culture Vultures: Is UK Arts Policy Damaging the Arts?*, London: Policy Exchange. Available at www.policyexchange.org.uk/Publications.aspx?id=164 [last accessed October 2008].

Sharp, J., Pollock, V. and Paddison, R. (2005), 'Just Art for a Just City: Public Art and Social Inclusion in Urban Regeneration', *Urban Studies*, 42(5/6): 1001–23.

CHAPTER 5

Design Client, Patron and Showcase: The Museum and the Creative Industries

Jane Pavitt

The development of debates concerning creativity and the social value of museums has followed a clear trajectory over the last ten years, since the Labour government's first defining statements on the 'creative industries' in Britain. The idea of the creative industries, in the late 1990s, was part of an attempt to create a strong identity for a post-industrial Britain, which had seen the decline of its manufacturing base to almost the point of non-existence, but also the rapid rise of service industries and creative professions specializing in what John Urry and Scott Lash have termed 'design-intensive processes' such as the fashion and style industries (Lash and Urry 1994: 123). Furthermore, a broadening American debate (marked by Richard Florida's influential book, *The Rise of the Creative Class*) has positioned creativity as an economic and social force (Florida 2002).

The subject of creativity has therefore also been at the top of the policy-making agenda in museums for some years now. In many ways, it has become the catch-all theme that unites the diversity of programmes and intentions offered by the museums and galleries sector. Creativity stresses the 'active' nature of museum-going – of not only looking, but doing. It has been used in shifting the idea of the museum away from the rather static conception of a repository of objects towards a more dynamic perception of an engaging and social space. The concept of creativity connects the functions of the museum to the wider world – based on the widely held idea that the cultivation of creativity can have widespread individual, social and economic benefits.

For example, a report commissioned by the UK National Museum Directors' Conference in 2004, entitled 'Museum and Galleries: Creative Engagement', examined creativity across the museum sector, exploring the ways in which museums and galleries 'create social capital [by] educating and empowering individuals and groups alike, creating networks and stimulating dialogue' (NMDC 2004: 2). The report goes on to argue that museums and galleries can contribute to social cohesion and to the regeneration of run-down areas, can work to counter the negative effects of disenfranchisement amongst some social groups, and can generally educate, inform and inspire people of all ages and diversities. In this context, 'creativity' is used to define means by which institutions have found imaginative ways to talk to audiences, work with the commercial and corporate sectors, and present their collections.

In 1998, the Department for Culture, Media and Sport (DCMS) published the first 'Creative Industries Mapping Document', the results of a study undertaken by the Creative Industries Task Force, a policy group within the DCMS. This hugely influential document detailed the contribution of the creative sector to Britain's economy. The taskforce estimated that the creative industries – an amorphous pool of talent drawn from the businesses of the arts, architecture, design, fashion, film, television and music, publishing and digital media – generated over £60 billion annually, employed over one million people and was growing exponentially.

The Creative Industries Task Force was one of New Labour's flagship initiatives in the arts after their first election victory of 1997. The term 'creative industries', which now underpins a broad sector of cultural policy and practice, was effectively launched by this report. The New Labour view of creative Britain was set forth amidst the short-lived attempts to re-brand the nation with the image of 'Cool Britannia'. The think-tank Demos (an independent organization which has done considerable work on the creative industries, and was in the late 1990s closely associated with the New Labour project) proposed a realignment of Britain's national identity in tune with this more modern and youthful attitude (Leonard 1997; Woodham 2000). Although the Cool Britannia moment of post-election fervour was short-lived (and one which many creative artists and politicians alike distanced themselves from quickly), the idea of 'creativity' has continued to be a basis for DCMS strategy in the arts ever since. Chris Smith, the Secretary of State for Culture, Media and Sport during New Labour's first term, set out a productive and inclusive view of culture in his 1998 book, *Creative Britain*, a celebratory account of Britain's potential for a successful creative economy supported by an arts-engaged government policy, written in more optimistic times than today (Smith 1998).

The late 1990s saw a number of design initiatives that reflected policy interest in the design sector. The first of these was the 1997 launch of the Millennium Products initiative, which awarded the Millennium Products marque to over 1,000 products displaying creativity and ingenuity (in design, engineering, business and science). Exhibitions featuring the products subsequently toured Singapore, Brunei, China, South Africa, Korea and Australia.

In 1998, an exhibition in London entitled 'Powerhouse:UK' was organized by the then Department of Trade and Industry (DTI) as a showcase for British design talent (and arranged to coincide with a summit devoted to Asian–European business and governmental cooperation). The exhibition was housed in a temporary inflatable silver structure designed by Nigel Coates, erected on Horse Guards Parade in London. Its contents were organized around categories of design for communication, networking, lifestyle and learning, and foregrounded an inventive and sometimes quirky British design 'character' (Catterall 1998). These initiatives were generally positively received, although overshadowed by the growing controversy surrounding the planning and organization of the 'Millennium Experience' exhibition in the Millennium Dome, Greenwich, which was frequently cited as a hollow and badly managed version of the Labour vision of creative Britain (Sinclair 1999; Bayley 1998). These events marked the start of a relationship between public policy and the creative industries, which has since continued in the museums and galleries sector.

The agenda for creative industries has had a decisive impact upon museums in Britain. First of all, there are more institutions that stress their links to the design sector than ten years ago. In Glasgow, for example, the Lighthouse (described as 'Scotland's centre for architecture, design and the city') promotes itself as a platform for the promotion of the Scottish government's policy on architecture. It also runs a programme devoted to 'creative entrepreneurship', a network for the creative industries. Museums and galleries have also become a more significant employer for the design sector. The Science Museum, for instance, has a reputation – established over a decade or more – for engaging designers such as Ben Kelly, Thomas Heatherwick and Graphic Thought Facility to present science subjects in inventive ways, under Head of Design, Tim Molloy. Put simply, museums are increasingly finding ways to claim themselves as 'client, patron and showcase' for design.

Here is how Britain's two leading museums devoted to design, the Design Museum and the Victoria & Albert Museum (V&A) signal their commitment to both the creative industries and to public creativity in their mission statements. The Design Museum (established with private funds, but the recipient of DCMS funding since 2000) summarizes its aim as 'to raise public awareness and understanding of design in every area of activity and by stimulating public debate' (Design Museum/DCMS Funding Agreement 2005–6 to 2007–8). The V&A's mission statement reads thus: 'As the world's leading museum of art and design, the V&A enriches people's lives by promoting the practice of design and increasing knowledge, understanding and enjoyment of the designed world' (V&A 2007). According to the funding agreements between museums and DCMS, museums are required to demonstrate, through evidence and evaluation, how these ambitions are achieved. This must also be evaluated in line with DCMS strategic priorities for museums and galleries (such as increased access, greater benefit to the economy and quality of experience), and measured against the key targets and performance indicators set forth in the funding agreement.

Taking the V&A as a central case study, this chapter examines how 'design' and 'creativity' have been foregrounded in the last decade, as demonstration of the links between a policy agenda and museum practice. My own involvement in this sphere of activity, since the late 1990s, has been as a research fellow and curator of several contemporary and late twentieth-century design exhibitions. The ground has shifted considerably in this time. When I arrived at the V&A in 1997, the museum was planning to build a dedicated contemporary design wing, called the Spiral and designed by Daniel Libeskind (for an account of the project's origins, see Benton 1997a and 1997b). Although the building itself was eventually cancelled, the project was the initial focus for the development of a strategy for the display, collection and interpretation of contemporary practice in the visual arts and design. The museum did not wait, however, for the provision of a new building, but implemented a new programme so that the idea of 'the contemporary' was gradually embedded into the museum. In 1999, a new department was set up to deliver a broad-ranging programme of contemporary visual arts. This Contemporary Team is now responsible for programming a dedicated contemporary exhibition space as well as events, talks, performances and web-based activities, which it does in collaboration with curators from other departments (such as myself), external curators and partner institutions. The V&A has also made the acquisition of contemporary design for its collections a priority. To quote the recently revised Collecting Plan for the museum: 'Contemporary collecting should reflect what is new, what is influential, what is innovative or experimental, and what is representative of contemporary social and artistic trends. Every artefact acquired will be the result of a creative process and should be culturally significant' (V&A 2004: 60–61). Finally, another shift is the placing of 'creativity' and the creative industries at the heart of the museum's educational and audience initiatives, as defined by the comprehensive learning strategy put in place by the V&A's Learning and Interpretation department. In 2008, the museum opened its newly designed Sackler Centre for Arts Education. The tag-line for Sackler Centre events, carried on every piece of its marketing, is 'Look, Think, Create'.

Like any cultural or corporate organization, the V&A sets out its strategic priorities in an annual report or review. These priorities can be read not only in the text and statistical data the report is required to contain, but in the design of the publication itself – recent editions have highlighted activities involving the creative industries. The cover for the 2005–6 Review is a glossy photograph showing the opening party for the Contemporary Programme exhibition, 'Anna Piaggi: Fashionology' (2005), showing Piaggi herself (the creative force behind *Vogue Italia*) dressed in Union Flag regalia and caught in the glare of flashbulbs. The report's foreword, titled 'Creative Industries and the V&A', declared 'The V&A is the hunting ground for Britain's design talent'. The Review for 2006–7 (which the artist Lucinda Rogers was commissioned to illustrate) opens with a quotation from the 2006 Report released by a consortium of cultural sector organizations: 'In the future, Britain's economic prosperity and well-being will not depend on industrial prowess, natural resources or cheap labour but on developing, attracting, retaining and mobilizing creativity' (NMDC 2006).

Creativity has arguably been at the heart of the V&A's ethos since its inception over 150 years ago. Established in 1852 from funds provided by the Great Exhibition of 1851, the South Kensington Museum (as it was then known) was founded with a mission to educate artists, artisans and the public alike, in matters of materials, skills, taste and decoration (Burton, 1999; Baker and Richardson, 1997; Taylor, 1999). The museum's founders saw its role as educational and social, serving a primary audience of designers and craftspeople as well as a broader public (much was made of how the museum would offer an alternative social space to the bar room or gin palace). At the same time, the establishment of a national system of design education, in which the South Kensington Museum played an important part, was meant as a vital commercial advantage to Britain's manufacturing industries. These origins are often cited when the museum's contribution to the contemporary creative economy is under discussion. A Demos report by John Holden, commissioned by the museum, makes this link:

> The V&A was conceived as, and continues to be, an engine room for the creative industries, but how does that conception translate into reality? What, one might ask, can a museum do that is relevant to a twenty-first-century economy? As we shall see, it can help designers by providing inspiration, learning, and access to technical expertise, and by giving them a showcase; it can create communities and networks of students, designers and manufacturers; and it can influence public taste, thereby affecting patterns of consumption and production. (Holden 2007a: 7)

Although this recent reassertion of the museum's role in encouraging contemporary creative practice is couched in a rather different language to that of the nineteenth century, it echoes the social and commercial arguments put forward at its inception. The V&A has adapted to reflect the changing economic and cultural significance of the creative industries, promoting itself as an institution central to the creation of a successful 'creative' Britain. In doing so, it has effectively returned full circle to the intentions of its founders, whilst modifying the museum's mission from the demands of an industrial age to those of a post-industrial age.

Spaces and Audiences

> In thinking about the relationship between culture and the creative industries – which is a relationship between structures, institutions and fields of policy as much as anything else – we need to hold on to the realization that creativity is generated by people. (Holden 2007b: 30)

An institutional strategy for 'being creative' may seem something of a misnomer. Creative practices and networks are often characterized by a culture of informality rather than legislation, as Holden (quoted above) pointed out in another Demos report, 'Publicly Funded Culture and the Creative Industries', the creative sector is 'micro, fluid, disaggregated – in many senses disorganized' (Holden 2007b: 2). Attempts to audit, qualify or quantify creativity can appear counter-intuitive. However, as the issue of creativity is often central to the funding agreements between the DCMS and museums, a significant proportion of institutional policy-making is devoted to the weighing up of outputs and benefits in relation to the creative sectors. This is certainly true of the V&A. Of its four current strategic objectives, three relate to broadening access, the worldwide reputation of the museum and its organizational efficiency. The other is 'To promote, support and develop creativity in individuals and in the economy' (V&A 2007).

The V&A can claim a wide audience in terms of the creative industries, and accordingly they are one of six key audience groupings employed by the museum. This model of visitor segmentation was put in place in 2004, but had been in development and under wide discussion for some time. In 2002, the V&A's Director of Learning and Interpretation, David Anderson, compiled the museum's 'Strategy for Learning', entitled 'Creative Networks: Knowledge and Inspiration'. Reflecting agendas for inclusivity and diversity in the museum, Anderson outlined a strategy that was audience-centred and committed to the idea of learning in all aspects of its programme. The strategy reasserted the idea that the V&A is a creative hub, helping 'everyone – adults, students, children – to enjoy and develop their own creativity'. In line with public policy, the V&A could contribute to the development of a successful, knowledge-based, creative economy by serving 'designers and other practitioners' as well as 'innovators such as business people, across the spectrum of the economy' (Anderson 2006: Section 3.3). A significant proportion of its programme is therefore tailored to the interests of this sector.

The emphasis on active and participatory engagement with creative practice has been made more possible by the provision of dedicated spaces in the new Sackler Centre. Designed by the architecture and design studio Softroom (within a nineteenth-century wing of the museum), the Centre includes workshops for artists/ designers in residence, an art studio and a digital media lab, as well as space for the display of work by artists and users of the Centre. The various programmes place emphasis on the Centre as a breeding ground for creativity. For example, a programme of workshops for teenagers entitled 'Create!' was intended to forge educational and career pathways in the creative industries. Another initiative, the residency programme, offers artists, designers, makers, writers and musicians a six-month residency in one of two dedicated studios. During the course of their residency, they offer open studio sessions and work with curators, educators and the public to develop new work and communicate their ideas. The first residencies of 2008 were for media artist Jo Lawrence, artist-jeweller Dorothy Hogg and product designer Lao Jianhua from China (as part of the HSBC cultural exchange programme). Overall, selective artists and designers are encouraged to take an active (even performative) role in the museum's educational programme. Finally, another major move to establish links between the education sector for the creative industries and the museum has been the establishment of the Centre for Excellence in Teaching and Learning through Design (CETLD) – a joint initiative between the V&A, University of Brighton, Royal College of Art and Royal Institute of British Architects. This research centre, funded by the Higher Education Funding Council, aims to embed the use of museum collections and archives into the learning experiences of design students, and develop innovative ways of teaching and learning across the partner institutions. The CETLD creates a wider platform for practice-based design learning in the museum.

Also, from a general emphasis on the social importance of creativity, the V&A aims to engage the creative industries in matters of professional debate. To give just one example, the first in a series of V&A think-tanks organized in 2008 debated 'the future designer' (organized in collaboration with the Royal College of Art's InnovationRCA programme). Speakers were asked to address the changing nature of the designer's professional, social and creative role – a discussion which resulted in such proposals as Daniel Charny's definition of the designer as an 'accelerator', Jeremy Myerson on the collaborative role of the designer, and Kevin McCullagh's counter-argument for the designer as 'synthesizer' of ideas (V&A 2008). Events such as the think-tanks are one means of building a professional audience (the debates are also disseminated online via the V&A's websites, for the benefit of students and other interested parties). They also provide a consultative role in gauging the expectations that creative professionals have of the museum (other think-tank subjects include 'the future museum' and 'the future object').

However, it is clear that the unified category of 'creative industries', whilst it has widespread use in government policy language, breaks down into a much more fragmented picture of needs and expectations when examined more closely. Although the Creative Industries Sector forms one of six key audience categories for the museum, the provision of a museum programme tailored to this constituency tends to also address smaller groupings or more specialist interests (these might be material categories, for example – such as textiles and ceramics). Recent research undertaken by the museum's Learning and Interpretation department supports the view that, within the Creative Industries Sector, whilst creative professionals might identify themselves with individual disciplines, they do so within a wide spectrum of activity which constitutes a shared community (Fritsch 2008). The scope of this spectrum, and the variations found within it, has enormous implications for the museum in terms of profiling its visitors and programming accordingly. Commonalities of experience, for example, included an interest in ideas and process, a collaborative outlook and a commitment to innovation. These are persistent themes given prominence by successive contemporary exhibitions and the site-specific commissions which have become a feature of the V&A's programme in recent years.

In the last few years, the V&A has therefore allocated a greater physical space to contemporary creative practice in the museum (a new gallery, learning spaces and a larger number of objects in collections). But how does it evaluate the impact this greater commitment has on government objectives for enhancing creativity and bolstering the creative economy? And how does it feed these objectives through to the exhibition and events programme?

Creative Collaborations

The most significant platform for engagement with the Creative Industries Sector is the exhibitions and events programme managed by the V&A's Contemporary Team, which tends to favour both cutting-edge practice and experimental methods of curation. The Contemporary Team was established to change public perception and expectations of the museum by offering a broad-ranging contemporary visual culture programme, which would attract new audiences, particularly a younger one. Without a dedicated gallery space at first, the Team devised various innovative curatorial strategies. One of these is 'Fashion in Motion' – a regular showcase for a selected designer to stage a 'catwalk show' in gallery spaces, with clothes worn by models. The idea was to take fashion out of the display case, off the mannequin, and present it on real bodies. Participating designers have included Issey Miyake, Alexander McQueen and Stella McCartney. Other inventive strategies for gallery interventions or displays have stressed the sensory and experiential nature of creative practice – such as 'Shhh … Sounds in Spaces' (2004). This was an auditory 'exhibition' (designed as a trail around the museum), in which commissioned artists including David Byrne and Gillian Wearing created soundscapes for different museum spaces (not only galleries, but corridors and cloakrooms). The installations could be 'toured' using MP3 players. As well as sound, the haptic qualities of design were explored in an exhibition entitled 'Touch Me – Design and Sensation' (2005).

Design curation has moved on from the largely celebratory accounts of company design policy (such as Sony and Ford – both the subject of design exhibitions in the V&A's Boilerhouse in the 1980s). Design curators are nowadays more likely to employ spectacular or emotive themes to unite sometimes disparate selections of objects. The Contemporary programme focuses predominantly but not exclusively on innovative works with a high creative content (the museum stresses this emphasis by using the term 'creative design') and often highlights the conceptual in design. Commercial imperatives for design are not entirely ignored – and were addressed in an exhibition I curated (with V&A colleague Gareth Williams) in 2000, entitled 'Brand.New' (which looked at the impact of branding on globalized consumer culture).

Another innovative strategy for exhibition curation was developed by Gareth Williams for his 2003 V&A exhibition, 'Milan in a Van', which highlighted the enormous commercial importance and creative influence of the Milan Annual Design Fair, revealing some of the mechanisms of the design industry (the selection of up and coming designers by manufacturers, for example) to a wider audience. Finally, there has been an increase in the commissioning of new work and site-specific installations by designers. Design commissions have become a regular feature of the V&A's programme, such as the installation entitled *Forever* – a large video wall of animations which respond to a changing soundtrack – by the multidisciplinary design group Universal Everything, shown in 2008. This followed another major garden commission, *Volume* (2006–7), an interactive installation of sound and light, responsive to human movement, designed by design collective UVA (United Visual Artists) in conjunction with Robert Del Naja of Massive Attack. Both works represent the growing presence of multimedia art and design in the museum, as well as the museum's increasing role as the 'client' for commissioned design.

Figure 5.1 'Milan in a Van' exhibition, Contemporary Space, Victoria & Albert Museum, London, 2002. © V&A Images.

Figure 5.2 'Forever' Light sculpture by Universal Everything, Madejski Garden, Victoria & Albert Museum, London, 2008. © V&A Images.

This kind of curatorial practice in contemporary design has become main-stream in museums in recent years. There are some key influential figures in this field: Paola Antonelli, curator in the department of design and architecture at the Museum of Modern Art in New York, has probably been the most important design curator in the last decade, from her landmark exhibition 'Mutant Materials in Contemporary Design' (1995) to the recent 'Design and the Elastic Mind' (2008). In Britain, the independent design curator Claire Catterall has worked for over ten years curating inventive design exhibitions for institutions including the V&A. Her exhibition, 'Stealing Beauty: British Design Now', at the ICA in 1999 brought many experimental designers to the fore (united by their interest in ready-made and everyday materials and objects). Her consultancy, Scarlet Projects, co-hosts the annual V&A 'Village Fête', a tongue-in-cheek, one-day festival of design which invites young designers to contribute their personal take on the village fête stall (selling goods or offering games and competitions). Another important cultural organization devoted to the promotion of British design is the British Council, which arranges international touring exhibitions of work by new designers, often highlighting quirky creative themes, prototype objects and the idea of the designer as the 'industry of one' – engaged in small-batch production for which he or she maintains overall control. In highlighting a kind of design practice with a high intellectual as well as creative content, these kinds of exhibitions have contributed to a more widely recognized idea of the 'creative' designer, privileging the processes of making and thinking. Such exhibitions have tended to showcase designers like Tord Boontje, Thomas Heatherwick and Paul Cocksedge (to name a few), whose work emphasizes interdisciplinarity and an interest in both innovative technologies and craft techniques. Although their work can have significant commercial impact (Boontje has designed products for Habitat), it is often the heightened aesthetic, technical or critical aspects of design that are foregrounded in exhibitions.

Nevertheless, museums also must have a productive commercial relationship with designers, as client as well as showcase. The V&A manages a broad portfolio of design projects, from the design of temporary exhibitions to the redevelopment of new gallery spaces. The selection of designers is usually the result of competitive tender, managed by the museum's Projects, Design and Estates Division (the in-house design team are also responsible for a proportion of this work, including exhibition and display design, graphics and marketing). Architecture and design consultancies used by the museum range from large practices such as Eva Jiricna Architects Ltd. and Casson Mann Design to individuals and small practices such as Gitta Gschwendtner or Graphic Thought Facility. Added to that, the V&A commercial wing, V&A Enterprises, employs a wide range of designers to produce goods from books to shop merchandise (recent shop commissions have included product designers Tatty Devine, graphic designer Daisy de Villeneuve and fashion designer Jonathan Saunders).

This broad range of collaborative activity between museum and the design sector shows how embedded the idea of the museum's role in the creative economy has become. Commercial, curatorial and educational activity alike is put forward as evidence of the V&A's strategic objectives towards the creative industries. The most significant form of evidential data is contained within the End of Year Report to DCMS, which matches the Key Performance Indicators (KPIs) of the DCMS Funding Agreement to museum outputs (exhibitions, displays, acquisitions, conferences and publications – as well as commercial outputs). For example, in order to show the scope of activities which promoted, supported and developed the Creative Industries Sector in 2007–8 (KPI 41), the V&A supplied evidence of engagement which ranged from the number of visits by creative industries professionals to the museum (388,000 or 17 per cent – with roughly the same number again of students) to image content and consultation supplied to TV and web projects. The museum worked with over 400 creative industries practitioners during that year – on creative and commercial collaborations that ranged from shop commissions for new products to exhibition design (some of which is detailed above) (Frampton 2007). The assessment of this every year is a laborious process, which also involves the gathering of anecdotal evidence of how designers have used the museum as inspiration or a source of information. It would seem that there is considerable overlap between the museum's roles of design showcase, patron and client.

As we have already seen, research undertaken by the museum's Learning and Interpretation department takes on a more complex view of the structure of and relationships *within* the Creative Industries Sector and the museum's relationship to this. Juliette Fritsch, Head of Gallery Interpretation in the V&A, has been engaged in ethnographic research that revisits the government-sanctioned definition of the creative industries, and questions its fit with current museum practice (Fritsch 2008). She points to the distinctions between how creative professionals define themselves, and the government's definitions of practice in the sector, preferring to see the creative industries as a 'community of practice' (based on shared and tacit knowledge, and around informal networks). In casting itself as a 'hub' of creativity, the Victoria & Albert Museum has adopted an open, flexible and cross-disciplinary notion of design, incorporating it both as object and process.

Conclusion

In showing how the V&A has responded to government policy in the creative sector in the last decade, I have also indicated how a complex programme of curatorial and commercial activity has developed within the museum. This is not merely a statement of how policy objectives overlap with museum interests, but shows the evolution of an alternative identity for the museum. The V&A has taken some pragmatic commercial decisions about its global brand in recent years, shifting it gradually towards something with a strong contemporary aspect. The V&A sees itself as *the* institution for and about the creative industries, and therefore well placed to put forward an increased understanding of how the creative economy operates in Britain. At the same time, the category of 'creative industries', which is frequently employed in government policy language, in fact presents a fragmented, heterogeneous profile with varying needs and expectations (as other essays in this book have shown). By following this thinking, the museum (with a foot in both camps) can offer up an adjusted view of design practice, which balances government 'creative industries' definitions with the concerns and experiences of those working in the sector today. The V&A has always been a difficult institution to categorize (design? art? decorative arts?) – but perhaps this has left it well placed to deal with the somewhat messy and open-ended proposition of defining creativity.

References

Anderson, D. (2006), 'Creative Networks: Knowledge and Inspiration, The V&A Museum's Strategy for Learning', V&A internal document, 18 June 2006.

Baker, M. and Richardson, B. (1997), *A Grand Design: The Art of the Victoria & Albert Museum*, exhibition catalogue, London: V&A Publications and Baltimore Museum of Art.

Bayley, S. (1998), *Labour Camp: The Failure of Style Over Substance*, London: Batsford.

Benton, C. (1997a), '"An Insult to Everything the Museum Stands for" or "Ariadne's thread" to "Knowledge" and "Inspiration"? Daniel Libeskind's Extension for the V&A and its Context, Part I', *Journal of Design History* 10(1): 71–89.

Benton, C. (1997b), 'Daniel Libeskind's Project for the V&A: Design and Context, Part II', *Journal of Design History* 10(3): 309–28.

Burton, A. (1999), *Vision and Accident: The Story of the Victoria & Albert Museum*, London: V&A Publications.

Catterall, C. (ed.) (1998), *Powerhouse:UK*, exhibition catalogue, London: Aspern Publishing in association with the Department of Trade and Industry.

Dept. of Culture, Media and Sport (DCMS) (2005), 'Design Museum Funding Agreement 2005–06 to 2007–08' (report). Available at http://www.culture.gov.uk/images/publications/fa_designmuseum.pdf [last accessed 10 January 2009].

Florida, R. (2002), *The Rise of the Creative Class – and How It's Transforming Work, Leisure, Community and Everyday Life*, New York: Basic Books.

Frampton, L. (2007), 'DCMS/ V&A Funding Agreement 2005–06 to 2007–08. End of Year Report April 2006–March 2007' (report). Available at http://www.vam.ac.uk/files/file_upload/49218_file.pdf [last accessed 10 January 2009].

Fritsch, J. (2008), 'Can a "Communities of Practice" Framework Be Applied to the Creative Industries as an Identified Audience for the V&A?', *V&A Online Research Journal* (1). Available at http://www.vam.ac.uk /res_cons/research/online_journal/journal_1_index/communities_practice/index.html [last accessed 10 January 2009].

Holden, J. (2007a), 'Useful and Suggestive: The V&A and the Creative Industries' (report), London: V&A/Demos.

Holden, J. (2007b), 'Publicly Funded Culture and the Creative Industries' (report), London: Arts Council England/Demos.

Lash, S. and Urry, J. (1994), *Economies of Signs and Spaces*, London: Sage.

Leonard, M. (1997), *Britain^{TM}: Renewing Our Identity*, London: Demos.

National Museum Directors' Conference (NMDC) (2004), 'Museums and Galleries: Creative Engagement' (report), London: NMDC.

National Museum Directors' Conference (NMDC) (2006), 'Values and Vision: The Contribution of Culture' (report), London: Arts Council England, The Museums, Libraries and Archives Council and the NMDC.

Pavitt, J. (ed.) (2000), *Brand.New*, London: V&A Publications.

Sinclair, I. (1999), *Sorry Meniscus: Excursions to the Millennium Dome*, London: Profile Books.

Smith, C. (1998), *Creative Britain*, London: Faber and Faber.

Taylor, B. (1999), *Art for the Nation: Exhibitions and the London Public, 1747–2001*, Manchester: Manchester University Press.

Victoria and Albert Museum (2004), 'V&A Collecting Plan, Including Acquisition and Disposal' (report). Available at http://www.vam.ac.uk/files/file_upload/26983_file.pdf [last accessed 10 January 2009].

Victoria and Albert Museum (2007), 'Strategic Plan' (report). Available at http://www.vam.ac.uk/files/file_upload/39718_file.pdf [last accessed 10 January 2009].

Victoria and Albert Museum (2008), 'Think-Tank: The Future Designer'. Available at http://www.vam.ac.uk/thinktank1/future_designer/index.html [last accessed 10 January 2009].

Woodham, J. (2000), 'A Brand New Britain?', in Jane Pavitt (ed.), *Brand.New*, London: V&A Publications, pp.56–7.

Part II

MANAGING DESIGN IN CONTEXT

CHAPTER 6

Routinized Labour in the Graphic Design Studio

AnneMarie Dorland

When clients ask me what kind of place a design studio is to work, they expect stories of playful days, an unpredictable and creative team of co-workers, and long hours filled with crumpled paper balls and ideas scrawled on walls. But for many of them, even our law, engineering and accountancy clients who work within highly systematized social environments, a day in the life of a designer in a studio setting would be surprisingly full of audit, measurement and management structures. In reality, the contemporary design studio is not a space of play and unstructured work, but one of regulation, measurement and multiple daily audit practices, where the time and output of individual designers is graded against a wide variety of metrics for success. Although the typical studio setting is a creative and generative space, designers are affected daily by a growing range of audit and measurement techniques. This chapter explores the demands placed on graphic designers by the internal structures of their workplaces, and by the framework of audit and accountability within which they are enmeshed.

Research Background

The research for this chapter was conducted while I myself worked as an account manager in a large Canadian design and branding firm, in a role that involved liaising between clients and a creative team of designers to ensure that design projects were delivered on time, on brief and on budget. I occupied a very specific place in the design studio setting: as a past graphic designer turned account manager, I had the daily task of implementing the wide range of management and auditing tools that directly impacted upon the practices and procedures that make up the creative work of graphic designers. The majority of the research for this study was completed between 2005 and 2008, and draws on interviews with six freelance graphic designers, six full-time studio-based graphic designers, and observational research conducted in graphic design studio settings in Toronto and Calgary.[1]

By interviewing these designers, and observing the unique studio settings, I have attempted to explore the topic of how auditing procedures required to manage creative design in a commercial context influence individual practice within what is understood as a 'creative space'. How are complex audit and time measurement systems used by studios to create value for clients? And how do time and financial pressures lead designers to devise various routines and forms of practice in order to accommodate the management restrictions within which they create?

Pubic Conceptions of Work in the Studio Space

The design studio is culturally imagined not as a space of audit, structure and management, but as a creative space of play, a conception fostered and nurtured by the design industry. In the promotional material created by design studios, graphic designers (and creative workers in general) are often positioned as playful subjects or adolescent adults playing at work; popular notions of the creative workforce feature an extremely youthful group of self-actualizing high achievers (Maslow 1954). Even the vocabulary used within the studio setting is centred around a playful practice: whether playing with software, playing with a concept, or playing out an idea with a client, the self-descriptive language of the studio-workplace suggests many spaces and times for unstructured play/work. A playful studio is also assumed to be a successful one. Many Canadian studios have marketed a description of their space as playful and unstructured to great effect. The most well-known example may be that of Bruce Mau, head of Bruce Mau Design (based in Toronto) who is such a proponent of the designer's work as a form of play that he published his incomplete manifesto for growth, encouraging play as a practice in 'serious' graphic design (Mau 1998). Other design firms, such as the American group Tolleson Design, market their success at developing creative work for clients as being *based on* an undirected, unmanaged, playful practice, explaining their group holidays, paintball tournaments, cook-offs and pyjama parties as important elements of the design process (see Tolleson 1999).

This description of the studio as a creative and playful space is not entirely unwarranted; many practices used by designers are intentionally developed to encourage unique response, collaborative work and original thinking. This development of 'play' techniques is often fostered in the design education system, where the term 'play' often replaces 'experimentation' as a methodology of creative exploration.

A 'playful' creative workspace can even be presented as a valuable element of a successful business plan. As Andrew Ross explains:

> In new media companies, neo-leisure [is] not simply tolerated as an unavoidable cost of doing business in the information age; it [is] actively encouraged as a way of adding value to an employee's output. Play [is] valued as an activity that [can] catalyse ideas and serve as a battery source for recharging flagging energies at the workstation. The permissive workplace [can] take a playful turn at any moment, and however spontaneous the result, it [is] still part of the business plan. (Ross 2003)

Although Ross is, in this case, critical of the idea that play is solely an organic and spontaneous creative tool, framing it instead as a business tool used to increase productivity, his argument is persuasive. It is not only the case that a 'playful' studio space is a productive one, but also that 'play' is a marketable feature in the competitive industry of graphic design, both as a differentiator of the type of work done within the studio space for client groups, and as a draw for creative workers and clients. Yet in many cases, the inclusion of 'play' in the work day often disguises the lack of more traditional or quantifiable benefits for creative workers in the design studio workplace. Ross's argument about 'play' as a productivity tool in disguise has been corroborated in every studio setting in which I observed.

But how does the practice of design within a studio setting actually work?[2] In my observation, the highly structured series of methodologies implemented by the design worker, and enforced by the studio structure, is very different from the intuitive creative process marketed to clients as the 'studio way'. Even design studios that present their process to the public as including more than just play or creative work often fail to mention the multiple layers of audit and management tools implemented during the design process. In internal guidelines and promotional writing, one Toronto-based design and branding studio very briefly describes their creative process as beginning with 'the creative briefing and end[ing] with the delivery of final art', but does not address the internal structures in place which guide and shape the work of the designers (SFP 2004b).

Contrary to the ways in which the 'creative workspace' is marketed by design studios, designers in the studio setting commonly work within an elaborate series of measurements and audit procedures. They are asked to continually record and project their time needs for each stage of the design process, to tailor their creative solution to the expectations and needs of diverse internal audience groups, and to find quicker and more effective work practices to substitute for lengthy explorations and creative generation practices. These processes are perhaps best described by outlining the journey of a creative project from initial client request to final solution and delivery to client.

The Intersection of the Creative Process and Audit Practices

A typical project in my own studio would begin not with the designer or creative director, but with the account management team, who would meet with the client and gather pertinent information about the project at hand (whether a new brand development, a piece of corporate communication, an annual report or any other printed, interactive or display project). This information is then translated into meeting notes and a creative brief document, which is approved in writing by the client and held as a quasi-legal agreement outlining the scope of work and specific expectations for the project. Having determined the budget for the general project (based on market value of the final designed deliverable, budget tolerance of the client, cost of previous projects, size and scope of project and size of team required), the account manager allocates a specific numbers of hours to each creative team member. During a weekly scheduling meeting, the account manager then plans how the creative team will use their time for various projects in the week ahead, a schedule that is then electronically generated and sent to designers. By the end of this stage, an average of two hours of conversation (on the phone and in meetings), seven e-mails and five key documents have been exchanged between the account management group and the client, constituting the initial stages of systematization and management of the designer's process.[3]

It is only now that the project itself is presented to the designer, in the form of two templated working documents: a budgeted allocation of billable hours, and a creative brief (most often presented in a briefing meeting by the account manager). The creative brief outlines the 'design objective', who the project is directed to (the end audience), and the deadlines and considerations that the design must meet. Also within this brief are the unspoken social and technical expectations entailed in the decision-making process, such as the secondary effects of the design work (a logo, for example, must not only convey the name of the company or product, but also the cultural position and aspirational values of the brand). The brief may also mention the 'tastes' to be indulged (whether of the client or the end-user) and the specific expectations of the client regarding the way the work will be realized.

Undocumented information, such as the working relationship between the design team and the client, assumed understandings of the behaviour or habits of the end-user audience, the aesthetic conventions acceptable for the type of work to be produced, the family of work that this project must fit into, and the working structures within the studio, are all conveyed to the designer though meetings with clients, with account executives and via the social environment of the studio as a place of practice. It is ideally with all of this information, documented and undocumented, that the graphic designer enters into the series of encoding and decoding couplets that constitute design work within a large firm (Hall 1980). Indeed, it is by defining the practice of graphic designers as, at least in part, one of encoding messages and information for a 'decoding' audience, or end-user (Hall 1980), that we can see how the work of graphic designers is distinct from that of their decoding 'audience'.[4]

At this point, the designer begins entering data into an online time-recording program (in six-minute increments), choosing one of hundreds of open dockets for internal and external work, documenting time spent on a project with a written description of activities and selecting sub-categories of tasks within which to list hours worked. With this, the designer begins work on the design of the communication solution to the presented brief. According to the designers I spoke to in one particular studio, there are three main activities that take place during this stage: group brainstorming, individual development of what the designers called 'the big ideas', and mood or concept boards.[5] However, brainstorming – despite being promoted as an ideal element of this studio's service offering by directors and company literature – is notably vulnerable to time and client restrictions, and thus is not always pursued for 'bread and butter' projects, such as repeat advertising based on templated designs, brochures modelled on past creative work, or other low-budget and quick turn-around work. In this studio, brainstorms frequently took the form not of large, formal meetings, but of informal gatherings around someone's desk or the collecting of inspirational material from other designers. Similarly, mood/ concept boards were likely to appear not as finished presentations, but as piles upon tables, collections of previous work, or doodles on meeting notes. In many cases, therefore, the highly valued practices of brainstorming and background research are in fact given far less time than is advertised or described to clients.

As the design project progresses, work is monitored by the account team, and creative workers design for an internal audience of co-workers from both the design and account management sides of the office, pitching their solutions by referring to the technical aspects of the work when addressing the production staff, the marketing and client-pleasing aspects when talking to the account management staff, the cost-effectiveness and ease of implementation when talking to the directors, and most frequently, the aesthetic or 'look-and-feel' when addressing co-designers. This stage of internal review and approvals reinforces the management and systematization practices at work in the studio, as well as the measurement process of time and budget allocations. It is worth noting that in the studio setting, designers must account for their work in many different ways, and to many different audience groups. However, such accounting practices also contribute to the way designers *think* about their practice, forming what I will later describe as a 'product image system' (Ryan and Peterson 1982).

At this stage, the design (or deliverable) will not yet have been shown to the client, but will have undergone several rounds of internal revisions. Two to three solutions are often generated, based on brand standards, understandings of audience profile and details provided in the creative brief. These solutions are presented through the internal decision-making hierarchy in the studio: project manager, account manager and creative director. Changes are requested at each stage, and made by the designer so that the design slowly becomes a collaborative effort involving one graphic designer and at least three outside sources. Throughout this process, the designer continues to complete timesheets, which are monitored by the account manager. Schedules are revised, budgets adjusted and scope of work documents updated by the account management team.

The updated design solutions are then presented to the client by the account manager (or creative director) perhaps, but not necessarily, with the designer in attendance. Questions and change requests are noted by the account manager in an update to the creative brief, and as a contact report that is sent to the client. The design is then revised as requested, and returned to client, a process that is repeated until the client is satisfied with the result. Although it is not often acknowledged as a practice, in studio settings I observed, the initial brief is quickly left behind as a guideline for design, and the client is held as the only arbitrator of success. This, in itself, presents a form of constraint on designers, since work initially done for multiple audience groups (such as the internal creative team, the creative director and, perhaps most importantly, the end-user), is ultimately selected and judged by an audience group who may be uneducated about the process, and who may be using personal criteria for judging success that have not been shared with the designers themselves. It was not uncommon, in my observation, to hear choruses of complaints about the ignorance of client groups from designers. One freelance designer described the process of client approvals as:

> A client is somebody who comes to you for your expertise and you give them your professional opinion, and but at the same time it's always a challenge [...] If I change something from red to blue, I don't know how that is going to affect the client [...] you are just using fuzzy logic, or just feeling your way through

things a lot of the time, and to use words to sell them to the client becomes really important. (Graphic Designer A 2005)[6]

Having presented several solutions, each with an elaborate rationalization, to the client-audience, a direction is chosen and the designer begins the development of a final solution. This stage often requires multiple presentations by the account management team to the client-audience, each with varying degrees of revisions, which are often undertaken by a junior designer and supervised by a senior designer.

Formalized Audit and Evaluation Techniques

Once the final design direction has been signed off, a formal approval form is submitted to the client, and the designer gathers his or her working files to be transferred to a production artist for a 'final build-out'. This includes a full overhaul and checking of the digital files provided by the designer, and preparation of those files for the printer or publisher. Timesheet entries are reviewed by an account manager, and if the designer has worked beyond the allocated hours, the billable time is reduced by the account manager to balance the budget, decreasing the designer's salary to profitability ratio, and impacting on his or her profit-sharing and salary negotiations in the future. Final files are generated, and archived in an online system. Clients are billed, using an invoice system that always reflects the budgeted value of the project rather than the hourly rate of the designer.

Design solutions are then put into practice by the client, and evaluated based on various testing metrics and internal/external feedback, including 'disaster checking' (used only to check for failure, rather than to evaluate success),[7] from which the client is able to assess the value of the end result. But other than this client-led 'disaster checking', what structures are used in the graphic design studio setting to measure, quantify and audit the final creative solution? In both studio settings, the value of the creative work was measured for client groups as a Return on Investment (ROI). This is calculated based on the value of the design 'investment' (measured by client and account management teams), and the value of the final solution from the client's perspective (increased share price, increased market awareness, improved employee recruitment or improved internal work procedures). According to one account manager, the majority of time spent on 'research' for a design solution is often not based on generating information, but on evaluating findings, focusing on justifying the price of an end product to a client group. As one account manager put it: 'No one wastes time they don't have on research before. You just need to show how good it was after. Then they come back. Do it before ... you can't get the money for that' (Account Manager A 2008).

Occasionally, design solutions are also evaluated (by both design studio and client) using the concept of the 'triple bottom line', a measurement of the environmental, economic and societal impact of a design solution (McDaniel 2003). This form of evaluation removes the labour of the designer from the equation completely, factoring in only the measured effectiveness (as assessed by the client using their own internal metrics) of the outcome. It is most often used in cases where the project involves public funding (such as government-assisted projects and not-for-profit or charitable work), and is usually delivered as a designed document and a formalized group presentation conducted by the design firm's account team. A final project evaluation is then completed by the account management group using a visual mapping program that allows the account manger to document variations in profitability based on size of team, time spent, and tasks completed. In many cases, clients assess the success of a project using very few factors, often tied directly to measured exit survey results. Increases in sales or issue awareness are often considered the only reliable markers of success from a client's point of view. These findings are fed back into the studio setting in one key way: through repeat business.

For the studio, success is evaluated using client feedback and testimonials, awards given by the design community, and the contribution a project can make to the overall studio portfolio. Projects are also evaluated based on their profitability ratio and speed of completion. Exit surveys are completed with clients, while standard testing of click through rates, in-market focus group testing, media survey analysis or user-survey feedback may be requested by the account team. In the studio settings in which I observed, the profitability of a project is the strongest indicator of success, as it determines whether projects of that specific kind, and for that specific client, can be taken on again without an increase in required team size or budget.

Technologies of Audit in the Design Studio Setting

This example of the lifespan of a typical project demonstrates clearly the multitude of auditing, management and measurement techniques that impact upon the creative process of designers. Designers are subject to time auditing practices (timesheets, budget allocation, work forecasting and scheduling meetings), internal hierarchy approvals (creative approvals, creative veto held by account managers, approval of creative work by clients), external hierarchy of approvals (testing, client feedback, disaster checking), budget management restrictions ('write-downs' or performance review punishment for overuse of time), and systematization in their design process (such as a lack of involvement with external audience research and the development of the brief and a dependence on design standards and brand standards). These practices of measurement, audit and management have a profound impact on the creative practice of designers.

The structures of audit and accountability also become a technology at work within the design studio. I use the term 'technology' here to describe the ever present computers and scanners that make up so much of the physical space of the design studio, as well as Ursula Franklin's definition of technology as a system, entailing 'far more than its individual material components. [It involves] organization, procedures, symbols, new words, equations and most of all, a mindset' (Franklin 1990: 12). In an industry where (billable, budgeted) time is literally money, these structures or 'technologies' can of course provide a profitable and beneficial framework for studio administration, allowing work to be done quickly, measured according to brand standards and assured of success, in turn guaranteeing repeat clients and dependable income for the studio. As one full-time graphic designer described it:

> It's not, you know, it's not what you would think at school, but it's the same for freelance, studio … you need to work in the system. And you need to work quickly, and to get it right the first time. [There is] nothing worse than having to go back and do it again and again: the client gets to be the creative at that point, and then you'll never get it right. So you use the timesheets and the budget and the rest to help you … (Graphic Designer B 2008)

But how do these individual structures come to collectively define the process of creative work? And what practices or structures have designers developed in order to successfully create work within this social context of audit and management techniques? Based on my observations, two key 'technologies' of practice emerge as a result of the structural conditions within which designers work. Firstly, designers describe their work in different ways to appeal to different audiences (both internal and external), thus speeding their creative process through the multiple stages of internal approval and demonstrating a constant awareness of budget and time constraints. Secondly, designers work to create solutions that adhere to expected brand or design standards, building on examples of previously accepted work and relying upon repetition of a library of ideas to create quickly and avoid costly time spent on creative generation.

A Re-imagining of the End Audience: The Product Image System

Let's first examine how designers use the expectations of their different audiences to make creative decisions within a structured hierarchy of approvals. One graphic designer described her hierarchy of audience groups, and its impact upon her working processes, as follows:

> You can't just make something you know the client will like; we don't have room to do a million versions, so you make a set of comps that you know can get past the account guys. Then, once you have that, you tweak them so that the creative director won't have too many changes. Then ... you know the client loves this or that, so you add a little of that right at the end. And if you are lucky, it gets through and you don't have to start from scratch or make some – you know – major changes. (Graphic Designer C 2008)

When working in this way, designers are employing a concept of 'the product image', as described by Ryan and Peterson (1982) in their study of country music songwriting. In this study, the concept of the 'product image' is presented as a system of creative production, whereby the creation of a single product is divided into a series of smaller products, each with a separate target audience in mind. Each of these stages then represents a product image: a defined imagining or set of expectations generated by a particular audience group (Ryan and Peterson 1982: 23). In this model, Ryan and Peterson describe the product image as the determining factor within the hierarchical decision-making chain, providing a space for the integration of various, equally important audiences into an understanding of creative production.

Using this model, we can divide the production of a design project, such as a book cover design, into smaller cycles of production. The project changes from a sketch to a pitch, a proposal, a comp and, finally, a proof before being described as a book cover. Each of these stages represents a product image: a defined imagining or set of expectations generated by a particular audience group. An analysis of production work as a 'product image' system also allows us to understand the emergence of standardization within creative practice. As Ryan and Peterson explain: 'The most common way of doing this is to produce works that are much like the products that have most recently passed thought all the links in the decision chain to become commercially successful' (Ryan and Peterson 1982: 25).

Referring to creative work as a series of products also provides a way of acknowledging the role of smaller routines of production at different stages of a project, as well as the various audiences invoked in the creative process. In the studio setting, and with freelance designers, this manner of producing work using pre-accepted strategies (or routines) can lead to the development of, if not a house-style, then certainly a common aesthetic tone throughout a design portfolio.

The breaking down and dividing of design work into smaller pieces, each meant for a separate audience group, is a defining aspect of the structure of creative decision-making followed by graphic designers. During my observations in one studio space, I attended a meeting between a senior designer and a junior account representative about a rebranding assignment for a post-secondary educational institution in Toronto. Throughout the discussion, the design work was never described as a whole, but as a series of stages. First, designers referred to the 'sketch' (for which the audience was the rest of the internal design team), then the 'comp' (which was produced for an audience comprising the client), followed by the 'proof' (which was directed at a high level within the client organization), and finally the 'deliverable' (a finalized piece directed at an audience of teenagers and their parents contemplating college choices within the Toronto area). By using the 'product image' system to work within the highly managed decision-making process of the design studio, designers are able to create work that satisfies their twin (imposed) goals of creative approval, and quick and efficient time use.

This reliance on the product image system can be seen particularly in the design of branded corporate communication pieces. As one studio-based designer described, creative innovation in many cases is not imperative, and is often trumped by the importance of previously approved brand standards, and accountability or time measurement metrics.

> For something like this, it looks like each thing would be so hard to come up with. But you don't have time for that, and if you did, this is just not the project you want to spend some of that time on. So you jam it through, make something that works for everyone along the way; you know what they all want, it's really not hard. Then you can get to the good stuff; I mean that's why God invented brand standards, right? (Graphic Designer D 2008)

In the studio spaces that I observed, designers implemented their own 'product image system' when confronted with routine, last-minute challenges, or with projects which strongly adhered to a previously developed brand standard, often working without the advantage of a clear brief (forsaken by the account manager for the sake of time or efficiency). Work in a design studio must be done quickly (on average, the freelancers I spoke to budgeted 45 per cent more time for a specific project than their studio-based counterparts), and is better assured of success if it is created using these structures.[8]

The Systematization of Creative Practice: The Use of Occupational Formulae

Although the system of 'product image' is one way in which designers are able to create design solutions that move quickly and expediently through the internal approval hierarchy of the studio, they also work within a system that encourages repetition of ideas in order to expedite the delivery of their solution to the client and to create in a more profitable manner.

In order to create work quickly, to present solutions that adhere to expected standards and to avoid spending costly time on creative generation, designers employ a range of practices. One corporate communications designer described the annual cycle of work through a studio as follows:

> Every year you come up against the same issues ... I mean, there are the same projects, you know: annuals, sustainability reports, same campaigns, new look. Which is fine, but ... so you have your list of bits, and you know this works for them, and this works for them. And you can guarantee that if you give them what got approved last year, with new lipstick on it, it goes through. (Graphic Designer E 2008)

In contrast to the common focus on originality and unique creative solutions for individual clients publicized by design studios and freelance designers alike, budget restrictions and client guidelines often forced the designers I observed to rely upon standard and tested solutions, pushing them towards what Negus has described as the 'habitual, un-reflexive and uncritical adherence to well-established production and occupational formulae' (Negus 2002: 510). In these cases, standardized and tested solutions may include the reuse of work that has been previously accepted or approved (by the client in question, or by another similar client group). This may also include formulaic or risk-free solutions such as traditional layouts, popular photo choices or current trends in colour palettes.

In this way, designers in studio and freelance settings employ what Negus (2002) has termed 'occupational formulae', a way of understanding creative practice as a series of repeated and formulaic steps within work. I use the term here to describe the systematically determined work practices of graphic designers, in conjunction with a similar term offered by Ettema (1982: 91), of 'routines of production'. Describing the working practices of television producers, Ettema uses the term to refer to the various shortcuts or corporate habits that 'energize the producer's creative abilities' (Ettema 2002: 47). Ettema builds here on the work of Hirsch (1977), who explains that what we commonly understand as individual 'creative' input is often in fact the result of a production routine. These routines of production, according to Ettema, serve to create a perspective in the workplace that is conducive to fulfilling specific tasks, creating a shared organizational vocabulary and socializing new recruits.

An example of such routines in the day-to-day practice of graphic designers can be seen in a typical project planning meeting that I observed at one studio, attended by an account manager, a project manager, a designer and a creative director. The project manger and account manager led the meeting, guiding a discussion about plans for a new Corporate Sustainability Report (CSR), to be designed by the designer in attendance and led by the creative director. The brief presented by the account team included information about the current initiatives and status of the client's company, their current activities that would be featured in the report, and the end uses of the document (presentation to government stakeholders, landowners and employees). The brief also included an outline of basic limitations, as well as the 'deliverable' elements of the design work (including page count, printing requirements, budgets and the availability of banked client images used in previous pieces). The choice of designer was based solely on the designer's experience in creating approved solutions for this particular client successfully and quickly in the past. It was the account team that suggested the general creative direction, and they who held the creative veto on behalf of the client. The 'look and feel' of the piece had been predetermined in meetings between account management and client, copy and headlines were pre-written, and previous examples of successful applicable work had been gathered and awaited review on the table.

This is striking, because it counteracts many assumptions about the creative process in major studios. One might assume that the creative team would present ideas to the account executives, and yet the design work here was prescribed by the account manager to the designer, who was tasked simply with 'making it happen'. The language of the meeting was at all times focused on marketing terms rather than on the design and aesthetic of the finished work. In this meeting, as in many others, the end-user audience was identified only in terms of their status in relation to the client group. Similarly, it was the case here, as in many other cases I observed, that designer engagement with the project, with background research, and with the client, was dependent on the budget allocated, and in this case was reduced to two meetings (both used to personally present proposed creative solutions to the client for approval). Moreover, continuous references were made to project work that had been done for the same client years before, which could be repackaged and updated for this particular task, and to designers who, having completed something similar, could offer guidance and suggestions for cost-cutting and timesaving strategies.

In this meeting, the structural imperatives of time and budget dictated the creative solution presented by the designer in more ways than just paper choice and time spent on outsourcing elaborate photography. The designer in this case was deliberately asked to engage in the use of 'occupational formulae', recycling previous solutions or previous concepts for use in this project. Since the designer was not given time to explore or to generate new creative solutions, he was forced to rely upon updating past work in order to satisfy the time and budget restraints. When asked about the end solution, this designer replied:

> Well, it's just ... it's what they want. And they pay the bills, don't they? And [they] would never go for something like that, so there is no point fixing what isn't broken. You just update: that's what design is. Accessing the library in your head. You get good at it: you can remember bits of other recipes and come up with something that feels ... you know, modern. New. Not like leftovers. That's what being good at this job means. (Graphic Designer F 2008)

This reliance on formulaic solutions for repeat or 'bread and butter' work extends to the freelance world as well: 'Sometimes, you know – I admit it – I do [work] like that too. You kind of have to, when you are banging out ideas and your time is billable', admitted Jon. He went on to explain:

> I think the worst thing that a designer can do... I think one of the worst things... is just scour through [*Communication Arts*] magazine or something like that. But a lot of people do, it's just what happens, you know, time constraints; they just want a sampling of... I call it – well [we] call it – 'turntablism', where it's like you are just looking for a quick style that they can ape. (Graphic Designer A 2005)

By employing these 'routines of production', freelance designers are able to hasten the process of creative production, reducing their workload and guaranteeing an acceptable design solution for their client. Only one of the freelancers that I spoke to expressed misgivings about relying exclusively upon their own personal 'formulae'. Other freelancers focused their concern primarily on over-reliance upon routines derived from design publications. In fact, by working alone, outside a social network of designers, freelancers are forced to rely upon such external sources (design magazines and samples of successful design from outside their group of colleagues and friends) to find their 'occupational formulae'. This differs from the practice of studio-based graphic designers that I spoke to, who also relied upon formulaic solutions, but were able to do this through discussions with co-workers and through the institutional structure of the studio space.

Conclusion

In order to have a more complete picture of the practice of graphic design in both traditional studio settings and, to a lesser extent, as a freelancer, it is necessary to supplement 'public' conceptions of the graphic design studio (as a space of irreverent 'play') with an understanding of the various audit and accountability structures that make up the contemporary studio space, including time restrictions, accountability metrics, multiple levels of hierarchy and approval, client constraints, and the necessity of reliance on routines of practice and occupational formulae. The ways in which design work is audited, accounted for and assigned, and the patterns of practice within the studio space, all shape the creative practice of graphic designers in ways that we are only beginning to uncover.

In fact, if one looks closely at the multitude of audit and management structures put in place to value and manage design work in a commercial setting, it is not surprising that the creative practice of designers is substantially shaped by its management context. To work within a structure of time and profitability audit, to generate creative work that will win approval by a complex and multi-layered hierarchy of audience members, and to create within a system that requires the reuse and borrowing of past concepts, directly affects the ways in which designers make choices and produce creative design work. This does not mean that such constraints go unchallenged, or that they do not elicit frustration and sometimes debate – but they are, for the most part, an accepted aspect of commercial design practice. As one designer put it, 'That's just how the studio works. It's just a few hoops ... not to say, you know, [that] you don't get tired of jumping through them' (Graphic Designer B 2008).

Notes

1. In this study, all full-time graphic designers were practising in traditional studio settings, consisting of production, design, creative direction and account management teams. All were between the ages of 24 and 50, with an even gender balance. The freelance designers ranged in their practice from full- to part-time, and were of similar ages and gender splits to their studio counterparts.
2. Ross has renamed the new corporate culture 'no-collar' in reference to the gold collar employee force, as well as the re-imagined corporate culture. This differentiation of the type of workplace as new and different has taken hold, and is naturalized in the promotional design of most large-scale firms throughout the USA.
3. These time measurements are based on an average of one month's worth of projects completed in the studio in one Canadian graphic design studio, as measured by account management timesheet entries.
4. In 'Encoding/Decoding' (1980), Stuart Hall provides a model for understanding the productive practices of designers, describing the communication of information not

as a straight line between sender, message and receiver, but rather as a series of articulations, or intersections, between spheres of production, circulation, distribution, consumption and reception. According to Hall, this process is completed through the transformation of produced information by decoders (in the case of the production of graphic design, by the audience or target market). In this model, a specific audience removed from the culture of production is held as the primary understanding of 'decoders'. Hall holds two events within the communication of information to be determinate: moments of encoding and moments of decoding. It is the moments of encoding, or the encoding work of the graphic designer (using Hall's terminology) that I am focusing on here in this research project, and it is primarily practices of encoding to which I refer when I discuss the practice of graphic design production. Using the two determinate moments of encoding and decoding, Hall explains degrees of understanding and misunderstanding of messages as degrees of symmetry within the process of media production and consumption – relationships of equivalency between the positions of the 'personifications' of encoder-producer and decoder-receiver (Hall 1980). The lack of symmetry between the interests, intentions and perceptions of encoder and decoder allows for a diversity of response to media texts – multiple readings that, while never individual and private, are simultaneously possible, defined by the social situation of receivers.

5. Concept or mood boards consist of swatches and sketches presented informally by the tasked team to an internal audience of co-designers in order to generate a unifying idea and aesthetic for the project.

6. At the request of designers interviewed, all names have been removed from their accompanying statements. All designers, account managers and creative directors are currently employed at one of two major Canadian design studios. Designers and creative directors interviewed have a minimum of eight years' experience working within a studio setting.

7. This 'disaster checking' or post-production research for preventative purposes was referred to at SFP as 'due diligence'. In the market in which the designers I interviewed worked, this type of research is often carried out by private companies, and was usually implemented by the production manager or the creative director, not the designer. The one area of design production that is *not* tested or 'disaster checked' is the creative process of the graphic designer. As we saw at SFP, the designer is asked to work in isolation, employing an unquestioned series of practices to emerge with a final solution for the first of their audiences. Methods of testing the effectiveness of the designers' practice are not used, and this lack of testing is unquestioned in the design industry.

8. This figure is based on a survey of the budgets and timelines of graphic designers who work within a traditional studio setting, but who have also worked freelance. In 2007, ten designers with a secondary freelance practice were asked to document what they would request from clients for fees and schedule as a freelance designer, and this was compared against similar projects completed within the design studio.

References

Dornfeld, B. (1998), *Producing Public Television, Producing Public Culture*, Princeton, NJ: Princeton University Press.

Ettema, J. S. (1982), 'The Organizational Context of Creativity: A Case Study from Private Television', in J. Ettema and D. Whitney (eds.), *Individuals in Mass Media*

Organizations: Creativity and Constraint, London: Sage.

Franklin, U. (1990), *The Real World of Technology* (CBC Massey Lectures series), Concord, Ontario: House of Anansi Press.

Hall, S. et al. (1980), *Culture, Media, Language*, London: Hutchinson.

Hirsch, P. (1977), 'Occupational, Organizational and Institutional Models in Mass Media Research: Towards an Integrated Framework', in P.M Hirsch, P.V. Miller and F.G Kline (eds.), *Strategies for Communication Research* , Beverly Hills, CA: Sage, pp.13–42.

Maslow, A. (1954), *Motivation and Personality*, New York: Harper.

Mau, B. (1998), 'An Incomplete Manifesto For Growth'. Available at http://www.brucemau.com.

McDaniel, J. B. (2003), 'The Paradox of Design Research: The Role of Informance' in B. Laurel (ed.), *Design Research, Methods and Perspectives*, Cambridge, MA: MIT Press.

Negus, K. (2002), 'The Work of Cultural Intermediaries and the Enduring Distinction Between Production and Consumption', *Cultural Studies*, 16(4): 501–15.

Ross, A. (2003), *No Collar: The Humane Workplace and its Hidden Costs*, New York: Basic Books.

Ryan, J. and Peterson, R. A. (1982), 'The Product Image: The Fate of Creativity in Country Music Songwriting' in J. Ettema and D. Whitney (eds.), *Individuals in Mass Media Organizations: Creativity and Constraint*, London: Sage.

SFP (2004a), *Spencer Francey Peters Celebrates 25 Years of Connecting the Dots*, self-published.

SFP (2004b), *Toolkit Document No 0.0, Creative Process*, unpublished document.

SFP (2004c), *Toolkit Document No 0.0, Brainstorming*, unpublished document.

SFP (2004d), *Toolkit Document No 0.0, Creative Set-Ups and Presentations*, unpublished document.

SFP (2005), *Creative Brief*, unpublished document.

Tolleson, S. (1999), *SpinRinseWashSoak: Tolleson Design*, New York: Princeton Architectural Press.

Interviews

Account Manager A (2008), personal interview, 4 May 2008.

Creative Director A (2008), personal interview, 8 January 2008.

Graphic Designer A (2005), personal interview, 3 May 2005.

Graphic Designer B (2008), personal interview, 2 February 2008.

Graphic Designer C (2008), personal interview, 2 February 2008.

Graphic Designer D (2008), personal interview, 12 April 2008.

Graphic Designer E (2008), personal interview, 12 April 2008.

Graphic Designer F (2008), personal interview, 8 January 2008.

CHAPTER 7

Auditing in Communication Design

Paul Springer

This chapter considers how creative working methods in communications firms have been systematized. In particular, it examines issues of policy, planning, measurement and routine by reviewing contemporary communications practices. The first section reviews the established practices of creative communications design, and considers how these processes are presented to prospective clients. The second section then addresses the impact of digitization on the creative process. Digital techniques have accelerated the pace (and expectations) of creative work, but how has digitization affected the different stages of the communications process itself? Examples reveal how customer databases and e-promotions have impacted on communication design practice by enabling messages to target people by name and personal preferences. The third section considers why clients are often brought into review stages by agencies. Does this involvement impair designers' and advertisers' sense of creative freedom? Agencies that use formalized review measures as a type of 'client PR' are also considered in this section. The chapter concludes by considering the impact of internal review and auditing processes on the final output of communications agencies.

Some of the chapter's perspectives may seem unusual on first reading. For instance, I argue that the location of creative 'lateral thinking' has shifted towards the early 'big idea' stage and away from the designed execution of an idea. Furthermore, far from hindering creative output, I suggest that formal review processes actually encourage clients to support creative and challenging communications *ideas* – although often at the expense of creative freedom in the campaign process. To outsiders, contemporary advertising now seems to be encompassing creative forms beyond conventional advertising boundaries, yet for practitioners the scope for creativity is more tightly focused.

Throughout the chapter I use the term 'communication design' to mean the combination of 'old' and 'new' advertising practices. This includes broadcast media, brand placement, sales-speak, online or on the street advertising – all now part of the promotional repertoire of twenty-first-century agencies. There used to be clearer demarcation between advertising, graphics, branding and marketing practices. However, today's media-saturated and advertising-wary consumers are seen as harder to persuade with conventional advertising alone, while digital technology has created scope to hone communications through both broadcast and narrowcast channels: both factors have been significant in driving the convergence of marketing and communications ('marcoms') with advertising and design practices. Under the new heading of Communication Design, approaches to promotions can incorporate wider influences. For instance, in 2000, the fashion label Van Heusen invited design firms, PR and marketing groups to compete with ad agencies for their communications business. In this context the scope for creative output is broader than ever.

The cases discussed here arose from my ongoing studies of advertising agencies from 2000. Common issues such as the client-company relationships and agency practices are also prominently featured in trade journals such as *Campaign*. These processes tend to be omitted from studies of creative communications design. Yet auditing and steering procedures are essential: every mass-media commercial image will have involved organized teamwork and planning stages in the effort to reach the right audience in the right way at the right time. Formalized processes reduce risk in commercial creativity, and the bigger the budget, the more necessary 'behind the scenes' processes are to ensure that clients get a worthwhile return on investment (ROI). Communications design is, after all, a commercial business.

Background: Working Models

Review processes have long been a recognized aspect of commercial communications practice. Agencies even implemented their own review tactics to underpin propositions in the late 1950s, when the American model of commercial communications, referred to as the 'Madison Avenue System', emerged. Much has been made of how business models were used to reshape creative ideas as commercial products (Mayer 1961; Tungate 2007) and how agencies used social sciences to 'legitimize' advertising's effectiveness in the eyes of clients (Reeves 1960).

In Britain from the late 1960s, planning was introduced within the advertising process to give it a more social-scientific underpinning. Stephen King (at J. Walter Thompson) is often credited with coining the term 'account planning' while Stanley Pollitt (founder of Boase Massimi Pollitt) is often acclaimed for incorporating detailed research into planning briefs, so that a campaign was 'on the strategy' before creative teams were briefed. Pollitt's method gave campaigns a context that was easily understood by clients, and his role became the archetype for other agencies to appoint account planners.

During the mid-1990s, some of the most prominent British independent agencies, including St Luke's Communications and Howell Henry Chaldecott Lury and Partners (HHCL), presented their creative *processes* as a unique selling point, rather than simply pitching on creative strategy alone. These agencies introduced phases to their creative process that involved their clients: client teams were invited to 'tissue meetings' (break-out sessions focusing on development), 'brand guardians' were appointed as client–agency go-betweens and creative teams were posted to work out of clients' offices, to get closer to the working culture of their projects.

Even agency offices were 'styled up' to remind clients they were in creative spaces. HHCL made a virtue of hot-desking (they called it a 'rapid operations moving programme', or ROMPing) while St Luke's introduced branded client rooms, which were spaces kitted out to embody the brands they represented. Chiat Day's famous (Pesche-designed) Manhattan office 'experiment' of the 1990s, with soft-walled offices, beanbags and brand-themed spaces, had tried

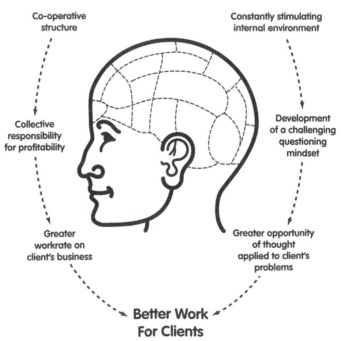

Figure 7.1 The creative process at St Luke's, as presented by the agency. © St Luke's Holdings Ltd.

to embody the spirit of new and different work. With the schemes at HHCL and St Luke's, it was the processes involving clients, not the space, that established creative difference.

The value of this for HHCL and St Luke's was that their processes also allowed creative ideas to be co-created and developed with clients, which meant that clients 'bought in' to ideas because they were involved in the key decisions early on. In terms of doing business, the agencies became skilled at shaping the creative *service* as a 'value added' activity paid for by clients. This reduced the risk of all-or-nothing client judgements later in the campaign process, as effectiveness became as much a test of the creative *process* as the finished graphic *product*.

Given that communications can move into the fields of product design, fashion and performance – for instance, collectable plastic dolls to advertise Britvic Tango fizzy drinks in the late 1990s, Comme des Garçons guerrilla store promotions in 2005, and organized flash-mob events to advertise iPods during 2007 – it is unsurprising that communications industries have been required to assert formal self-audit and client review stages. The wider the opportunities have become for choosing media, the more certain agencies need to be that they are choosing the right approach. Thus self-audit has been a way of 'scoping' communications. However, only a few texts (e.g. Leadbeater 1999; Dru 2002) discuss current revenue-earning methods of creative businesses. This is partly because processes are not as compelling as the finished visual results, and also because creative businesses have tended to publish their own working practices to vindicate the approaches being sold. Examples of this include *Under the Radar* by Jonathan Bond and Richard Kirshenbaum (founders of Kirshenbaum Bond), *Lovemarks* by Kevin Roberts (CEO of Saatchi & Saatchi) and *Beyond Disruption*, by Jean-Marie Dru (CEO of TBWA).

Approaches to Managing Creativity

The processes of creative production have tended to be linear in medium-sized agencies (50–250 employees), but have become more sophisticated since the turn of the millennium. After winning accounts at pitches during the late 1990s, agencies normally had three periods that required client 'sign-off': the creative brief, selection of the final concept, and agreement that the final campaign was ready for launch. Between these key stages, agency planners would shape a creative brief around target markets, the media to be used and the 'personality' of the brand. An agreed brief would go to the 'creatives' – teams of art directors and copywriters – who would produce creative responses to the tasks set. Account handlers would operate as go-betweens with staff and client representatives, usually a brand manager, in conjunction with an agency's 'new business' manager, whose role it is to liaise with clients. Media buyers would work with creative directors and when the creative output was near completion, they would begin to negotiate with venues for the placement and timing of the creative work. The process was – and still is – directed by project managers in a role called 'traffic': their responsibility is to ensure that the various stages of projects are delivered on time and, in conjunction with account handlers, on budget. It is the function of 'traffic' to manage the process of creativity and ensure that agency processes and standards are upheld. It is also their role to make sure unique creative review stages, such as client–agency brainstorming sessions, are developed as a feature of the service being provided.

While this system of roles and operations is still the norm, communications companies founded more recently tend to incorporate further opportunities for client involvement throughout the process. Apart from sampling various stages in the development of the creative brief, brand managers are often involved in focus groups and ideas generation meetings to ensure they 'buy in' to the creative process. According to Tim Allnutt, head of the communications planning unit at London-based agency Clemmow Hornby Inge (CHI), in newer agencies the role of traffic sits alongside that of new business, since both involve nurturing the process and serving as points of contact for clients. Social events, such as away-days with clients, marketing and management teams, are incorporated so that agencies can get a closer feel for the company's personality and ethos of the brand, via its staff. This is not unique to CHI; the worldwide brand innovation company, ?Whatif!, base themselves in clients' offices and require their clients to participate in extracurricular activities so that they get closer insights into company personnel. Such work-oriented net-working and client insights become useful when 'challenging' campaign ideas need to be communicated to clients.

What Drives Tracking Procedures?

Although communications agencies today tend to present in-house review and tracking procedures as part of their commercial service, the demand to formally manage creativity has been driven by clients from both the public and private sectors. Even during the early days of commercial television advertising during the mid-1950s, clients had reason to be wary of their advertisers. Agencies and media owners had routinely charged clients fifteen per cent commission to absorb what clients were told were typical production costs.

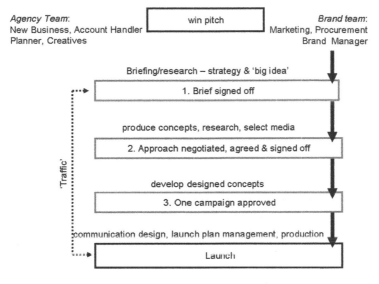

Figure 7.2 Stages during campaign construction: a conventional media agency's model identifying key decision-making stages.

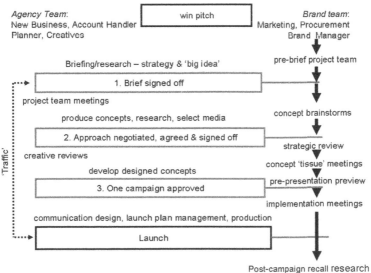

Figure 7.3 A 'media-neutral' model contains more informal meetings to facilitate client involvement and closer tracking procedures.

However, agencies were able to negotiate discount deals with media owners for volume deals without clients being privy to the arrangements. When disclosure acts forced media owners to reveal their true costs, clients started to demand greater transparency throughout the process of advertising production (Brierley 1995).

However, many of the current checks, measures and tracking processes were introduced as a consequence of industry recessions during the late 1980s and early 1990s. Clients demanded greater operational transparency from an industry where developmental work did not form part of the final output and the labour involved was not immediately apparent. The pressure from clients for accountability was most pronounced during the stock market crash of 1987, when brands were looking to 'push the pound' and get better returns on their capital outlay. Interim reports and budget reviews had, after all, become the norm in other sectors.

In the early 1990s brands from fashion, automotive and food retail sectors started to get a better understanding of their customers through the use of data technology to capture customer information. As this chapter goes on to illustrate, Land Rover and the data analysts Dunn Humby (for Tesco) were instrumental in leading other brands to consider researching their customer data to assess how it could inform their advertising and marketing practices. This provided valuable evidence on the motivational factors of niche market groups. It also gave marketing departments enough material to question their communications agencies' effectiveness, as much of the outlay appeared to be wasted. Although mass-media channels – television, radio, cinema, billboard and press – still had the widest audience reach, their potential to reach a mass audience diminished during the 1980s due to greater competition. For instance in 1981, ITV – then the UK's only commercial network – had an audience share of 49 per cent; by 1991, ITV competed with two other terrestrial commercial channels but was still the largest, with an audience share of 42 per cent; by 2001 its share had dipped to under 30 per cent, when satellite and cable networks further dispersed the concentration of viewers (BARB 2003). Mass-media channels also lost their ability to convert awareness into sales. Spending patterns on broadcast advertising reflected clients' move away from advertising practices towards methods associated with marketing: between 1996 and 2006, spend in the UK on broadcast commercials increased by little more than 27 per cent compared to a 40 per cent increase in direct mail services. Similarly, spend on new 'outdoor media' promotional techniques rose by 54 per cent in the same period, compared to a mere 23 per cent increase in spending on press advertisements (figures derived from the Advertising Association's Advertising Statistics Yearbooks 1996–2006). The capability of interactive billboards – in the form of streamed video at metro stations, skywalk boards on pedestrian walkways, transvisuals on escalators and digital advertising hoardings – were developed for outdoor advertising firms including J. C. Decaux and CBS Outdoor as a way of reinvigorating outdoor advertising media. However, developing digital platforms required a large outlay of capital that could only be recouped through charges for the service. Direct marketing and other forms of one-to-one selling required less design expense than conventional advertising and generated higher ROI. As a consequence, marketing and advertising correspondents often questioned the effectiveness of mass communications campaigns.

A difference of opinion as to what constituted 'effective advertising' also encouraged clients to regularly re-tender accounts. Marketing Direct's award scheme, amongst others of its ilk sponsored by services and manufacturers, acknowledges the impact and value of communications (Kover et al. 2005), while most agencies subscribe to schemes that recognize excellence through peer-reviewed awards, acknowledging creativity and craft rather than ROI. Prestigious trophies such as the Cannes Gold Lion, Design and Art Direction Gold Pencil and the One Show ('Gold') are still prominently featured on the shelves and walls of agencies.

Many brand managers also felt that re-tendering addressed the need to take control of their company's identity. In many cases, agencies had held client accounts for a longer period than client teams had been in the post, so creative agency staff had developed a closer understanding of brands' characteristics than their clients. Some communications agencies had even publicly declared themselves to be 'brand guardians' on behalf of their clients. By contrast, brand managers tended to operate in a job cycle that lasted between two to five years and habitually pushed creative agencies to produce *famous* rather than *effective* promotions for immediate impact and personal advancement. This had repercussions, particularly in the fizzy drinks and fast-moving consumer goods sectors during the late 1990s, with client–agency power struggles over the creative direction of campaigns. Established accounts were re-tendered, and communications tasks were split and put up for re-pitch in different sectors of the industry to prevent the situation from arising again.

Such changes impacted on the ways in which agencies operated. The economic downturn from 1992 prompted many clients to reappraise long-standing accounts. Heinz and Coca-Cola were typical of many brands in moving their promotional budgets from advertising to marketing (Zyman 2002; Tungate 2007). 'Marlboro Friday' in the USA, where on 3 April 1993 the company Philip Morris slashed their promotions budget to fund a 20 per cent cut on cigarette prices, led pundits to believe that big budget, big brand advertising was dying and prompted many large advertising firms to downsize. Agencies remodelled their staffing around shorter project-based contracted work, which reduced the need to pay full economic costs (including pensions) and enabled account handlers to closely time-manage project staff. Many employees on permanent contracts were made redundant and a greater percentage of communications workers became contracted to projects, requiring an ability to constantly prove their worth to their employers.

The change of employment conditions in agencies made workers more aware of their own accountability, and prompted changes in the way designers, art directors and copywriters tended to operate in the workplace. They discovered that it paid to show 'face time' in studios by working longer hours than they were paid for, while simultaneously developing their portfolios and registering with recruitment agencies for further work.

The Impact of Digital Profiling on Creative Processes

The communications agencies able to exploit data technology were those with a balance of marketing, advertising and design expertise at their disposal. Land Rover's 'Adventures' campaign in 1993, by Craik Jones Mitchell Voelkel, London, was one of the first campaigns to utilize a client's customer profiling data creatively. A total of 100,000 existing Land Rover customers (plus registered 'prospects') were targeted with a mail-shot that included a stylized brochure and membership pack. The campaign later expanded to include branded 'away-days'. The objective was to instigate an 'active membership culture' around Land Rover and motivate potential owners to 'join the club'. The idea of involving customers opened up creative possibilities for design work. Publications (including a *Freelander Little Book of Freedom*) and expensively packaged gifts were all commissioned to engender a sense of brand loyalty.

Other customer-focused communications schemes soon followed, also connecting creative design with marketing know-how. A bigger breakthrough came with the launch of Tesco Clubcard, the world's most successful store loyalty card scheme, which interlinked quantitative customer data, qualitative evidence of consumption habits and communication processes in a fluid information-communication cycle. Launched throughout Britain in 1995, Tesco Clubcard utilized communications design in a strategic way: information received at the checkout was profiled against customer data that had been gleaned when shoppers applied for the reward card; the material provided enough information to profile and position customers within niche market segments, which in turn shaped the content of the creative brief for designers. Designers then created mail-shots that stimulated sales – and the generation of more customer data.

Data analysts Dunn Humby had been able to segment Tesco's Electronic Point of Sale information and define customers more closely than the National Readership Survey (NRS) social demographics standards, by referring to frequency and timing of visits as well as specific patterns of consumption (Humby, Hunt and Phillips 2003). Customer insights included motivational aspects such as value for money, and recognized life changes such as family growth and changes in taste. The information enabled Tesco's communications agency, Evans Hunt Scott (EHS), to produce targeted communication strategies: EHS designed adaptable schemes that incorporated brochures, personalized letters and offers. These became the basis of a quarterly mail-shot that included discount vouchers for promotions and a lifestyle magazine.

In using a different approach to customer targeting, Land Rover Adventures and Tesco Clubcard required a broader application of designers' skills. In such campaigns, design briefs were becoming less concerned with design differentiation and more concerned with securing a 'share of customer and lifetime value' (Dru 2002), and with Clubcard the shift in emphasis was significant. They believed that they were honing a deeper and more interactive customer relationship. This approach reaped dividends as it drove longer-term brand loyalty while motivating immediate sales, as regular customers shared their experience of Tesco's benefits with friends. Designers at EHS were required to produce adaptable schemes that could be shaped through any number of themed iterations, predetermined by niche customer profiling. The scope for creativity lay in shaping the tone of voice and art direction for differing market segments.

Adventures and Clubcard needed less 'hands-on' management during their creative processes because checks and measures were built into the tight brief, which was closely attuned to the delivery of sales-oriented strategic goals. Communications design has become an increasingly tailored activity as brands produce far closer profiles of prospective and existing customers. The advantage for clients is that there is less chance of inappropriate creative decisions and less time (and money) is wasted through the creative process. For clients, it is clear where their promotional budget is being spent and for customers, this approach to promotion appears to offer benefits as reward for brand loyalty. However, the flip side for creative practitioners is that creative work is so closely targeted and defined that it leaves little scope for personal creativity in the design execution. There is no longer the creative freedom that many used to expect in design communications work. Instead, the creative scope for designers in such tightly regulated processes is in making the execution appear unconstrained.

Form Follows Funds

It is clear then that digital tracking technologies and customer databases have enabled promotional communications to be more focused within the design of campaigns (the rise of digital databases and 'e-tailing' is discussed in Lindstrom 2001). In recent years, the one-to-one communication opportunities afforded by mobile devices has further encouraged manufacturers to reappraise the appropriateness and effectiveness of their advertising media.

In agencies, the role of media planning has expanded to appraise all available media. According to Ian Howorth, Global Chief Creative Officer of 'media-neutral' group WWAV Rapp Collins, multimedia agencies often employ planners to specialize in the client's media choice, market or target consumer. It is therefore no longer creative teams that decide on strategy *and* media; it is planning departments, in conjunction with the marketing departments of clients, that dictate the choice of media. For creative problem-solvers in communications agencies, this reduces the scope for creative decision-making to creative execution stages. For instance, if a product is being launched, the choice of mass media – press, television, radio and billboard – is likely to be specified in the brief along with a suggestion of how it connects with other forms of promotion produced by other agencies. This was rarely the case during the early 1990s, where numerous creative outputs were managed by a single agency. The difference is that where agencies used to present completed problem-solving briefs to their clients, teams constructing a brief today – usually involving client's senior marketing representatives with senior agency staff (account handlers, planners and client handlers called 'new business') – tend to agree details such as the scope, key tasks and use of media up front. A creative brief for art directors and copywriters (and later graphic designers and illustrators) now tends to arrive with facts and statistics, suggestions for creative inspiration, a detailed profile of the target market and the most appropriate media to use in reaching them. Briefs therefore tend to reach creative teams in a detailed form further along in the creative process.

However, in other cases the creative opportunities for designers have grown, particularly where communications require graphic flexibility – schemes that can operate as a kit of options for use in other media, as part of an integrated multimedia campaign. Within multimedia schemes, visual communication needs to be as appropriate in communicating to individual customers via SMS or video messaging as it would be in a mainstream commercial. Less time is spent on the campaign idea, and more time is spent on designing the communication system, ensuring consistency across media. One of the most successful examples was Nike's 'Run London' multimedia project, which grew into a network of ten-kilometre running events around the world. The scheme was conceived as a means to develop closer engagement with customers and the first run was in 2000. AKQA, the agency that created Nike's 'Run London' communications, dovetailed a website, tailored SMS texts and e-mails with offline communications including on-site signage, race packs, banners, billboards, press advertisements and even a winner's medal (Springer 2007). The strength of the scheme was its flexibility, with the graphic identity easily transferred through a number of iterations across a range of media.

As 'Run London' demonstrated, multimedia campaigns can widen the remit for designers further along the creative production line. Spin-offs – such as Britvic Tango's doll, and social network sites such as Unilever Dove's worldwide 'Campaign for Real Beauty' in 2004 – can create ongoing opportunities for designers during the run of a campaign. There are also visual and text-based design opportunities within computer game promotions. 'In-game advertising', where paid-for communications form part of the rendered scene of a computer game, incorporate virtual advertising sites. Games such as DTI Race Driver incorporate a structured and measurable costing hierarchy based on screen exposure (the amount of time a brand is featured in the screen frame), where the placement of brand logos is ranked according to the performance levels of characters within games. In the context of in-game promotion, media buyers are able to provide clients with an accurate estimate for the amount of time their spot will be seen. Within tightly regulated digital spaces therefore, there is creative scope for designers, although there is little opportunity for creatives to deliver a higher than expected ROI.

Checks and Measures as Promotional Tools

Although digital platforms seem to contain the scope for creative communications, opportunities still exist for lateral thinking in the production of a campaign idea. An overarching creative idea tends to be the common aspect that fuses all parts of a campaign, more so than design style. Since an overarching idea needs to operate through a variety of linked design, advertising and marketing situations, producing a 'big idea' is central to the creative process. In recent years some agencies have repositioned the process of producing a 'big idea' into a promotional tool, by positioning their brainstorming stages at key review and reflection points in the communications process. Furthermore, by involving clients, these research and development stages may become an interactive part of an agency's self-promotion. Clemmow Hornby Inge, a leading UK agency, made a virtue of their creativity in strategy development by opening up a 'Big Ideas Floor', which occupies an entire level of their London headquarters.

Figure 7.4 The 'Big Ideas Floor' at Clemmow Hornby Inge. © Clemmow Hornby Inge, London.

From an agency perspective, Tim Allnutt of CHI makes the case that brands need a 'big idea' rather than an advertising solution, because brand marketing directors are not in the post long enough to be true to the brand (Allnutt 2008). Their short-term view, he claims, means they are inclined to change the direction of their advertising too frequently, whereas longer-lasting big ideas 'stay true' to consumers' experiences of a brand. CHI's office space and 'Big Ideas Floor' are designed to be conducive to staging group events, since client and agency teams can use them to review ideas and creative work 'in the round'; on the wall the agency's creative processes are mapped out with defined stages including Client Briefing, Product, Customer, Company and Corporate Ambition Reviews and a Big Ideas Day spelt out across the walls. The building's structural columns bear mottos including 'The best way to get a big idea is to get a lot of ideas', which serve to instil the sense that the space is at the heart of producing structured original creative ideas. The Big Ideas Floor helps to promote the working practices of the agency to existing and prospective clients. It reinforces the notion that innovation is managed through a set of agency-specific policies and processes, and that there is a rigorous method to the 'madness' of creative production.

In a similar vein, Jean-Marie Dru made TBWA's creative methods distinctive by introducing a Connections Theory Wheel to TBWA Disruption (brainstorming) Days (Dru 2002). The aim of the wheel was to pinpoint moments in the consumer's day when they were more likely to be swayed by commercial messages. The agency's final communications output would normally take the form of PR, digital, 3D, advertising, graphic design or any of these in combination. The advantage of publishing creative processes is that it brings clients into the fold of communication design practice, to experience the process of campaign construction as it emerges. It imbues in clients the sense that they have co-created a campaign at key stages, which makes them more sympathetic to the work that is produced at the end of the process. Therefore brand managers are more likely to champion the output, feel that they have experienced their agency's creative process management and, as a consequence, are less likely to quibble with the final results.

The logic behind such developments is that the closer clients and agencies work, the greater the share of accountability. Allnutt notes that while it is not always the case that all communication processes are audited, there is always a pressure on clients and agencies to prove the work they have done (Allnutt 2008). Extra research is often produced, both qualitative (focus groups, bespoke research, sales figures) and quantitative (data supporting research), to vindicate decisions made on strategy and creative direction.

Of all the benefits of making creative practices and their management transparent, perhaps the greatest has been to engage those outside the agency with a communication agency's working processes. It enables client contacts to explain to others further removed from a creative agency how their money is being spent. More often than not, the authority to sign off budgets rests with procurement departments, so the cost of production, labour and indirect benefits is subject to financial metrics. As marketing directors tend to be the signatories in signing off creative work before production, their role in reasoning work on behalf of their agency is crucial. In practice, therefore, selling the process to clients during the stages of production ensures that projects are 'signed off' and reduces the risk of the agency being asked to alter work. Less time is wasted but, as a consequence, the scope of creative freedom is necessarily restricted to staged moments.

Conclusion

Modern agencies promote their creative processes and their evaluation practices to make themselves distinctive and to establish smooth client relationships. Client involvement is increasingly designed into creative processes on the basis that the more clients work with their creative agents, the more 'socialized' the client–agency relationship becomes. Client teams are likely to

1960s	• Creative teams and Sociologists involved in campaigns • Analysis of market segmentation • Agencies success measured in terms of brand awareness, sales and creative craft
1970s	• Planning developed as a discreet practice to create a context for creative work • Analysis of products • Agency success measured in terms of brand awareness and advertising recall
1980s	• Planning highlight lifestyles in campaigns, Multinational brands demand ROI • Analysis of brands and consumers • Agency success measured in terms of advertising recall and awards
1990s	• Awards for effectiveness. Relationship Marketing develops • Analysis of brand cultures and media • Agency success measured in terms of ROI and 'talkability'
2000s	• Creative production presented alongside design solutions at pitches • Analysis of media, one-to-one communications and customer-brand relationships • Agency success measured in terms of ROI and depth of consumer engagement

Figure 7.5 Development of creative production processes by decade. © Paul Springer.

champion their agents because, as co-creators, they have first-hand experience of the processes involved. Openly accountable stages also help agencies; where client audits may question strategic direction or value, agency-directed review processes involving clients ensure that the creative rationale is championed right through the infrastructure of their paymasters. Therefore socializing review processes has become a means of 'training' clients to appreciate creative content. Clients become better equipped to understand creative decisions from an embryonic stage, so that strong ideas are less likely to be quashed early on. Consequently, strong creative ideas have actually been able to flourish in a period of tighter fiscal control.

There are other consequences of socializing the creative process. Review meetings are not equally balanced, in the sense that clients have the ultimate say, so in many respects it is clients rather than agencies who have creative freedom, despite lacking the skills to deliver campaign artwork. In this respect 'educating up' clients can actually weaken the authority of creatives. Such a conclusion cannot be taken as a general rule, however. St Luke's, CHI and TBWA have all devised formats that allow their creative departments to flourish without being constrained by the first-hand experiences of their clients. For these agencies, closer audit processes work well, yet for others, systematic checks and greater client involvement have confined the spirit of creative freedom to the beginning of the creative process, to the 'big idea' rather than other parts of the campaign.

It is therefore fair to conclude that the augmentation of review measures has further compartmentalized the stages of the creative process, making the design content of mass communications less 'creative' overall. More frequent reviews and clearer lines of accountability have limited the potential for under- and over-estimation of ROI, and this has led to greater client satisfaction. Although advertising is still not as measurable as digital marketing in terms of ROI (digital click-through tracking is more of a 'science' than advertising,) closer control of creative working methods has at least raised the industry standard enough to convince brands to engage with consumers through mass communications.

Are such changes to the communications process unique to the communications industry, or are they symptomatic of convergent creative practices? The jobs in large design practices correspond with communications firms of similar size. For instance, the roles of new business (handling clients) and traffic (project process management) in communications firms correspond with client services and design managers in design firms. Global creative holding companies with a mix of design and communications firms (such as WPP, Omnicom, The Interpublic Group, Publicis, Havas and Dentsu) often encourage the sharing of good practices and working methods across different types of creative agency. As the Van Heusen example earlier in this chapter illustrated, there is increasingly an overlap between the types of work that creative houses take on. Similar modes of accountability, work measurement and client involvement would be a logical step in standardizing (if not fully systematizing) commercial creative practices.

Costing is also a practice that appears to have been standardized between design and communications firms. Itemised stages allow clients to see what they are being billed for – and to assess its value. In most types of practice, concept work and brainstorming stages (sketching out rough 'scamps') tend to be billed separately from market analysis, planning and development stages, which are also separated from design iteration and storyboard phases. This is similar across product design, interior design, architecture and communication practices. One could therefore make the case that advertising, branding, media and communication design have converged with design practices through commerce: by shaping creative practices as a series of costed commercial processes, different disciplines can increasingly be measured by their processes rather than their output.

References

Allnutt, T. (2008), interview with Tim Allnutt, London, 27 May 2008.

Brierley, S. (1995), *The Advertising Handbook*, London: Routledge.

Dru, J-M. (2002), *Beyond Disruption*, New York: J. Wiley/ Adweek.

Goodkind, G. (2006), 'Buzzworthy PR' in J. Kirby and P. Marsden (eds.), *Connected Marketing*, Oxford: Butterworth Heinemann.

Hartley, J. (ed.) (2005), *Creative Industries*, Malden, MA: Blackwell.

Humby, C., Hunt, T. and Phillips, T. (2003), *Scoring Points*, London: Kogan Page.

Kover, A. J., Goldberg, S. M. and James, W. L. (2005), 'Creativity vs. Effectiveness? An Integrating Classification for Advertising', *Journal of Advertising Research*, 35(6): 29–40.

Leadbeater, C. (1999), *Living on Thin Air*, London: Penguin.

Leadbeater, C. (2008), *We-Think*, London: Profile.

Lindstron, M. (2001), *Clicks, Bricks and Brands*, London: Kogan Page.

Mayer, J. (1961), *Madison Avenue, USA*, London: Penguin.

McIlrath, S. (1997), 'A New Creative Manifesto' in *Admap*, Issue 378, Bucks: World of Advertising Research Council.

Reeves, R. (1960), *Reality in Advertising*, New York: Alfred A. Knopf.

Roberts, K. (2004), *Lovemarks: The Future Beyond Brands*, New York: Power House.

Springer, P. (2007), *Ads to Icons*, London: Kogan Page.

Tungate, M. (2007), *Adland*, London: Kogan Page.

Zyman, S. (2002), *The End of Advertising As We Know It*, New York: J Wiley & Sons.

CHAPTER 8

Researchers in the World of Product Design

Nitzan Waisberg

Introduction

Over about the past twenty five years, the world of product design has integrated a group of professional researchers into its practice. This group includes anthropologists, psychologists, statisticians, market researchers and others – people people – who specialize in the human factor of the design process. These researchers collect information about people's behaviour, needs and dreams, make sense of it and communicate their understanding to others involved in the design process. They contribute to the design and development of a wide variety of products, for example computer software, medical devices, mobile phones, infant car seats, soap packaging and potato crisps. Also, they contribute to the design of spaces, services, strategies, messages and experiences. Indeed, it is the researchers' expertise in figuring out people – *not* in making artefacts – that enables them to find a common denominator among all of these. Their work anchors the constraints of design in the realm of human experience, and their activity in the world of design casts doubt on the usefulness of traditional disciplinary distinctions such as 'product design', largely defined through technological conventions and constraints. These researchers are located at a turbulent and strategic intersection of worlds and sensibilities, and their impact on design is substantial. This said, as supporting actors their contribution is generally marginalized, and little is known about their role in the social world of design.

Discussing the social world of art, sociologist Howard Becker (1974: 770) wrote that 'producing art requires elaborate modes of cooperation amongst specialized personnel' (see also Shibutani 1955, Becker 1982). He argued that conventions of the art world which guide both artists and supporting actors are real constraints that shape what a work of art will ultimately be. The size of paintings, for example, correlates with the size of canvasses (obviously) as well as museum walls (less obviously). A sociological view of art as collective action makes apparent that any work of art would not exist as it is were it not for the particular conventions that guide the various individuals and groups involved in its production. A profound appreciation of these conventions, and a mastery of social interactions that make up a social world can help an artist leverage them and transcend their limitations.

This same idea can be extended to the discussion of product design, a social world related to art, engineering and business. Studying the individuals responsible for crafting and conveying knowledge about specific groups of people to others in the design world reveals that contemporary product design is a truly collaborative, interdisciplinary practice. This collaboration is characterized by ongoing negotiation, unlike the type of well-defined and controlled collaboration characterizing editorial design practice, as described by Sarah Owens in her chapter in this book. I will present this thesis even more provocatively: it is impossible to allocate 'ownership' of any element of the design process, including form and function, to any one type of actor. All decisions in today's design process are explicitly or latently influenced by complex modes of cooperation between people who don't necessarily have much in common apart from working on the same project. Researchers are just as much of a creative force as designers and, for all practical purposes, research and researchers influence what a product is just as much as design and designers. In fact, researchers might be described as 'cultural intermediaries', preoccupied with linking production and consumption, in the same way that designers have been described (Bourdieu 1984; du Gay et al. 1997).

I have referred to research and researchers without specifying what these terms mean. Though sometimes called human-centred design research, the research I refer to might best be described as a specialization within the field of market research. Market research is the field devoted to identifying, understanding and influencing the motivations and barriers that impact on a specific category of human behaviour – consumption. We have incredibly complex and evolving relationships with artefacts, which makes consumption far more than just the physical act of buying something (Ariely and Norton 2009). It is, in fact, a central and engaging activity in contemporary society (Chapman 2005). Market research has evolved to cater to this, significantly through its growing presence in all stages of design and product development, from generative exploratory research into future needs to evaluation of finished products, services, spaces, experiences and so forth.

The incorporation of market research into the design process marks an important change in the idea and practice of contemporary product design. In *The Substance of Style*, writer Virginia Postrel (2004: 4–5) claims that 'Aesthetics has become too important to be left to the aesthetes.' Citing David Brown, former president of the Art Centre College of Design in Pasadena,

California, she writes: 'Design ... is moving from the abstract and ideological – "This is good design" – to the personal and emotional – "I *like* that."' This is clearly an oversimplification, and designers and others interested in innovation rightly distrust the idea that 'I like that' offers a legitimate evaluation of their work. Many people do not warm to new products instantly, and almost everyone changes their likes and dislikes based on what others around them are doing. The idea that design must cater to an empirically based interpretation of adequacy ('I like that') rather than to what designers know at a gut level to be optimal, is a source of contention and conflict within the world of design. This conflict manifests itself in tensions between the ideal and the contingent, between the systematic and the intuitive, between the analytical and the creative. These are the polarities that characterize much of the social interactions that bring together design and research, and they will surface throughout this chapter as I explore the sub-world of researchers.

I begin by outlining two important trends that lead to the incorporation of researchers into the world of design: the trend to see systematic study as a path to innovation and the trend to humanize technology. These trends, though they will take us momentarily away from understanding how researchers impact on design, are important for establishing the 'rationale' (Becker 1982) of their activities in the design world. Then I explore the sub-world of research in the world of design by looking at the backgrounds of researchers and at the tasks they tend to perform, those of crafting knowledge, communicating knowledge and communicating status. I rely on my own experience as an industrial designer and qualitative market researcher, having done research for companies such as LG, Procter & Gamble and El-Al Airlines, as well as on eight in-depth interviews I conducted with experienced researchers, and two open-ended discussions with experts and educators in the field of design research.[1]

The Incorporation of Research into the World of Design

Systematic Study as a Path to Innovation

The idea that growth within the business world is increasingly reliant on a company's ability to bring innovation to market – the 'innovation imperative' (Rhea 2006; see also Huston and Sakkab 2006) – has become increasingly widespread. Consequently, it has created opportunities for those who claim to innovate systematically, methodically and on demand. This has sparked a tremendous interest in designers who have a reputation for being professional innovators and in design as a general process for innovation and a catalyst for growth. Furthermore, it has focused attention specifically at the design and innovation culture of the Silicon Valley in California (Hammel 1999; Moggridge 2006).

In *The Sciences of the Artificial* Simon (1969: 111) wrote that 'Everyone designs who devises courses of action aimed at changing existing situations into preferred ones ... Design, so construed, is the core of all professional training.' In *The Reflective Practitioner*, social scientist Donald Schön explored design as an iterative form of practice-based research and, like Simon, suggested that it is a phenomenon worth studying systematically in itself. He noted that design was beginning to embrace intangible things and that disciplinary distinctions in the design world were eroding. He proposed that through empirical observation of design in practice, 'We may also discover, at a deeper level, a generic design process which underlies ... differences' (Schön 1983: 77). The hunch that there is something important which characterizes the way designers design is the base for what has been labelled 'design thinking', now an established – indeed marketable – idea. 'Simply put, it is a discipline that uses the designer's sensibility and methods to match people's needs with what is technologically feasible and what a viable business strategy can convert into customer value and market opportunity' (Brown 2008). 'Design thinking' expresses the process in which elements of the tacit knowledge exhibited in the work of designers have undergone formalization, becoming an explicit business tool for innovation.

Design firms such as IDEO have relied on this idea to reposition themselves as innovation experts who apply 'design thinking' and human-centred design methodologies (essentially human-centred design research, brainstorming and prototyping) to tangible and intangible objectives. Jane Fulton Suri, chief creative officer at IDEO Palo Alto, listed some of the innovation challenges IDEO is facing today (Fulton Suri 2008: 54):

> How can we leverage the value of this brand to increase its reach? Here's an amazing new technology – what applications would be good business opportunities? There hasn't been real innovation in our industry for a decade or more – what can we do to change that? We already own this market category – what's going to be our 'next big thing'?

These are fairly traditional objectives in the worlds of market research and of management consulting, and have now become what Becker (1982: 9) refers to as the 'bundle of tasks' that designers and researchers carry out, with varying degrees of division of tasks between designers, researchers and others. Consultancies with design capabilities such as IDEO and Frog Design might compete with strategic consulting and market research firms such as Cheskin

Added Value, design research firms such as SonicRim, and even large management consulting firms such as McKinsey & Company or Booz Allen Hamilton. These companies conduct their work differently and have different deliverables: IDEO may ultimately design a new product for their client, conducting in-house research, perhaps selecting only highlights to present to their client for buy-in. SonicRim will deliver a report with specific recommendations for the design team chosen by their client, trying to make their report reflect their expertise in research, and their understanding of design through attention to visualization tools. McKinsey may deliver a PowerPoint slide deck connecting various data points, ultimately recommending downsizing and restructuring, for example.

Each type of consultancy will promote their particular approach to the division of labour in creating artefacts, and each will display a very different view of design and of designers in the process. Thus Steve Diller, head of the Experience Design Studio at the Silicon Valley office of Cheskin Added Value, claimed that:

> One of the problems with a lot of design-centric companies is that they still privilege design. They say they are going to do [research] to inform the design process. We say, we are going to bring designers, researchers and consultants into a process together of understanding what is going on in the world and coming up with an experience strategy based on that. Then that group will develop a set of design principles that can guide the development of new offerings ... We don't do industrial design ... Once you've got the design principles, it should be easy to spin off a brand positioning or a product design from those principles, because they are just tools for delivering the experience.

In contrast, Jason Severs, senior design analyst for the industrial design department at Frog Design's New York office, emphasized the importance of having design and prototyping capabilities integral to the collaborative process:

> Communicating an idea, especially something wrapped around design or services, to get buy-in is critical ... [but] we also make sure these things are actually feasible and build-able ... To do that you have to have the skills of designers and mechanical engineers, which we have in the office; business analysts, which we also have in the office. To make sure we are doing things that are actually going to be valuable to [the] client.

As Becker (1982: 9–10) suggests, 'Nothing in the technology of any art makes one division of tasks more "natural" than another.' Specializing in research or having research and design combined under one roof are equally valid divisions of tasks in the making of artefacts. To a large extent, clients will choose a consultancy based on a hypothesis of what kind of output they want. The underlying premise of all these firms is that research, and the consequent analysis, synthesis and implementation, is the systematic path to innovative breakthrough solutions for their clients. In the process, design and research become somewhat interchangeable.

Much in the same way as the boundaries between design disciplines have been blurred, similar boundaries have collapsed in relation to research. Designers have been a notably enthusiastic group of amateur researchers, incorporating human-centred design research into their bundle of tasks. Some have even turned into professional researchers themselves. This is what happened to me: a product designer turned qualitative market researcher.

This process is now institutionalized: The MoMA exhibition, 'Design and the Elastic Mind' (2008), has presented some of the expressions of this affair between design and research as the most significant trend in contemporary design. Design educational programmes around the USA offer training in human-centred design research to designers as well as students from business schools and other disciplines. These include the California College of the Arts' Graduate Design Programme and the MBA in Design Strategy; the Illinois Institute of Technology's (IIT) Master of Design, Master of Design Methods and Master of Design/ MBA programmes; and the Hasso Plattner Institute for Design at Stanford's (known as the 'd.school') classes and workshops, which are open to all Stanford graduate students, and offer executive education courses to train industry executives in human-centred design and the 'design thinking' process. The Design Management Institute (DMI) offers regular seminars about human-centred design research and innovation to executives and managers.

The romantic notion of inspiration, the cultivation of creative genius or the enabling of divine intervention no longer dominate our theory and practice of design and creativity. In product and service design, systematic study, as the foundation of both information and inspiration (Fulton Suri 2008), often supplants these and is seen today as the path to innovation. As such, this provides the rationale (Becker 1982) behind the collective action in the world of design, specifically as it involves research.

Humanizing Technology

Barry Katz, Professor of Humanities and Design at the California College of the Arts, and fellow at IDEO, explains that 'During the 1980s, radically new technologies began drifting into the market from corporate laboratories' such as Xerox PARC (Palo Alto Research Center). Designers and others who sensed that something big was happening gravitated to the area. In *Designing Interactions,* designer and IDEO co-founder Bill Moggridge describes the Silicon Valley he encountered after moving to Palo Alto from London in 1979:

> The innovation was certainly there, with connections between Stanford and the industry that emerged from it, a rapidly expanding venture capital community, and start-up companies all over the place. It was very exciting for me to discover that the valley was evolving from a place where electronic chips and printed circuit boards were invented to a product development community with the chips included in the products; this meant that they would find themselves needing good industrial designers. (Moggridge 2006: 10)

While for much of the twentieth century, industrial design work comprised largely of styling existing technologies to make them more visually appealing, innovations such as the personal computer or the mouse required that designers give form to things that had never existed before. No one knew how people would respond to them, because they were both new and complex. Katz draws a comparison between designers such as Peter Behrens at AEG, who designed electrical products that had never existed before electrification during the early twentieth century, and designers who worked in Silicon Valley during the 1980s.

The comparison is insightful and thought-provoking, and allows the tracing of similarities as well as of differences. If, as philosopher Martin Heidegger (1977) suggested, we commonly perceive technology in one of two ways – an instrumental approach and an anthropological approach – I would argue that the instrumental approach guided the efforts to promote electrical technology (think of the term 'labour-saving device', for example), while so-called human-centred design embraces both the instrumental and the anthropological approaches. The point of this synthesis is to humanize technology while continuing to ensure it serves its function. Human-centred design achieves this through the interdisciplinary collaboration of designers, engineers, anthropologists, psychologists and others, who as a team approach new technology both as a means to an end and as human behaviour. All work together to devise courses of action 'aimed at changing existing situations into preferred ones', but they go about this in very different ways, working with different mindsets of constraints.

The Sub-World of Research

Coming into the World of Design

To contextualize the activity of researchers in the world of design, it is useful to understand a little about their background and how they came to practise human-centred design research. This is particularly significant because as a group, they have rather eclectic training and experience. Many of the people I spoke to described their path to research in the world of design as a personal journey of discovery rather than a clearly delineated career choice. As such, they pollinate the world of design with ideas from other social worlds, with their own unique interdisciplinary experiences, and with the fresh take on design work that their outside perspective enables.

Liz Sanders, a social scientist and design researcher, describes how she was hired in 1981 by the design firm Fitch (then Richardson Smith) as 'an experiment in interdisciplinary design', to work on a strategic project with Xerox. She had an undergraduate degree in psychology and anthropology, and a Ph.D. in experimental psychology with no training or experience in design or engineering. At Fitch, Sanders moved between different groups of designers such as graphic designers and product designers, and today she works with architects in her own consultancy. Her view of design has made this kind of path natural to her. She said: 'Really, they are all working with people and so from a research point of view, it is relevant to all of it. Designers just have different embodiment skills.'

Kelley Styring, an independent consumer strategist, began her career as a product designer in the early 1980s, intuitively conducting research to inform her designs at school and later at Black & Decker and NASA. She discovered market research while doing an MBA and shifted her focus to research out of the belief that her design background would make her a more effective researcher for creative people. She reflected on the situation today: 'The interesting thing, though, in working with creative organizations, is [that] there is fear and loathing of researchers ...' Styring believes that this is the result of researchers' abuse of their position, specifically of the fact that they tend to offer opinions on design details rather than guide the team according to principles based on research into people's needs.

Jason Severs of Frog Design began his design research career in fine art. He worked as a Flash developer in the early days of Flash and became curious about the link between new media and behaviour. He received a Master's in education research and focused on instructional design and usability research: 'That's when I got my first dose of what it meant to be a designer, not in the sense of a graphic designer, but to do design thinking, iterative design thinking.'

Researchers, with their varied and interdisciplinary backgrounds, are seasoned at negotiating disparate ideas and experiences. They draw on observation, experience and intuition to craft their rather open-ended and changing roles. Importantly, although they are charged with research, a process not generally identified with creativity, they tend to be creative, original, often nonconforming individuals with a talent for synthesis.

The Tasks of Researchers in the World of Design

Different researchers, with different skills and background, may have different tasks in their bundles, and yet some tasks are ubiquitous: crafting knowledge, communicating knowledge and communicating status. These constitute key reasons for why researchers are an important part of the design process today. I discuss them in turn.

Crafting Knowledge, Systematically Dealing with Intuition. People, Needs and Motivations

According to most researchers, their main task is to ensure that design serves the real needs of people. Sanders explained:

> I've found if you don't give designers any information they just make stuff up. They have no trouble making stuff up. So, I'm just there making sure the stuff they make up has some connection to the people they are serving. And I do see design as serving the needs of people.

'Serving the needs of people' may mean anything between serving existing, explicitly articulated functional needs to latent experiential needs. Furthermore, needs can be unique or universal and can be met at various levels. Different researchers will craft knowledge about people's needs in different ways, depending on their philosophical approach, background and intuition, as well as the methods in which they specialize.

The first step to crafting knowledge about people's needs is defining whose needs will be served. This is often done by conducting quantitative surveys that ask samples of a population many different questions about their income, age, opinions, habits and even hopes and dreams. The analysis involves looking for groups that seem to have more things in common than differences. Such a cluster might be called a segment. The segment might then get a name, to make it easier to relate to and design for – for example 'Baby Boomers' or 'Fashion Junkies'. The way a segment is defined (be it through quantitative or qualitative research) will have a tremendous impact on how the people that design is meant to serve are understood and consequently what will be seen as serving their needs.

The weakness of this system is twofold: the first is that it is possible to identify a group of people with lots of stuff in common, but all this stuff may not be relevant to identifying needs and motivations or shared meaning. The second weakness is that human beings have a compulsion to reify things, that is, mistake an abstraction (which is what a segment is) for a real thing. Although it is researchers who come up with ways of framing and abstracting people and their behaviour in order to study them and draw conclusions that are true for more than one individual, a large part of their work actually involves fighting this reification tendency.

Severs says that while defining a segment, identifying the outliers ('people who are relevant to, but lie outside core audience demographics') is crucial 'to get that surprise point of view'. Brenda Laurel, a designer, researcher and writer with an eclectic background in theatre and computers, founded Purple Moon, a company that developed successful interactive media for girls, 'emotional rehearsal space for social interaction', at a time when computer gaming was a boys' market. Now Chair of the Graduate Design Programme at the California College of the Arts, Laurel begins her trans-disciplinary human-centred design research course by ensuring her students are wary of the terms often used to lump people into abstract categories. She lists 'Seven Dirty Words' which include 'consumer', 'users' and words that equate people to animals – such as 'targeting'. Alexandra Zafiroglu, an anthropologist in the Domestic Designs and Technology Group at Intel, wrote that the first principle guiding her research is that she studies people rather than users (see Zafiroglu 2007). Obviously, studying people and studying users might involve exactly the same human beings. These semantic distinctions are important because they show a struggle against the reification tendency: approaching the subjects of research with a clean slate upon which it becomes possible to trace opportunities for how design might serve a group's latent needs. However, defining the conditions under which unbiased research can take place begins and ends in the researcher's approach.

Paul Holtzman, a senior statistician and director of methodology for the global market research firm Synovate's MarketQuest division, develops research tools for the product development process from initial concept development to pricing, packaging and ongoing performance monitoring. Holtzman sees the market as an indicator of how artefacts meet the needs of people: 'What good is an object that exists just for design or statistics? ... One must begin with a need ... [In free markets] bad ideas die and good ideas thrive, as opposed to regimes where bad ideas are put on life support.'

Holtzman draws on eclectic sources such as economic theory and philosophy to design statistical models that express causal relationships, help to identify unmet needs of large groups of people, and help to evaluate how products and services meet those needs. Holtzman uses the market as a source of knowledge about needs and this impacts on the models he designs. At Synovate and other research firms, the ability to formulate 'branded' models and routinize the work around them is essential for both speed and consistency. For example, a client may want to repeat a study on a quarterly or yearly basis, or conduct the same study across markets. Substantial inconsistencies may render a comparative analysis between periods or across the globe meaningless. Because these models are used by other researchers in the firm's offices round the world, Holtzman's interpretation of need and how it can be researched is replicated in different studies around the world and across industry sectors.

Kerry O'Connor, an anthropologist with an MBA, is a fellow at the Hasso Plattner Institute for Design at Stanford. She heads executive education workshops, which give corporate executives some experience with human-centred research and 'design thinking'. While O'Connor agrees that bad products will tend to fail in the marketplace, mediocre ones abound. She claims that the role of research is to turn products and services from something that meets needs adequately, to something that delivers experiences that satisfy and inspire beyond what is currently imaginable. O'Connor believes that opportunities for innovation lie in the gap between what people say and what they actually do, that is, in contradictions. O'Connor's research relies on observation and intuition to generate insights into what may serve needs that cannot be articulated. However, insight is not easy to arrive at. Identifying friction at the interface between behaviour and artefacts is an important method that researchers use to locate possible unmet needs and to arrange the information gathered into research findings. Contextualizing needs and collaborating with people with different points of view may help set excellent conditions for arriving at insights, but like inspiration or talent, insight has an elusive dimension and there is no sure method of attaining it.

Understanding need goes only part of the way to devising courses of action that may meet needs exceptionally in practice. Understanding motivation, what draws people to meet particular needs in a particular manner, and understanding barriers – what may deter them from meeting those needs in a particular manner, are also part of the work of researchers.

Holtzman described his view on price in this context:

I see price as a barrier, and we understand how to balance that barrier. The price of something has to be a reaction to perceived function, form ... I don't necessarily think of it in a monetary sense. Price is a voting system ... it is a trade-off system. Am I willing to part with something dear in order to obtain [something else]?

Today researchers can offer simulators that 'prototype' trade-off scenarios in which design parameters can be balanced against business outputs. These simulations can, in turn, inform detailed specifications for design. Thus, elements such as colour, texture, or the location of a button become human and business factor issues just as much as they are design or form factor issues. Holtzman stresses that simulations can run amok unless used by someone able to interpret the output. The abstractions used in market research by research professionals must be fleshed out and contextualized to avoid the fear and loathing of researchers to which Styring alluded. They must be woven into a narrative of human motivation and experience that all collaborators in the design process can relate to.

Unlike needs which may be quite specific, motivations may be much more general. These are themes that help researchers to make a coherent story out of the information they gather about people. The Synovate Censydium division operates using eight so-called mechanisms of universal human motivation. These are: vitality, enjoyment, conviviality, belonging, security, control, recognition and power. Each mechanism is allocated a colour, imagery and string of related stories. The mechanisms and associated research methodology (a very long and rather odd version of focus groups) were originally developed in the late 1980s by two economists, Jan Callebaut and Hendrik Hendrickx, but rely heavily on ideas from psychology and philosophy. Censydium is, in fact, a branded model marketed to research clients interested in motivational market research. Interestingly, one of the ideas Censydium promotes is 'systematically dealing with intuition' through computerized diagnostic tools for qualitative findings. This is part of a growing trend within qualitative market and academic research to routinize and systematize the craft, intuition and experience that dominate analysis of findings in the field today.

Diller, Shedroff and Rhea (2006) describe fifteen experiences with global appeal (only a fraction of possible meaningful experiences) namely: accomplishment, beauty, creation, community, duty, enlightenment, freedom, harmony, justice, oneness, redemption, security, truth, validation and wonder. Unlike Censydium, these experiences are not a branded model. The authors discuss them in their book, *Making Meaning: How Successful Businesses Deliver Meaningful Customer Experiences*, promoting a sense of the company's experience in research by offering that these were arrived at as a result of thousands of interviews with people over the years. This knowledge, though arranged and articulated, is still left at a 'know-how' level, communicating that Cheskin

Added Value's insight into human motivation relies on skill and experience, on the craft of research.

Researchers rely on systematic study, routinized work processes and formulated frameworks for analysis (branded or not), but they equally rely on their intuition, empathy and experience to weave stories that serve as guides for others in the design process.

Communicating Knowledge

Researchers tell, write, illustrate and animate empirically inspired stories about our relationships with the artificial to communicate the knowledge they assemble through research. Christos Eliades, a statistician and research director at Synovate, explained that 'Numbers have their charm, but they need to tell a story in a succinct and comprehensive way.' An important offspring of the affair between design and research is the increasing emphasis on visualization as a tool for analysis, and on visual storytelling as a means of communicating knowledge to interdisciplinary teams (Bernstein 2007). This has been particularly important in convincing designers that their intuition might benefit from some information. An early example appeared in a 1983 paper describing the human factors testing of the Xerox 8010 office workstation, known as 'Star'. The authors explain that user research was necessary because 'the background of the targeted users was very different to that of Star's designers; the designer's intuitions could not always be used as criteria for an acceptable system' (Bewley et al. 1983: 72). The authors emphasize in their conclusions that 'Videotaping was a very important tool ... the designers were more convinced by videotapes than by our dry numbers that people were having trouble with their system' (1983: 76–7).

Although human-centred design research is more commonplace today, persuading designers and others of the validity and significance of findings is still a challenge, mostly because collaborators in the design process often disagree about crucial things such as 'What is this product for?' or 'What would make this product better for the people who use it?' To overcome this, researchers may rely not only on their storytelling abilities, but also on their ability to step back and act as *mediators* rather than actors with their own agenda.

Sanders, for example, envisions the blurring of discipline boundaries in what she terms 'post-design', a shift from designers designing *for* people by using their input, to designing *with* them, as creative partners through the use of participatory and co-design tools. She describes how her role has evolved into a mediating role between designers and people:

When I first started in the 1980s, I felt my job was to cover the gap, to translate between the users and designers. So my job would be collecting information and making sure to get the relevant information and putting it in a form that designers would find useful. About ten years ago, I realized I could have a much greater impact on design if I stepped out of that role and instead focused my energy on developing a language that designers and end-users could both use to ideate and express themselves with. So, I'm not translating or providing insight, I'm providing experiences or events that they participate in using this language to talk directly to each other.

Ken Miller, an innovation consultant based in New York, started his career with an MBA and worked for several years in product development at American Express. He then founded his own branding agency and after a few iterations he started an innovation consultancy. Miller, who communicates with creative and business functions, also described his role as mediation:

My job is basically to facilitate theirs and provide a bridge for 'What is right for the project?' to 'How can we generate the creative output that will serve that?' … It calls for mutual respect and it calls for design direction methodology that

Figure 8.1 Marketing and design processes, as seen by Ken Miller. © 2008 Ken Miller Group. Reprinted here with permission. 'Insight for Innovation' is a registered trademark of the Ken Miller Group.

identifies very distinct, clear innovation platforms that can be functional and perceptual and emotional ... Once you put [up] those guard rails, they become not a constraining factor, but an enabling factor ... I've always called them innovation platforms: basically what we are solving for, before we go about solving it.

Miller notes the differences in the way in which designers or creative people approach their work as opposed to business people, and sees his role as creating structured interventions that compel the different actors to cooperate.

The Symbolic Role: Communicating Status

One important role that researchers play is a symbolic one: they communicate status. This role enables design institutions such as design firms, innovation consultancies and universities to align themselves with the two previously discussed trends – systematic study as a path to innovation and the humanizing of technology. One of the benefits of aligning oneself with these trends is status.

Firms that publicize their use of research as an integral part of the design and product development process are singled out, and enjoy an aspirational status in the design and business worlds (Rawsthorn 2008; Kalins 2003; Borden et al. 2008). Michael Marks, CEO of Flextronics, the world's largest manufacturing service provider (which amongst its many assets owns Frog Design) claimed that 'Design is no longer a competitive advantage. Design is a commodity' (Engardio 2005). Design firms use research – and importantly they communicate this use – as a means of differentiating themselves and emphasizing their service orientation in a global market with fierce competition.

Thus, Frog Design's three-part process – Discover, Design and Deliver – begins with research. Their website explains that 'Analysis becomes insight. Through intensive design research and strategic evaluation, Frog Design gains insight into a brand's identity, consumer base, existing assets, and key market opportunities'. Research, or rather an idealized version of what research in a design firm might be ('traditional research methods are used in unconventional ways'), is emphasized disproportionately to other supporting functions (accounting, for example!) in the overall process of design. It is apparent that research is now more than just a stage in a process – it is part of the Frog Design brand. However, the integrity of a brand should not be mistaken for a homogenous workforce or seamlessly peaceful cooperation. Research may be emphasized, but who conducts it and how others in the design process accept, reject or modify the constraints that researchers propose, remains elusive. As

I have suggested throughout this chapter, the collaborative design process is not seamless, the actors involved anything but homogenous. The collaborative process is a series of negotiations and mediated interventions because it is riddled with conflict. It is a practical debate about the constraints of design, which is to say, about design itself.

Conclusion

Researchers anchor the constraints of design in human experience and as such, these individuals and their practices have a substantial impact on the products of contemporary design practice. Researchers craft and communicate knowledge about people; knowledge which nourishes the design process with human-centred information, insight and inspiration. They create and routinize frameworks for thinking about people, what characterizes them, what motivates them and what is important in their lives. They systematically weave stories about our complex relationship with artefacts and, through collaboration with others in the design process, they enable the telling of new stories through new artefacts.

With varied and eclectic training and background, researchers adapt and customize their 'bundle of tasks' to support and mediate different approaches to the division of labour in the design of new artefacts. Furthermore, their involvement in any particular design process implies a culture of creative collaboration aimed at systematic, informed, risk-reduced innovation. The integration of research into the broad spectrum of product and service design – from conceptual 'design for debate' to branded design and innovation methods – has become central to defining the forefront of design activity today.

Design, framed as collective action, is a mosaic of human interactions characterized by new kinds of cooperation as well as conflict. Researchers must negotiate ideal goals and contingent realities, systematic study as well as intuition and analysis, as well as creative synthesis in order to generate insight into human needs and evaluate how design may meet those needs. Exploring the sub-world of the 'people people' in the world of product design brings to the surface the ambiguous and intermingled natures of design and research in one of the creative industries.

Note

1. I thank my informants Barry Katz, Brenda Laurel, Liz Sanders, Steve Diller, Christos Eliades, Paul Holtzman, Ken Miller, Jason Severs, Kelley Styring and Kerry O'Connor.

References

Antonelli, P. (2007), 'TED Talk'. Available at http://www.mefeedia.com/entry/tedtalks-paula-antonelli-2007/5946418/5/5/08.

Ariely, D. and Michael I. Norton (2009), 'Conceptual Consumption', *Annual Review of Psychology*, 60(1): 475–99.

Becker, H. (1974), 'Art As Collective Action', *American Sociological Review*, 39: 767–73.

Becker, H. (1976), 'Art Worlds and Social Types', *American Behavioral Scientist*, 19: 703–18.

Becker, H. (1982), *Art Worlds*, Los Angeles: University of California Press.

Bernstein, A. (2007), 'Transfer Through Entertainment Talk at IIT Design Research Conference. Available at http://video.google.com/videoplay?docid=2980481075503396161.

Bewley, W., Koherts, T., Schrnit, D. and Verplank, W. (1983), 'Human Factors Testing in the Design of Xerox's 8010 "Star" Office Workstation', *CHI '83: Proceedings of the SIGCHI Conference on Human Factors in Computing Systems*, pp.72–7.

Borden M., Breen, B., Chu, J., Dean, J., Fannin, R., Feldman, A., Fishman, C., Hochman, P., Kushner, D., Lacter, M., Levine, R., Lidsky, D., McGirt, E., Sacks, D., Salter, C., Svoboda, E. and Tischler, I. (March 2008), 'The World's Most Innovative Companies', *Fast Company*. Available at http://www.fastcompany.com/magazine/123/the-worlds-most-innovative-companies.html.

Bourdieu, P. (1984), *Distinction: A Social Critique of the Judgement of Taste*, trans. Richard Nice, London: Routledge & Kegan Paul.

Brown T. (2008), 'Design Thinking', *Harvard Business Review*, 86(6): 84–92.

Chapman, J. (2005), *Emotionally Durable Design: Objects, Experiences and Empathy*, London: Earthscan.

Diller, S., Shedroff, N. and Rhea, D. (2006), *Making Meaning: How Successful Businesses Deliver Meaningful Customer Experiences*, Berkeley CA: New Riders.

du Gay, P., Hall, S., Janes, L., Mackay, H. and Negus, K. (1997), *Doing Cultural Studies: The Story of the Sony Walkman*, London: Sage.

Engardio, P. (2005), 'Design Is a Commodity', *BusinessWeek* magazine, 21 March. Available at http://www.businessweek.com/magazine/content/05_12/b3925609.htm [last accessed 25 January 2009].

Fulton Suri, J. (2008), 'Informing Our Intuition: Design Research for Radical Innovation', *Rotman*, Winter: 52–7.

Hamel G. (1999), 'Bringing Silicon Valley Inside', *Harvard Business Review*, 77(5): 70–84.

Heidegger, M. (1977), *The Question Concerning Technology and Other Essays*, New York: Harper & Row.

Huston, L. and Sakkab, N. (2006), 'Connect and Develop', *Harvard Business Review*, 84(3): 58–66.

Kalins, D. (2003), 'Design Gets Real', *Newsweek Magazine*, 27 October. Available at http://www.ideo.com/images/uploads/news/pdfs/Reinventing.pdf. [last accessed 25 January 2009].

Kelly, D. (2002), 'TED Talk: The Future of Design is Human-Centred'. Available at http://blog.ted.com/2007/05/ideo_founder_da.php. [last accessed 25 January 2009].

Laurel, B. (2003), *Design Research: Methods and Perspectives*, Cambridge MA: MIT Press.

Moggridge, B. (2006), *Designing Interactions*, Cambridge MA: MIT Press.

Nisbet, R. (1980), *History of the Idea of Progress*, New York: Basic Books.

Norman, D. (1990), *The Design of Everyday Things*, New York: Doubleday.

Pine, B. J. and Gilmore, J. H. (1999), *The Experience Economy: Work Is Theatre and Every Business a Stage*, Boston, MA: Harvard Business School Press.

Postrel, V. (2004), *The Substance of Style: How the Rise of Aesthetic Value Is Remaking Commerce, Culture, and Consciousness*, New York: Harper Perennial.

Rawsthorn, A. (2008), 'Can Design Solve Social Problems?', *Fast Company*, November. Available at http://www.fastcompany.com/magazine/130/mission-critical.html.

Rhea, D. (2006), 'The Innovation Imperative'. Available at http://hubmagazine.com/?p=85 [last accessed 25 January 2009].

Sanders, E. (2002), 'From User-Centred to Participatory Design Approaches', in J. Frascara (ed.), *Design and the Social Sciences: Making Connections*, London: Taylor & Francis.

Sanders, E. (2006), 'Design Research in 2006', *Design Research Quarterly*, 1: 1–8.

Schön, D. (1983), *The Reflective Practitioner: How Professionals Think in Action*, New York: Basic Books.

Shibutani, T. (1955), 'Reference Groups as Perspectives', *American Journal of Sociology*, 60(6): 562–9.

Simon, H. (1969), *The Sciences of the Artificial*, Cambridge, MA: MIT Press.

Styring, K. (2007), *In Your Purse: Archaeology of the American Handbag*, Bloomington, IN: AuthorHouse.

Zafiroglu, A. (2007), 'Sideways Glances: Thinking Laterally and Holistically About Technology Placement in the Innovation Process', *Intel Technology Journal*, 11(1): 1–10.

CHAPTER 9

The Turn to Service Design

Lucy Kimbell

At the close of the twentieth century and beginning of the twenty-first, the already busy category of design saw several new fields emerge, entangled in different ways with the development of new information and communications technologies (ICTs) and with the changing role of design in organizational life. Interaction design, experience design, service design and transformation design, to name four, are clusters of ideas and practices around which practitioners have organized themselves, won clients and written manifestos. Of this list, only service design maps directly on to established categories within economics, which divides up productive activities into the extraction of raw materials, manufacturing and services. Pine and Gilmore's (1999) argument that value creation is about creating experiences is not matched by conventional ways of analysing gross national product. Experiences don't feature – yet – as measurable and governable economic outputs, but services do.

The emergence of service design accompanies two developments. The first is the way in which networked media technologies have changed the traditional outputs of design, which now include electronic products but also arrangements of interfaces to distributed devices through which services can be delivered. These include Internet-based technologies such as the web, e-mail and chat, and resources for collaboration and interaction; mobile and fixed telephony; accessible and affordable resources for the creation and distribution of rich media, especially video and high-resolution graphics; the miniaturization of hardware; and the development of networked connectivity. Services do not necessarily require these technologies in their design and organization, but many do involve them.

The second is the increasing attention paid by management theory and practice to the role of design in organizing production and consumption, and in particular to its role in creating new or innovative products and services. Researchers from the fields of design management and innovation studies have recently found empirical examples in which designers and design practices played important roles in creating value for organizations (Bruce and Bessant 2002; Borja de Mozota 2006). One study found that some design consultants were involved in making strategy even while others worked within the bounds of more traditional conceptions of design (Seidel 2000). The involvement of designers in new product development has increasingly been seen as linked with innovation, whether incremental or radical (Perks et al. 2005), while another study saw design consultants as catalysing cultural change (Feldman and Boult 2005).

In these accounts, the creative input of designers is observed in three main ways: through their insights into consumers and end-users, evidenced in their human-centred approach and methods; through their iterative processes of idea generation, modelling and prototyping, testing and selection, often involving multidisciplinary teams; and through their competences in working with aesthetics and with visual forms. Whether hired as external consultants or operating internally within an organization, organized as a stand-alone function or as part of multidisciplinary teams, designers and design managers are seen as making creative contributions that are sometimes formally organized and systematized, but sometimes not. In fact, while design consultancies talk a lot about their routine processes and methods to clients, it is often the case that on closer inspection they also allow considerable space for unexpected outcomes and for surprise (Downs 2006). More generally, it is clear that designers are no longer expected to confine their creative processes to the development of discrete products but can apply their skills and knowledge across a wider range of organizational activities. Overall, the role of design can be seen as shifting from being about giving form to or decorating manufactured commodities to locating them within flows in which production and consumption are blurred (Thrift 2008).

Against the background of these developments in technologies and the changing role of design within organizations, this essay will focus on the emergence of service design as a field of practice and as a discipline. During the development of a new area of knowledge, one is unlikely to find formal routines firmly established in practice, nor clear modes of accountability to service providers, users and other stakeholders. As might be expected, the service design consultants discussed here do not show significant evidence of systematization and formalization in their work. However, a number of factors external to design consultancies may lead to the profession, or discipline, of service design becoming more formally established. Through the possible incorporation of service design into management and design education curricula, its adoption within a 'services science' promoted by corporations such as IBM, and the dissemination of its methods and processes among clients such as those in the public sector, what is at present novel and tacit may become routine and explicit. Situated against this background, this essay explores what the designers who call themselves service designers do. It reflects on these observations in the light of current thinking about design and considers the consequences of the turn to service design and the prospects for it becoming a discipline.

What Is Distinctive about Services?

If one studies the websites of design schools, the pages of design magazines, the catalogues of design fairs and proceedings of conferences, it is clear that service design is not yet an established area of practice or theory. It shows signs of becoming a discourse community (Krippendorff 2006), but even among designers its vocabulary, methods and approaches are not well understood. In everyday conversation, the term 'service design' usually needs explaining and has to be illustrated with examples: you call your bank to discuss a mortgage, or receive a text message with your account balances, or transfer funds online, or get cash from an ATM in a shop on the High Street, and all of these can be seen as components in the service your bank provides. In many organizations, the arrangement of these interactions with a customer may well be handled by a number of different departments, replicating the conventional divisions in management thinking between operations management, marketing and IT, for example. A service design approach, by contrast, would see all of these inter-faces or 'touchpoints' with the customer (or other end-users) as something to be thought of holistically, and it would seek to offer an intentionally designed experience of the organization.

Services are typically conceived of as what products are not.[1] They are seen as intangible, having no physical form, and are distributed in time and space. They cannot be owned, although of course the artefacts involved in delivering services are owned. They cannot be stored or perish. Services are consumed as they are produced and sold, and the customer typically needs to be present for the service to be delivered. Partly because of that customer involvement, services are considered to be heterogeneous, unlike the standardized outputs of manufacturing.

Services are highly varied. To the example of banking, outlined above, we could also add hairdressing, going to a restaurant, taking an aeroplane, or pro-fessional services such as accountancy. A brief consideration of each of these throws up the realization that services are diverse in terms of where they happen, the level of skill and organizational complexity involved in designing and delivering them, the extent to which the experience of a service is an important part of the value added, the involvement of people or technologies, and the extent to which a service can be customized and personalized. Services include activities at both the very top and the very bottom of the economic spectrum, offering some of the best and the worst jobs in contemporary economies, from consulting to cleaning (Salter and Tether 2006).

Economically, services are dominant: they account for three-quarters of gross value added in developed economies and are often growing at a faster rate than other parts of these economies (Salter and Tether 2006). Depending on how you distinguish products and services – an area of some considerable debate – some companies such as General Electric, IBM or SAP are now garnering larger revenues from services than from products (Cusumano et al. 2006). Indeed, services are such a large category, with such internal diversity, that it is questionable whether it is helpful to bundle them together at all. One way of dividing them up distinguishes between traditional services which are often traded locally by small firms, such as construction; systems firms, such as insurance or supermarket retailing with highly developed divisions of labour and reliance on technology; and knowledge-intensive and professional service firms, often undertaking project work with ad hoc organizational structures (Salter and Tether 2006).

Recent awareness of the relative lack of academic knowledge about innovation in services compared to products (Salter and Tether 2006) has prompted questions about how services are designed and how this design process can or should be organized. But before service design practitioners appeared and started to argue that services should be intentionally designed by designers, who was designing them?

The Design of Services before Service Design

A ready answer comes in the phase 'silent design', from the field of design management (Gorb and Dumas 1987). This phrase suggests that much of the designing going on within organizations is undertaken by people not educated in design, or not considering themselves to be professional designers. Services may have been designed in-house or with the help of external consultants, perhaps with responsibility for one particular component of a service, such as the design of a call centre or a website. Since there is not, as yet, any clearly identifiable service design profession with associated institutions such as professional bodies, and few universities teaching service design, it may well be easy to claim that the designing of services going on in organizations must be silent design. But the picture is a little more complicated than that. Within operations management textbooks, for example, there are chapters on how to manage product and service design. Work on new service *development* includes discussions about new service *design* (Fitzsimmons and Fitzsimmons 2000). Examine other literatures that emerge from management faculties and there exist bodies of knowledge within the sub-discipline of services marketing, which has generated ideas and methods such as blueprinting (Shostak 1984) or serviscapes (Bitner 1992). Within computing, there is also a literature on how to design services, where the service is enabled by ICT and the approach is informed by science and technology rather than the arts and humanities. Standards bodies have also paid attention to service design, with a British standard first published in 1994 offering a guide to managing the design of services (British Standards Institution 2006). So a profusion of diverse services exist, designed by all sorts of people with a range of knowledge and intellectual traditions, but typically not people who have been to design school.

In recent years, however, self-named 'service designers' educated in design schools have begun to organize themselves into consultancies offering service design. Some of the first such companies include live|work, a London-based dedicated service design and innovation consultancy founded in 2001 (Løvlie et al. 2008), discussed in this chapter; and the international design and innovation consultancy IDEO, which has a service design practice (Jones and Samalionis 2008, Moggridge 2006). They have clients, large and small, established and entrepreneurial, public sector, non-governmental and commercial. They have informal and formal networks through which they exchange ideas (Saco and Gonsalves 2008). Some of them are involved in making public their work through speaking at conferences, teaching and publishing where they connect with academics working in this area, including the faculty from the Köln International School of Design (Saco and Gonsalves 2008). And some of them at least have a desire to formalize their knowledge, skills and methods into a discipline to build their market (Downs 2006). What is it these practitioners do? What is distinctive about service design as a field of design practice? What are the consequences of the emergence of this field? And what are the prospects for it becoming more systematized and more visible?

Research Study

In what follows I address these questions by drawing on an empirical study into the designing of services in science and technology-based enterprises (Kimbell and Seidel 2008). The observations made below are informed by theoretical and empirical literature concerned with how people work and consume, their practices and arrangements, and the artefacts they create and use (Orlikowski 2000; Schatzki et al. 2001; Reckwitz 2002; Orlikowski 2007;

Shove et al. 2007). Briefly, the study involved three service design firms under-taking several days' paid consultancy for three science- and technology-based enterprises. Five workshops attended by all participants offered opportunities to discuss what the consultancy–enterprise pairs were doing together, and reflect on existing knowledge about the designing of services. Interactions between the pairs were filmed and observed, drawing on ethnographic research methods.

For the purposes of this chapter, one of these three projects will be dis-cussed. This involved the service design and innovation consultancy livelwork's undertaking of a review of a personalized smoking cessation service being trialled in pharmacies offering National Health Service (NHS) facilities and making proposals for improving it. The service is based on research that originated at Oxford University, which found that people respond differently to some medical treatments depending on their genetic profile. At the time of the study, the enterprise was in a growth phase, seeking another round of investment and undertaking a trial in the UK led by the National Institute of Clinical Excellence. The enterprise's core service involved doing a finger-prick blood test on a smoker who wanted to give up, to find specific genetic markers.

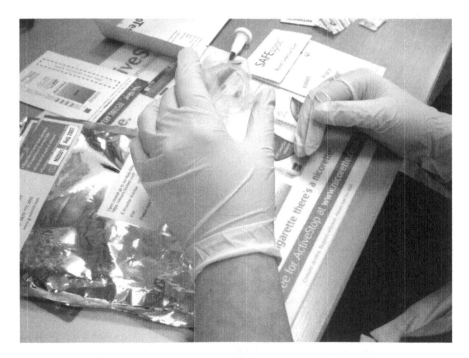

Figure 9.1 Artefacts forming part of the smoking cessation service studied by designers. © University of Oxford.

Depending on his or her molecular profile, the smoker would then be advised which dose of nicotine replacement therapy would work best, the research having shown that the right dose was linked to an individual's molecular profile and that taking it would significantly increase the chances of giving up permanently. This test was bundled into a broader smoking cessation service with other components to help the quitter give up and stay off cigarettes, including a website with information and chat rooms, and a phone service offering personal advice and support and text messages.

This was an exploratory project and the observations made here about service design practice cannot necessarily be generalized, although they may be applicable to other types of context.[2] They are that the designers paid detailed attention to both the artefacts and experience of a service; they made artefacts such as the customer journey diagram that rendered the service tangible and visible; they assembled humans and non-humans into sets of relations; and the designers were also involved in considering and proposing business model innovation.

Paying Attention to Both Artefacts and Experiences

The service designers' approach to redesigning the smoking cessation service involved observing at first hand the way it was delivered, in order to generate insights. Following an initial information-gathering meeting with managers from the enterprise, two designers spent a morning at a pharmacy where the service was being trialled and conducted a 'walk-through' with the pharmacy assistant.[3] In addition they accessed the website through which the service was partly delivered. Enacting a human-centred design approach (Krippendorff 2006), the designers paid considerable attention to the interfaces with which the various stakeholders (the person trying to give up smoking, the pharmacy assistant) engaged with the service – what they called the service 'touchpoints' – and what people did with them. These included a poster in the pharmacy window appealing to would-be non-smokers, the test kit used in the pharmacy to take blood and sputum samples, the website where data were logged by the pharmacist, the letter the quitters received with their test results and recommendations for what treatments to take based on their profiles, and the website, text messages and phone service offering support to smokers whilst giving up. Each of these was scrutinized, documented and criticized.

What was striking was the detailed attention the designers paid to every element of the service, starting before the potential user had even made the decision to quit. For these designers, the service was an assembly of artefacts and experiences that were organized in time and space, operating in a number of locations including the pharmacy and people's own homes. In their work, the designers managed to be attentive to the design of many different touchpoints as well as holding in mind the service as a whole.

Rendering Services as Tangible and Visible

Typically conceived of as intangible, services are nonetheless experienced by end-users through engagement with artefacts that are in fact distinctly material and tangible. These designers used methods that made visible and tangible the service from the point of view of its end-users, for example a diagram of the 'customer journey'. In contrast to the enterprise's operations diagram of the service, which took the form of a flowchart showing the key steps in delivering and supporting it, the service designers created a more rough-and-ready, human-centred representation of the service, incorporating visualizations of its touchpoints and notes about the way service users and stakeholders engaged with them.

Assembled in the studio by the two designers, this customer journey covered an entire wall, comprising photos and screenshots showing the designers' understanding of the pharmacy assistant's and the smoker's engagements with the touchpoints over time. When they were joined by a colleague and began their critique of the trial service, this assemblage was added to with comments

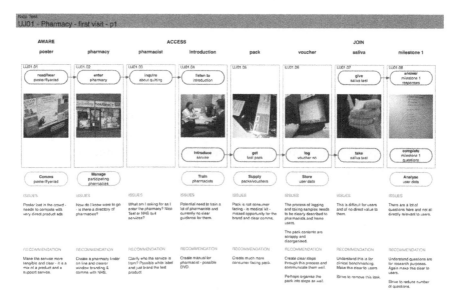

Figure 9.2 Diagram of the customer journey. © University of Oxford.

and suggestions written down on Post-it notes. At the end of the session, the designers took photos of this collection of images and text – their annotated representation of the customer journey. Once this diagram was created, it became an important boundary object (Star and Griesemer 1989) in the exchanges between the designers and the enterprise managers, reframing what constituted the design of the service. At this early stage of the project, this visual representation played a distinctive role in articulating what was and was not known about the service (Whyte and Ewenstein 2005–7). In this project, costs did not feature as part of the diagram but in a later interview, livelwork's Ben Reason said the company had subsequently added a line for cost or revenue per user to their customer journey blueprint. This was not data that livelwork had gathered, he said, but on some projects they had worked with specialists to include costs and revenues in the diagram.

Assembling Sets of Relations

In their discussion of the artefacts and practices involved in constituting the service, the designers seemed to view the service as a fluid arrangement of human and non-human artefacts, rather than a fixed, intangible entity (Latour 2005). As articulated in their verbal and visual representations, the service could not exist without the social dimension or the material dimension: the touchpoints and the ways stakeholders engaged with them. In their discussions they seemed confident, even forthright, about their views on what users wanted or needed. Yet at the same time they emphasized how partial their knowledge was, how their design proposals had to be tested and iterated in context through methods such as experience prototyping (Buchenau and Suri 2000), and that users and stakeholders were essential parts of conceiving of, and constituting, services. Their ways of thinking about the sociality and mate-riality of services seemed, in other words, to be guided by both non-routinized tacit knowledge and slightly more formalized processes of user testing and pro-totype development.

Designing Business Models

Throughout their engagement with the smoking cessation service trial and the enterprise offering it, the designers repeatedly commented both on the artefacts that constituted it and the business models underlying it, what they referred to as the '(value) proposition'. Discussions about value, business models and strategy became more pronounced when the designers started sketching after having assembled the customer journey. Some sketches

Figure 9.3 Designer's sketch showing a new way of thinking about the service. © University of Oxford.

suggested improvements to the existing service trial; some proposed an alternate way of conceptualizing the service, in turn implying a different business model for the organization. In one sketch, the designer proposed a boxed version of the test kit to be sold in pharmacies, which would also include patches to help the smoker give up. Combining the test with patches to be retailed in a box was a new service concept (Goldstein et al. 2002), and was seen as a new way of balancing customer needs and organizational intent. But it also implied a new business model. Selling a test to determine the right patch, alongside support for giving up smoking, together with the patches, would require partnering with patch manufacturers; it also implied different customers, and the need to develop a consumer-facing brand, among other things. When the chief executive of the enterprise saw this sketch, he queried where the designers had got the idea. The designer said they had combined knowledge gained from conversations with the managers with their insights gathered from the pharmacy visit.

In producing that sketch, the designers were not advising the chief executive to take a particular path – it was just one of several sketches they brought to that meeting. Nor had the designers systematically thought through the detail of how this service concept might require the enterprise to reorganize itself. Rather, the sketch functioned as a stimulus to help clarify what the service could or should be: what the concept was, who it was for, and what the nature of that experience would be – how usable and how accessible. This research suggests that, in their work, service designers are deeply concerned with the concept being put to the customer by the organization and that they are therefore attentive, albeit indirectly, to the business models underlying a service. This observation is consistent with recent research into innovation in experiential services (Voss and Zomerdijk 2007).

Discussion

These observations emerged from an empirical study into what designers from one service design and innovation consultancy did during their short project within a larger study. The next section raises questions about what these findings might mean for current understandings of design.

Recent theory has argued for a semantic turn in design (Krippendorff 2006), arguing that human-centred design must pay attention to meanings ascribed by stakeholders to artefacts in use and in language. Contrasting this kind of design with a more technology-centred design, Krippendorff emphasizes the importance of language within design and the ways that designers and stakeholders create meanings about artefacts during the design process, in use and within a wider ecology. This argument foregrounds the need for designers to be aware that they have competences in working with meaning. In this study, the designers seemed aware that in redesigning the service, or part of it, they would be proposing artefacts which would have meaning for the various users.

Where these designers' practice challenges conventional ideas about human-centred design is that their work is not so much concerned with designing artefacts, but rather on arranging entities into sets of relations (Latour 2005) and thinking about the practices of users and stakeholders (Shove et al. 2007). Consider the iPod and its success. Since the iMac desktop computer, Apple has been considered a company that is good at manufacturing desirable products that balance functionality and aesthetics (Buxton 2007). Informal discussions about the iPod in its various instantiations often focus on its 'great design', where 'design' means visual and tactile appeal and ease of use. Commentators have pointed out that there were several iterations of its design before sales grew significantly (Buxton 2007). The design of the device is typically seen as being a core value for consumers and a contributor to the rise in Apple's stock price. But as Hargadon (2005) has argued, what makes the iPod successful is not just the pleasing and usable design of the tangible artefact, but the intangible network within which it is situated and the venture as a whole. The great design job is the design of the iPod as an assemblage of user-device-software-network, situating the device within a network of practices of non-human (web-based databases, music files, coding for preferences, online purchasing) and human actors (the iPod owners, their friends, other music lovers, executives in music companies, musicians). The iPod can exist and be used without the networked services enabled by iTunes, but its value to many owners and users is higher when the free and paid-for web-based services are assembled in relation to the product. The creation of such product-service systems relies on the ability to arrange the assemblage, not the skill in designing an individual artefact.

A possible implication of this is rethinking the roles that service designers play in constituting these sets of relations. Callon's (1987) study of engineers designing electric cars described them as engineer-sociologists, emphasizing how their ideas about the potential uses of the vehicles were inscribed into their designs. Building on this, it might be helpful to think of service designers as designer-sociologists, as a way of foregrounding the ways in which designers' assumptions and hypotheses about human and non-human activities together constitute services.

The final section will consider the possibility of service design practice becoming more routinized and more visible and, indeed, forming a discipline. It would be foolish to make concrete predictions, since any attempt to consider the stabilization and development of service design depends on how the reader understands technology development and innovation. The most relevant actors in the further development of service design are likely to be the designers themselves; managers and entrepreneurs in organizations offering services, especially those involved in service management, operations, marketing and innovation; institutions, such as design departments in education, government bodies and policymakers; academics studying services, especially those with an interest in design and innovation; service users; and technologies, which may support new arrangements of services and the involvement of users, for example in open innovation. As Henderson (1999) has argued in relation to engineering designers, visual representations play an important role in standardizing, codifying and ordering knowledge. It may be that service design as a distinctive area of practice stabilizes over the next few years around concepts and devices such as the customer journey and stakeholder diagrams. Alternatively, its approaches and methods may be diffused through organizations and into the competences of other kinds of professional, including managers, where they may well become routinized.

At least three factors may impact upon these developments. Firstly, the attention paid to design and design management within organization theory and practice. Recent developments in some business schools demonstrate a growing interest in 'design thinking' (Dunne and Martin 2006), 'designerly ways of knowing' (Cross 2006) and 'managing as designing' (Boland and Collopy 2004) as approaches to problem-framing and problem-solving, offering tools for managers facing complex, fast-changing markets. Another factor is the wider attention being paid to service innovation by academics and practitioners coming from a range of orientations. For example, the global IT services company, IBM, includes service design as part of its efforts to construct a 'services science', an interdisciplinary approach to the study, design and operation of services systems which it calls Service Science Management and Engineering (SSME) (Spohrer and Maglio, n.d.). This initiative is about precisely the kinds of routinization, replication and systematization that the service designers discussed here are only slowly beginning to organize in their work.

A second factor is the context of public services. Service designers have already had an impact in the UK on public services from education, health, and transport to welfare provision operating nationally, regionally and locally. Manifestos published by a think-tank (Parker and Heapy 2006) and a research and development unit of the UK Design Council (Burns et al. 2006) have crystallized an ongoing debate about design practice and its relationship to social problems and public service provision. Although they have different approaches – the former calling it 'service design' and the latter 'transformation design' – they share the idea of using designers educated in the design school tradition to be involved *as designers* in tackling social and economic issues. They propose that designers' skills, methods and user-centred approaches can enable improvements in services so that they become more effective and get closer to people's day-to-day lives. Furthermore, they argue that design approaches can inspire and generate innovations which offer solutions to problems facing policymakers working in areas – such as rural transport or diabetes – that span existing institutional structures. Public services in developed economies make up an important area of activity in the UK and many other countries. Driven by political agendas around choice, participation and value (see Moor, and Julier and Moor, in this volume), there may well be opportunities for designers to get much more involved in (re)designing public services. The research cited above involving the smoking cessation trial is one example, even though the starting point was a technology-based enterprise.

A third factor is the exchange of knowledge, methods and tools between designers and their clients. Service designers are already finding themselves facing the opportunity of diffusing their intellectual property, knowledge and skills among their clients. Ben Reason of livelwork says that part of the service they offer is in helping clients, especially public sector organizations, to develop a service design capability of their own, by transferring skills and knowledge. Other consultancies also see this as part of their work. For example, IDEO has created a 'transformation design' practice as one of its core offerings, helping its clients develop human-centred design capabilities internally (IDEO 2008). It is too early to say what the implications might be of helping clients develop service design capabilities in-house. It may lead to the formalization of service design practices, as organizations seek to systematize and protect their investments in developing this resource. Yet if such developments lead to consultancies' revenues being cannibalized, this may result in changes within consultancies' approaches to service design itself.

Conclusion

This essay has explored one of the new design fields that have emerged in the past twenty years alongside the rapid development of ICT and the increasing attention paid to the role of design in management practice and theory. A vast area of economic activity, services have not been seen as something to be created by designers educated at design school, although of course they have always been 'designed', at the very least in the sense of someone arranging separate service components, perhaps designed by others. The development of consultancies offering something called service design is a departure from existing traditions that conceptualize design as based on tangible products or interactions with technologies. The service designers discussed here have practices that are recognizable as design, but which also pay attention to both artefacts and users' practices, render intangible services tangible and create arrangements of human and non-human actors. Implicated in their (re)designing of services are discussions of existing services and proposals to create new service propositions, which may in turn require new business models for an organization.

At this early stage in the development of an area of practice not yet formalized into a discipline, which lacks the associated institutions that typically govern professions, these designers are reflexive about their need to develop vocabularies and methods and for a discourse community to stabilize. While service design consultancies are niche, and their practices dependent on informal, tacit knowledge, their profession may remain emergent. But their practices and methods may stabilize or diffuse depending on the influence of at least three factors: the attention paid by management theory and practice, such as the IBM services science initiative; investment in design by public services; and the transfer of knowledge, methods and tools between service designers and their clients. All of these may lead to increased systematization, professionalization and routinization in service design practice. If so, just as product design is closely associated with industrialization, then service design may turn out to be the current century's emblematic set of design practices.

Notes

1. The distinction between products and services is an area of considerable debate. The standard features of a service are briefly introduced here without qualification, but those interested in a critique of the definition of services as being unlike products are referred to Vargo and Lusch (2004: 324–35).
2. In the time it had available to undertake the project and its artificial nature (driven by a research agenda rather than a client's), the consultancy was not able to undertake the full range of activities it normally would have, such as creating prototypes or a service specification. Secondly, this particular study focused on services in science- and technology-based enterprises including business-to-business services rather than consumer or public sector services.
3. The designers also planned to observe and interview smokers who wanted to give up engaging with the service, but this was not possible with the resources available.

References

Bitner, M. J. (1992), 'Servicescapes: The Impact of Physical Surroundings on Customers and Employees', *Journal of Marketing*, 56(2): 57–71.

Boland, R. and Collopy, F. (eds.) (2004), *Managing As Designing*, Palo Alto, CA: Stanford Business Books.

Borja de Mozota, B. (2006), 'The Four Powers of Design: A Value Model in Design Management', *Design Management Review*, 17(2): 44–53.

Bruce, M. and Bessant, J. (2002), *Design in Business: Strategic Innovation Through Design*, Harlow: Pearson.

British Standards Institution. (2006), *BS 7000-3: Guide to Managing the Design of Services*, London: BSI.

Buchenau, M. and Suri, J. F. (2000), 'Experience Prototyping', in *Proceedings of the Conference on Designing Interactive Systems: Processes, Practices, Methods, and Techniques (DIS2000)*, New York: ACM Press, pp.424–33.

Burns, C., Cottam, H., Vanstone, C. and Winhall, J. (2006), *RED Paper 02: Transformation Design*, London: Design Council.

Buxton, B. (2007), *Sketching User Experiences: Getting the Design Right and the Right Design*, San Francisco: Elsevier.

Callon, M. (1987), 'Society in the Making: The Study of Technology as Tool for Sociological Analysis' in W. Bijker, T. Hughes and T. Pinch (eds.), *The Social Construction of Technological Systems*, Cambridge, MA: MIT Press.

Cross, N. (2006), *Designerly Ways of Knowing*, London: Springer.

Cusumano, M., Kahl, S. and Suarez, F. (2006), *Product, Process, and Service: A New Industry Lifecycle Model*, background paper for Advanced Institute of Management (AIM) Research's Grand Challenge on Service Science, Oxford: Saïd Business School.

Downs, C. (2006), Unpublished interview from workshop held at Saïd Business School, University of Oxford.

Dunne, D. and Martin. R. (2006), 'Design Thinking and How It Will Change Management Education: An Interview and Discussion', *Academy of Management Learning and Education*, 5(4): 512–23.

Feldman, J. and Boult, J. (2005), 'Third-Generation Design Consultancies: Designing Culture for Innovation', *Design Management Review*, 16(1): 40–47.

Fitzsimmons, J. and Fitzsimmons, M. (2000), *New Service Development: Creating Memorable Experiences*, Thousand Oaks, CA: Sage.

Goldstein, S., Johnston, R., Duffy, J. and Rao, J. (2002), 'The Service Concept: The Missing Link in Service Design Research?', *Journal of Operations Management*, 20(2): 121–34.

Gorb, P. and Dumas, A. (1987), 'Silent Design', *Design Studies*, 8: 150–56.

Hargadon, A. (2005), 'Leading With Vision: The Design of New Ventures', *Design Management Review*, Winter: 33–9.

Henderson, K. (1999), *On Line and On Paper: Visual Representations, Visual Culture, and Computer Graphics in Design Engineering*, Cambridge, MA: MIT Press.

IDEO (2008), 'Transformation Design Offering'. Available at http://www.ideo.com/about/offerings/info.asp?x=6 [last accessed 10 July 2008].

Jones. M. and Samalionis, F. (2008), 'From Small Ideas to Radical Service Innovation', *Design Management Review*, 19(1): 20–27.

Kimbell, L. and Seidel, V. P. (eds.) (2008), *Designing for Services in Science and Technology-Based Enterprises*, Oxford: Saïd Business School.

Krippendorff, K. (2006), *The Semantic Turn: A New Foundation for Design*, Boca Raton, FL: CRC Press.

Latour, B. (2005), *Reassembling the Social: An Introduction to Actor-Network-Theory*, Oxford: Oxford University Press.

Løvlie, L., Downs, C. and Reason, B. (2008), 'Bottom-Line Experiences: Measuring the Value of Design in Service', *Design Management Review*, 19(1): 73–9.

Moggridge, B. (2006), *Designing Interactions*, Cambridge, MA: MIT Press.

Orlikoski, W. J. (2000), 'Using Technology and Constituting Structures: A Practice Lens for Studying Technology in Organizations', *Organization Science*, 11(4): 404–42.

Orlikowski, W. J. (2007), 'Sociomaterial Practices: Exploring Technology at Work', *Organization Studies*, 28(9): 1435–48.

Parker, S. and Heapy, J. (2006), *The Journey to the Interface: How Public Service Design Can Connect Users to Reform*, London: Demos.

Perks, H., Cooper, R. and Jones, C. (2005), 'Characterizing the Role of Design in New Product Development', *The Journal of Product Innovation Management*, 22: 111–27.

Pine, B. J. and Gilmore, J. H. (1999), *The Experience Economy*, Harvard, MA: Harvard Business School Press.

Reckwitz, A. (2002), 'Towards a Theory of Social Practices: A Development in Culturalist Theorizing', *European Journal of Social Theory*, 5(2): 243–63.

Saco, R. and Gonsalves, A. (2008), 'Service Design: An Appraisal', *Design Management Journal*, 19(1): 10–19.

Salter, A. and Tether, B. (2006), *Innovation in Services: Through the Looking Glass of Innovation Studies*, background paper for Advanced Institute of Management (AIM) Research's Grand Challenge on Service Science, Oxford: Saïd Business School.

Schatzki, T.R., Knorr-Cetina, K. and von Savingny, E. (eds.) (2001), *The Practice Turn in Contemporary Theory*, London: Routledge.

Seidel, V. (2000), 'Moving From Design to Strategy: The Four Roles of Design-Led Strategy Consulting', *Design Management Journal*, 11(2): 35–40.

Shostack, G. L. (1984), 'Designing Services That Deliver', *Harvard Business Review*, 62(1): 133–9.

Shove, E., Watson, M., Hand, M. and Ingram, J. (2007), *The Design of Everyday Life*, Oxford: Berg.

Spohrer, J. and Maglio, P. (n.d.), *The Emergence of Service Science: Toward Systematic Service Innovations to Accelerate Co-Creation of Value*, Almaden, CA: IBM Almaden Research Centre.

Star, S. L. and Griesemer, J. R. (1989), 'Institutional Ecology, "Translations" and Boundary Objects: Amateurs and Professionals in Berkeley's Museum of Vertebrate Zoology, 1907–39', *Social Studies of Science*, 19: 387–420.

Thrift, N. (2008), *Non-Representational Theory*, Abingdon: Routledge.

Vargo, S. L. and Lusch, R. F. (2004), 'The Four Service Marketing Myths: Remnants of a Goods-Based Manufacturing Model', *Journal of Service Research*, 6(4): 324–35

Voss, C. and Zomerdijk, L. (2007), 'Innovation in Experiential Services – An Empirical View', in DTI (ed.), *Innovation in Services*, London: DTI.

Whyte, J. and Ewenstein, B. (2005–07), *Do You See? Visual Representations As 'Artefacts of Knowing'*, EBK working paper.

CHAPTER 10

Cinema by Design:
Hollywood as a Network Neighbourhood

Damian Sutton

We are all engaged ... in creating a world for an audience, and it's a narrative world. And I think design is coming front and centre to all this.

Alex McDowell, production designer

It may seem a predictable conceit that Hollywood production designer Alex McDowell, whose credits include *Fight Club* (Twentieth Century Fox, 1999), *Minority Report* (DreamWorks SKG/Twentieth Century Fox, 2002), *Dr Seuss' The Cat in the Hat* (DreamWorks SKG/Universal, 2003) and *The Terminal* (DreamWorks SKG/Amblin, 2004), should identify cinema design as being on the front line of film production in the contemporary industry (Schorow 2006: 8). As production designer on these and other projects, McDowell has a privileged position handed down through cinema history. The production designer has personal creative contact with the director and cinematographer of the movie he or she is working on, in a relationship which is still known in Hollywood folklore as 'the trinity' or, more soberly, as 'the creative triangle' (Longwell 2007). Whilst directors who work with McDowell (David Fincher, Steven Spielberg) get headline awards when a movie does well, McDowell might feel the hard work of those movies – *Fight Club*, *Minority Report* and *The Terminal* – was done in developing their stunning sets and action sequences. As the production designer of a major motion picture, McDowell is responsible for overseeing the entire look of the movie, communicating that to the director and cinematographer, unit designers and other department heads, as well as generating the right material data that will see that overall look turned into sets, and which will be used by the advertising and franchise arms of the studio. It is perhaps for this reason that production design offices such as McDowell's have become a movie's 'natural operations centre through the whole of the production process' (Garrett 2006: 20).

However, this assertion should not be seen as a radical departure. The cinema industry, as a creative industry reliant upon collaboration and joint enterprise, has long necessitated the development of a central department that will carry the production from the drawing board and storyboard through to shooting and marketing. In the heyday of Hollywood's 'golden age' of the 1930s, with its seemingly Fordist production line practices, this department was the art department. As we shall see, in a contemporary industry reshaped by information technology and digital processes, this production line has been replaced with a *pipeline* of creative output, whose responsibility for administration is left in the office of the production designer. In a diversified industry, with production material exchanged by independent companies working with the studios, the working practice becomes focused around a continuous flow of material enabled by information and communication technologies. Creatives take companies' material from this central resource, and return it for use by others. The result is a production workflow as well as a creative resource, with copy continually circulating between creative companies as the production progresses. New paradigms of creativity include collaboration as the joint enterprise of individual talents, the value of systems and workflow practices over signature design, and the central role of the conference table or studio space where decisions are taken and communicated collectively. These are paradigms of the design studio which cinema adopted early in its industrial history, which is why we, as scholars, might find that the study of cinema by design methods quickly reveals that the industry creates cinema by design processes. We can also see new principles of creativity, which the changes in technology and market have necessitated, such as the development of a metadata *pipeline*, the importance of networked *involvement*, and the production of continuous *working copy* as extendable Intellectual Property (IP).

This chapter will demonstrate how these principles have so easily proved necessary in the entertainment industry at large, and why they are particularly appropriate to industrial situations where *networked* creativity is an organizational necessity. In the Hollywood of the contemporary blockbuster, the film as seen in the cinema is now a very small part of a broad range of products under the umbrella of a 'movie'. Cinema and DVD packaging as sales points are now extended to include multiple franchise elements (books, CDs, games and toys) as well as continuation elements (material for spin-offs such as television shows). With a diversified range of revenue streams from any single cinema franchise, and with copy circulating continuously between creative teams and individuals throughout production and after, the necessity of effective networked management is clear. The chapter examines the development of cinema as a networked *design practice* in one of the industry's leading regional and critical centres – Hollywood – in a study informed by historical and analytical film studies, cultural and economic geography, as well as theories of our contemporary network society. By alloying these with an understanding of design processes and the creative environment of the studio, a distinctive picture of collaboration in the creative industries can be drawn.

Hollywood: From Factory to Neighbourhood

To aid an understanding of the change in design management in Hollywood, it is useful to look back at the popular concept of Hollywood as a Fordist production line. For many, this image is a legacy of the studio system of the 1930s – Hollywood's 'golden age', the heyday of Greta Garbo, Bette Davis, Clark Gable, and Fred Astaire and Ginger Rogers. It was in the 1930s that West Hollywood, Beverly Hills and Burbank, suburbs of Los Angeles, began to assume a regional relationship with the industry on a par with Dearborn in Michigan for car manufacture, or the San Francisco Bay Area and Silicon Valley in California for computer software. It was at this time that the industry appeared to adopt a Fordist approach to production, but one that relied upon an emerging network of locally situated corporations rather than one or two large manufacturers. The industry was dominated by a small number of large film companies, the 'majors', who still form the neighbourhood of Hollywood. These included Fox (now Twentieth Century Fox), Metro-Goldwyn Mayer, United Artists and Columbia (now all subsidiaries of Sony Corporation), Warner Brothers (now a subsidiary of AOL Time-Warner), Paramount (now part of Viacom) and RKO, the last of which is the only 'major' studio no longer making films. Smaller companies, then as now, produced specialist films, appealing to niche markets. Famous examples include Disney, whose films such as *Snow White and the Seven Dwarfs* (1937) were distributed by RKO, and Miramax, who began by making low-budget 'indie blockbusters' such as *Scandal* and *Sex, Lies and Videotape* (1989) and were purchased, as a venture to continue this practice, by Disney in 1993 (Perren 2001: 30).

Scott (2002) has argued that the moniker 'Fordist' is an unhelpful description of the industry as it developed, since

> ... its technical and organizational configuration was marked by quite high levels of scale and a degree of routinization, but nothing equivalent, say, to the typical Detroit automobile assembly plant churning out identical models by the thousands. (Scott 2002: 960)

Nevertheless, the popular image of Hollywood is that of the mass production of generic films designed to appeal across a wide variety of audience demographics, creating the appearance, in passing, of an identical product.

Given the demand for cinema as a regular weekly (sometimes many times a week) activity in the 1930s, and the global reach of US cinema distribution (Fred Astaire movies, for example, were a big hit in India), the scale of production in West Hollywood was immense. In one season, 1935–36, the region's majors produced 433 films between them (Ramírez 2004: 43). In comparison, the region's entire feature film output in 1980 was only 191. This has risen in recent years, with the growth of small independent companies, so that Hollywood is once again producing in excess of 400 films per year. However, the majors only account for 40 per cent of this, including the films produced by their niche market subsidiaries (such as Fox Searchlight, New Line) designed to cash in on the indie boom.

High turnover of production amongst the majors during the heyday of the studio system led to a refinement of both production and aesthetic practices, as studios came to rely upon film series, marketable ensemble casts (such as the Marx Brothers) and the development of genre pictures which could begin to develop demographically discrete audience groups. Memorable hits such as RKO's *King Kong* (1933), which could create momentum and financial cover for a corporation's business year, came to be known as 'blockbusters' (after the Second World War) and more recently as 'tentpoles'.[1] In order to service this production, each studio in the 1930s had discrete departments devoted specifically to the various tasks involved in making movies in-house. Movies would have an assigned producer and a core unit of personnel, but would pass through each department as it progressed through shooting to editing and distribution. A designer working in a studio art department might work on a number of films in any given week, and even unit art directors themselves might work on six or seven movies in any year. Any creative continuity was often developed through the office of the supervising art director for the studio. In some cases, supervisors such as Hans Dreier at Paramount, Van Nest Polglase at RKO, and Cedric Gibbons at MGM, earned names for themselves, even a considerable star quality, due to their ability to develop a coherent studio look across any number of different features a studio might produce. To talk of the 'individual' style in 1930s Hollywood it is more appropriate to talk of the studio look, headed by the supervising art director. It was the supervising art director's responsibility to involve directors, cinematographers and producers, but also the carpenters and electricians who would be expected to make suggestions and/or objections. As Ramírez notes, in 'completely overseeing visual production at their respective companies, [art directors'] hierarchical and specialized work methods closely resembled those already established in major American architectural studios by the first decades of the twentieth century' (Ramírez 2004: 38). The process depended upon a network of highly specialized designers who were responsible for various stages of the elaboration of a film's settings. The success of Gibbons at MGM, for instance, was ensured by his reliance upon designers who "'should have enough knowledge not to have to depend on the research department to tell him what a Corinthian column looks like'" (Gibbons, cited in Eustis 1937: 797). Given the technical and logistical challenges involved, the office itself played an important role for conferencing and discussion, and also as the home of the filing cabinet and its critical metadata. Metadata is the information attached to film rushes, designs, script treatments and scripts, sets and props, and other principal sources of data. It might include exposure and laboratory directions, a script's margin comments, or a prop storeroom inventory. As Gibbons himself pointed out, with a studio requiring as many as 2,300 sets in any production year, the archive files were central to the running of the studio (Gibbons 1938: 47). Ultimately, of course, historians primarily work with metadata in order to understand how and why creative decisions were made. For instance, a budget account from the filming of a 1936 RKO Astaire and Rogers hit, eventually called *Swing Time*, reveals how Fred Astaire took a fixed fee (he also got a percentage of the film's gross take) whilst Ginger Rogers was still on a daily rate.[2] Thus it is the metadata which helps reveal the inherent gender bias in the development of star teams in studio projects. Famously, Rogers refused to turn up to the shooting of the following year's *Shall We Dance* until her contract was reviewed.

The dominance of the major studios came largely through their vertical integration of movie house real estate (exhibition) with rentals (distribution) and movies (production). With the films themselves as relatively intangible, the integration was rather like an inverted pyramid, as Tino Balio has described, with the vast real estate empire resting on the seemingly risky product of a movie (Balio 1995: 5). It is also not surprising, then, that studios came to rely upon relatively assured chances of success, such as certain stars and particular types of film. In the days before widespread television, corporations could rely upon high attendance through a week's run for a movie in any town (the average exhibition period at that time), but what the production companies were really after was the all-important *holdover*: when a movie hit really big and a second or even third week of screenings was guaranteed. It is important to remember at this point that the success of any movie, past and present, is quite difficult to gauge, especially if we just rely on ticket sales. In the 1930s, for example, holdover rentals were only one possible measure, but may not indicate widespread appeal as opposed to a returning fan audience. The contemporary analogy we might draw is with websites. Counting website 'hits' is not the same as counting unique visitors, and neither will yield qualitative information on why a website is visited or what people think about it. At least return visits, just like holdovers, offer analysts and historians a potentially a clearer picture of what might be called great or successful ventures. A better comparison perhaps is between 1930s holdovers and contemporary DVD rentals and sales. In contemporary Hollywood, exhibition accounts for only 15 per cent of a corporation's revenue, with DVD sales and rentals making up as much as 55 per cent (Currah 2007: 363). This means that blockbusters may only break even when DVD sales are taken into account, and *success* might only be made clear once DVD sales have started to improve on this percentage. In the 2000s, as in the 1930s, success depends on how audiences return to a movie after that first viewing.

Another way the majors ensured success in the 1930s was through exploiting their network of theatres and distribution: block booking packages of A- and B-pictures (the best features with what we now call 'B-movies'); owning and pooling theatre chains; and enforcing 'blind bidding' on independent theatre owners who could easily be outbid on major pictures (Gil 2008: 3–4). The US Department of Justice campaigned against these uncompetitive practices in the 1930s, and in May 1948, the US Supreme Court decreed the theatre 'divorcement' of the major studios (the so-called 'Paramount decree'). Gil argues that, contrary to accepted film scholarship, this did not have a material effect on economic outcomes for the studios since they had already started to move towards fewer, longer movies (Gil 2008: 12) – the era of the big colour epic was already under way. However, we might argue that the 1948 decree had a significant effect on how the industry changed in its structure as a process of design and manufacture. The studios also divested themselves of specialized production personnel, many of whom nonetheless remained in the area to work on films. In this way, the capacity of Hollywood as a *neighbourhood* became essential to its success as designers and other creatives went solo, or set up their own small, specialist companies. Studios themselves became, as Scott describes, 'nerve centres of vertically disintegrated production networks' in 'transaction-intensive congeries of small and specialized but complementary firms' (Scott 2002: 959).

More Than Just a Movie

The pressure that studios put on 'tentpole' pictures led to the growth of the franchise, for which the movie was just one constituent part. Early examples of franchise include *Jaws* (Universal, 1975), which was one of the first to properly exploit merchandising and particularly the tie-in novel, *Star Wars* (Twentieth Century Fox, 1977–), *Indiana Jones* (Paramount, 1981–) and *Batman* (Warner Bros., 1989–). The success of franchises, and the way they exploit the widespread potential for consumer interaction, has drawn sub-stantial analysis ranging from the study of their beginnings in other texts (Meehan 1991) to global corporate entities in the late modern period (Wasko 2001) and on to contemporary cinema and branding in the present (Grainge 2007).

Whilst all films involve artistic direction and most films involve production design in a coordinated manner, it is the franchise that has come to stand for the global reach of Hollywood and its ability to mobilize consumer activity. Intellectual property (IP) in franchises is exploited across film and television (such as TV spin-offs, print works (comic-book and graphic novel franchises), through graphic design and packaging (fast food tie-ins), gifts and leisure (toys and special-edition gadgets) as well as the web and interactive campaigns (user-created content). Designers working on a suitable movie project thus feed into an IP pipeline that can be used to output to a variety of different, distributed areas, and thus realize value from multiple revenue streams. In the late 1980s and early 1990s, this type of franchise was ironically dubbed 'high concept', since it was intended to appeal to the broadest audience base (as the lowest common denominator) and to do this through simple elements: the look, the hook and the book (Wyatt 1994: 20). Archetypal franchise movies have a heavy emphasis on style ('the look'), have easily recognizable plotlines pre-sold on the value of designer stars ('the hook'), and have great potential for extended sales beyond core audiences through CD music compilations, novelizations, video/DVD sales and rentals, as well as toys and games ('the book'). High-concept movies, under this useful definition, are films likely to appeal across age ranges and which are likely to tap previously underused adult revenue streams.

One such example of the development of franchise IP, even in its simplest semiotic form, was the 'reboot' of James Bond in 2006 for *Casino Royale* (Sony/MGM) and later for *A Quantum of Solace* (2008). The Bond franchise was already what marketing analysts call 'toyetic', in that it had potential in both subject matter (spies and spying) and material form (cars, gadgets) to spin out to toys and games (Anon., *Selling to Kids* 1999). For *Casino Royale*, merchandising included toy and collectible versions of both the new 6-litre Aston Martin DBS and the 4-litre 1964 Aston Martin DB5 (made famous by Sean Connery's Bond), both of which the 'new Bond', Daniel Craig, drives in the movie. The screen time for each vehicle is minimal (he drives the vintage Aston around a parking lot) compared to his special edition Tonic Blue 2.6-litre Ford Mondeo ST, but which was not issued as a collectible. The Aston Martins were crucial, however, for Sony Ericsson's marketing of the 'Bond' edition k800i mobile phone, in matching Aston Martin silver, in time for a movie whose plot hinges at several points on the receiving of text messages (again on Sony Ericsson phones). For *A Quantum of Solace*, British TV spots in the weeks running up to the movie's premiere carefully mixed Sony's franchise elements: advertisements for back catalogue Bond DVDs; a specially commissioned action sequence with Daniel Craig advertising the Sony high-definition television range; and a trailer for pop band Scouting for Girls, whose debut album includes the track 'James Bond' (the band are signed to Sony subsidiary SonyBMG). In addition, as specific tie-ins, the company released a numbered, limited edition VIAO TT notebook computer, 007 USB 'micro vault', as well a game for its PlayStation platform. The approach of 'toyetics' – exploiting the subject or material from a franchise – works on the principle that audiences relate to movies through objects and practices, in a manner little different to children and convention-goers playing at dressing-up. The difference with franchises such as James Bond is the relative sparseness of the design signifiers (the '007' logo, the silver from the car) required to develop this in the more lucrative market offered by more mainstream and adult audiences.

Corporations such as Sony, who as owners of MGM also own Bond, therefore invest in the flows of information upon which IP travels, including the production pipeline for the movies themselves. Their financial power arises less from the IP elements as marketable knowledge, and more from their ability through infrastructure, ICT and film audiences, to recombine the elements in which the IP is invested. This is an ability that Manuel Castells has described as separating contemporary 'informationalism' from a broader, longer information age (Castells 2005:8). Where power has always been invested in information and the ability to control it, in a contemporary network society the power is invested in the ability to exploit information and recombine its elements in new forms. For instance, where in the past studios advertised through trailers, billboards and 'hoopla' (lobby cards, stands, magazine articles etc.), this relied on a one-way flow of information from the centre in Hollywood out to theatres across the world. Contemporary Hollywood makes greater use of ICT technologies: when fans re-cut trailers of Bond movies on YouTube, they engage with the text in a similar way to the producers themselves, since the technology of the network gives them the 'ability to experiment in real time in combining knowledge' (Castells 2005: 11). This dovetails with the large body of freelance designers who now feed working copy into a digital pipeline which might output to a variety of production and manufacturing uses controlled by studios and, above them, by umbrella corporations able to operate across viewing platforms and leisure and consumption activities.

With Hollywood established as a dispersed network economy, it is difficult to develop a sufficient *'redundancy* of information' between interdisciplinary designers – the necessary overlapping of knowledge and ability to talk the same common technical language and overcome common practical problems – in order to collaborate well (Nonaka and Takeuchi 1995: 80–82). When working teams get together, the act of sharing redundant information – perhaps better known as 'shop talk' – provides the conditions of active collaboration from which new knowledge can be created, since it can be used to improve the chances of easy exchange of ideas between otherwise differently trained colleagues. This is why corporations often use ice-breaking sessions, away-days and intramural events to bring together disparate departments whose working relationship is strained. Therefore the industry relies on 'social networks of trust and face-to-face interaction' to bind together the network of hubs and clusters, with ICT providing a way to manipulate space sufficiently enough to bring London and other hubs into the geographical neighbourhood (Currah 2003: 71). The diffusion of clusters of designers and companies within this network as nodes of operation, rather than as subsidiaries to larger industrial corporations, is evident in their independence from the film industry in a manner which allows their collaboration with filmmakers to work to their practical advantage as designers outwith the film industry. For example, the architecture and design company Roman and Williams, fronted by Robin Standefer and Stephen Alesch, have established themselves at the slicker end of contemporary interior design, handling prestigious and complex projects such as the redesign of Phillippe Starck's original lobby interior for the Royalton Hotel in Manhattan, and the residences of stars such as Goldie Hawn and Kate Hudson, and Ben Stiller. Previous to this, they had been a creative team in production design and art direction working with Stiller, most notably on his comedy *Zoolander* (Paramount, 2001). The success of Roman and Williams in moving from production design to interior design is not necessarily representative of a new mobility for designers in the wider industry. They are taking advantage of a mobility often exercised by design houses, but which is rare in the 'intangible' construction industry of cinema. Their wholesale move from cinema to architecture and interiors reflects the independence of new creative clusters from the subsidiary relationship with the industry that dominated even in the years following the 1948 decree.

Mainstream Cinema as a Network Enterprise

The network economy is, for Castells, the result of the growth in ICT technologies in concert with the social movements of the 1960s and 1970s as well as the reorganization of capital and state after events such as the break up of the Soviet Union. These three factors led to a philosophy of independence and counter-culture, with a global perspective, enabled by advancing networked technologies. Thus the economy privileges start-up companies, effective

freelancing and flexible specialization. On a corporate level, industry and production has been replaced by the 'networked enterprise', in which labour is
distributed over the network and financial/economic power is held by those
who supply the connections and who create the physical and technical infrastructure for social interaction (Castells 2005: 26). In addition, we might characterize this change as a move from disciplinary and interdisciplinary division
of labour to multidisciplinary collaboration. Where in the past the industry
required specialized designers working under panoptic supervision (e.g. art
directors, set designers, set builders, prop masters), the industry now thrives
on autonomous individuals choosing to working together, feeding into a
pipeline, to realize projects from the conceptual drawing to the detailed model.

The ability to manage parallel workflows, not to mention the development
of a pipeline of commodifiable information as digitally transferred IP,
depends heavily on the standardization of metadata as much as had been the
case under the studio system. Where art directors relied upon the filing
cabinet to marshal the extensive backlot of a studio, here the metadata within
the material in the pipeline becomes essential to the success of a networked
enterprise. We might understand the role of metadata if we are familiar with
tools such as 'track changes' in Microsoft Word, or if we have ever used
custom colours in Adobe Photoshop. Metadata adds information to files

Despite the temptation to see the pipeline as the reinforcement of a linear
production process, in actual fact it is more likely to create non-linear workflows and even a small amount of uncertainty and chaos in production. As
movie production after 1948 became more project-focused, the natural
passage of a movie from pre-production, through production to post-production was established. A contemporary blockbuster shooting in multiple locations, might take six to twelve months to film, with the pre- and
post-production periods being up to four or five times that in total. (This is
vastly different from the studio-bound production schedules of the 1930s:
Astaire and Rogers's *Swing Time* began casting in May and premiered in late
August 1936.) Thus projects grow organically from collaborations as disparate
personnel come to know one another, teams can be assembled (placing greater
creative power in the hands of producers and agents as well as directors), and
production can be refined once the shooting is completed. Production schedules became oriented around any adverse effects on this process (actors'
schedules, script delays, public holiday release dates). With a digital pipeline,
cinematographers and production designers have been able to establish parallel workflows since the exchange of working copy can begin much earlier,
and a movie may be in pre-, post- and production at the same time whilst
digital effects, shooting and script are still being worked on (Williams 2007b:
27).

The ability to manage parallel workflows, not to mention the development
of a pipeline of commodifiable information as digitally transferred IP,
depends heavily on the standardization of metadata as much as had been the
case under the studio system. Where art directors relied upon the filing
cabinet to marshal the extensive backlot of a studio, here the metadata within
the material in the pipeline becomes essential to the success of a networked
enterprise. We might understand the role of metadata if we are familiar with
tools such as 'track changes' in Microsoft Word, or if we have ever used
custom colours in Adobe Photoshop. Metadata adds information to files

which is unlikely to be misunderstood after modification or misrepresented by poor workstation screens. Metadata in digital pipelines involves the use of common file formats, common software languages, and applications that can work across platforms or can generate outputs to different media. In the past, the correct use of laboratory instructions ensured differently shot film could be cut together to create a seamless montage. For example, where this information has been lost on classic films, as was the case with redistributed versions of Francis Ford Coppola's *The Godfather* (Paramount, 1972), the project of restoration has involved viewing archive reels for colour reference and interviewing the film's original cinematographer Gordon Willis. 'New' metadata meant the restoration team was able to reinstate the film's lyrical dissolves (lost in the 1980s reissue) and even correct lab mistakes from the film's original processing (Argy 2008: 78–80).

In contemporary production, metadata can facilitate the coordination and useful parallel development of modelling, shooting and post-production, and this has meant that various software packages such as Maya, Antics, SketchUp and Lightwave are common tools for working across specialisms, rather than within or between disciplines. Visualization technologies such as Antics and SketchUp use the same basic language for film as they do for gaming, and these publicly available software packages are ideal for both user-created animation and, for filmmakers, for movie storyboards. Lightwave, an industrial design virtualization tool, can produce models that can be exported to animation packages such as Maya, which are used for virtual filming. This was employed, for example, by illustrator Daren Dochterman to create a seamless shot in Wolfgang Petersen's remake of the classic *Poseidon* (Warner Bros., 2006), in which the camera flies around the digitally created ship and closes in actor Josh Lucas running on a real deck (Williams 2007a: 10). The clearest illustration of metadata as the lingua franca of the digital pipeline is that of pre-visualization, or 'previs'. Previs programmes, including SketchUp and other proprietary packages, allow production design departments to quickly model and render sequences, and sometimes whole films, including settings, props, actors, lighting and camera, which can then be viewed as a lo-fi version of the real film to be shot. As a communication tool in the studio conference situation, the value of being able to work with the previs in front of the team, and even manipulate it in real time, is obvious. But the real advantage is that metadata from the previs can be exported to the studio lot as set dimensions, colour registers and style guides – at the same time changing the way we understand the concept of 'computer-generated imagery'. Previs is therefore dominating the production process as both a creative and communication tool. Whilst there is a temptation to see modern production schedules as being faster than those in the past because of the development of new technology, this is not necessarily the case; new technologies have enabled more sophisticated parallel production schedules facilitating pre- and post-production in technology hubs (New York, London) alongside shooting in new, cheaper locations (Canada, Czech Republic).

Production Design as a Well-mannered Operations Centre

Let us return to the example of production designer Alex McDowell and his approach to contemporary practice, which is often prized as innovative. Encouraged by his work on science fiction movies such as *Minority Report*, McDowell established a research and development cluster called Matter Art & Science, which pools diverse knowledge from different disciplines to create bespoke solutions to the various film projects that he works on. It was just such a 'think-tank' approach that contributed to the sophisticated vision of the future that *Minority Report* achieved, including Maglev car concepts developed with John Underkoffler from the MIT Media Lab (Garrett 2006: 24). In expanding Matter Art & Science as a networked cluster of changing personnel, McDowell has realized virtually what the sociologist Bruno Latour has described as the network capability of the office as 'star-shaped oligopticon' (Latour 2005: 182). The designer's office uses its technology to enact spokes and hub, and is constantly open to new connections and new networks.

After being introduced to previs by director David Fincher, McDowell developed it as a workflow tool with Ron Frankel of Proof Inc., who was largely responsible for the visualization of *Minority Report*. For its Maglev chase sequence, each shot was composed in previs, which then provided raw data for virtual modelling and rendering. For later projects, such as Steven Spielberg's *The Terminal*, the same process was used to visualize a chaotic, present-day airport terminal, and indeed previs stood in for the traditional storyboard. With more traditionally minded directors, such as Bo Welch on *Dr Seuss' The Cat in the Hat*, previs was employed to generate in 3D virtual sets with data that could then be manipulated with the modelling package FormZ. This could then be output to AutoCAD, which in turn could print tooling patterns to create the full-size set in polystyrene. At the same time, as with production of *The Terminal*, other personnel could be brought in early on who would work on later stages of the project, such as matte painters for *The Terminal*, or game and DVD packaging designers for *Dr Seuss' The Cat in the Hat* (Desowitz 2003). The pipeline for *The Terminal* connected the three production companies (DreamWorks SKG, Amblin Entertainment and Parkes/MacDonald Productions) with the distributor (United International Pictures) and the twenty-four different specialist companies working on the film, which included Proof Inc. and another studio, Twentieth Century Fox, which provided specialist post-production.

With previs as the pipeline mechanism, and useful practices of parallel and circular production development established, it is easy to see why McDowell tends to view people and talent as the actual 'raw materials' of movie production (Garrett 2006:19). However, given our historical perspective, a clearer-sighted observation of contemporary production practices offers a view of mature networks of social interaction, in which objects (as software and meta-data) have a considerable agency. With Hollywood under the studio system, for example, the filing cabinet was more than simply a repository or conduit of metadata, and probably had an effect on creative decisions. For Latour it is still the office which has an agency of its own, in the sense that it is given the capacity to organize the critical acts of 'interference, dispatching, delegation, articulation' which make creative decisions possible (Latour 2005: 198). In a traditional business, these critical acts of decision-making are smoothed over by the furniture, decor, attire and official hierarchy. Interference is kept to a minimum through careful line-management and delegation, dispatching is routine, whilst articulation is made through instruction. Interruptions to this smoothing constitute *disruption*, even though they often create new ideas or ways of working. Alternatively, the place where the exposure of these acts is crucial to decision-making is the design or architecture studio. Studio spaces often mix furniture and activities inappropriate to business but which facilitate social activity (sofas, games, loud music and even bars), and involve elaborate methods of high-quality visualization (the drawing board, graphpad, data projection) to generate working copy that will be produced by a collaborative team of individuals rather than subordinates.

The studio space therefore relies on the visible entanglement of activities, and the production design office is just such a space. Critical decisions are made, for instance, when cinematographers interfere with agreements between directors and their production designers. Storyboards, and now previs, provide methods of articulating ideas in progress, involving personnel such as lighting and set technicians who each contribute (and will go away to complete) particular elements of the whole. As McDowell describes, 'It's about transfer of information and keeping a library of digital images that's available through a network to all departments' (Calhoun 2004: 2). The marketing of movies and moviemaking smooths over this messy, networked productivity, giving the appearance of a continuous, linear workflow as the image of movie magic. This commoditization serves to extend the possibilities of consumption (in the form of special edition DVDs with TV-spot production featurettes) and 'disentangle' the finished product from the real processes involved in creative decisions, especially those that are difficult to market (Callon 1999: 189–90).

In DVD extras, there are interviews with principal production personnel working in tidy offices alongside motivated colleagues whose work is more like play – energetic interactions with technology, as well as with costume and props and on set. Similarly, they often feature specially commissioned video clips animating the production of characters and sets from clay, through wireframe, to rendered shading and texture. The DVD extra rarely show rows of unhappy renderers hunched over identical computers, or fractious discussions about script readiness or whether mistakes can be 'fixed in post', as is commonly heard.

Even so, the need and emergence of a truly 'well-mannered' workplace also is recognized in both industry analysis (Currah 2007: 360) and in practice (Williams 2007b). Workflows tend to gather their own momentum, and this is no different to the non-linear, networked pipeline that dominates production in Hollywood. The critical difference is that, with technical information and working copy entering and exiting the pipeline, the dangers of material going astray, or being corrupted, or being locked in firms' own software language, is very high. In any networked creative environment, small firms, start-ups, student projects and midnight workers are likely to produce highly disruptive innovation which, when combined, push technology and practice forward. The industry's problem is therefore how to get different technologies to work together, such as when digital images, digital-intermediate processes and filmed material are all required to become part of the same whole in the production of a movie. Different companies will use different formatting, compression and transmission standards, and the information that is required to translate these. This 'dark metadata' is critical in the archiving of film material, or in updating technologies, but also gives companies owning it a market advantage if they keep their processes secret (Kaufman 2003: 93). The American Society of Cinematographers and the Art Directors' Guild (ADG) Technology Committees, which represent cinematographers and art directors (production designers) in Hollywood, have therefore tasked themselves with a job of smoothing the information pipeline. As Currah notes, the industry uses 'inter-firm' networks, such as the guild committees, to create a closed 'sphere of innovation' in which they act as a kind of neighbourhood watch protecting the industry as a whole from restrictive practices and disruptive or 'bad' behaviour (Currah 2007: 377).

Conclusion

Currah's view is that the approach taken by the guild committees is to dampen the effect of disruptive innovation and protect the power base of a Hollywood oligopoly – corporate capital invested in the major studios as management centres. It is a difficult view to take issue with, as the future of even the smallest, most avant-garde design start-up is often wedded to the notion that it will be discovered and produce IP for a major franchise. We thus have a simple dichotomy of innocent industrial pragmatism versus political power exercised through the formation of capital: it is practical and advantageous for the industry to promote innovation and even anti-corporate sentiment, and then adopt it as part of a further cultural expansion, and the development of 'indie' subsidiaries as part of the major studios is an example of this. Creativity and disruptive innovation are controlled and enclosed by the acceptance of standards. However, that does not negate the opportunity such a view gives us of understanding how creative practices change in an industrial neighbour-hood, one which is extended to include lo-fi and user-created content through information and communication technology. The work of Alex McDowell and Matter Art & Science is illustrative of how inter-firm networks take advantage of the existing social networks of the industrial neighbourhood (McDowell also serves on the ADG Technology Committee) and the changes effected in this neighbourhood by their expansion as informational networks. It is the concern to keep the collaborative process at the heart of this neighbourhood that has led to the need for, and development of, joint metadata protocols to facilitate previs, as well as the potential to bring in external specialists from other fields in order to provide expert knowledge in response. Established net-works evolve quickly into systems houses: 'large-scale production units turning out limited numbers of extremely variable and complex products (like space satellites or blockbuster films)' not unlike the example of Roman and Williams (Scott 2002: 960). Whilst these have evolved since the 1970s, perhaps even as early as the 1950s, it is in new technologies such as previs, and in the need for an effect of metadata, that we can see how design practices – such as the use of the studio as office – are central to the networked creativity which has always been latent in the cinema industry. In addition, it is the growing use of technologies such as previs that articulate the distribution of creative decision-making which feeds off and sustains a production pipeline. These illustrate, by throwing history into sharp relief, how cinema as a network enterprise has based itself on a principle of design in response to economic concerns as well as creative briefs. This is the principle of *involvement* of collaborating indi-viduals, producing a *pipeline* of continuous *working copy*.

Acknowledgement

I would like to thank Philip Drake, University of Stirling, and Gordon Hush, The Glasgow School of Art, for their advice and comments on the ideas and their presentation in this chapter.

Notes

1. Movies such as Paramount's fourth Indiana Jones film – *Indiana Jones and the Kingdom of the Crystal Skull* (2008) – are classic tentpole projects, designed to prop up the studio in order to allow it to release lower-budget movies or, in some circumstances, recoup the costs of slower-performing films such as Mike Myers's *The Love Guru*.
2. RKO Pre-budget estimate for 'I Wont Dance' (sic) – 29 April 1936.

References

Anonymous. 1999. 'Case Study Kids 0–12 Dinosaur Mummies on the Titanic! How to Spot a Hot Property: Marketers Share Visions', *Selling to Kids*, 23 June. Available at: http://findarticles.com/p/articles/mi_m0FVE/is_12_4/ai_54983445?tag=content;col1 [last accessed 14 October 2008].

Argy, S. (2008), 'Paramount Restores *The Godfather*', *American Cinematographer*, 89(5): 78–82.

Balio, T. (1995), *Grand Design: Hollywood as a Modern Business Enterprise, 1930–1939*, Los Angeles: University of California Press.

Calhoun, J. (2004), 'Lounge Act: Production Designer Alex McDowell Recreates JFK On a 75,000 sq. ft. Set for *The Terminal*', *Entertainment Design*, July: 2.

Callon, M. (1999), 'Actor-Network Theory – the Market Test', in J. Law (ed.), *Actor-Network Theory and After*, London: Blackwell.

Castells, M. (2005), *The Network Society: A Cross-Cultural Perspective*, Cheltenham: Edward Elgar.

Currah, A. (2003), 'Digital Effects in the Spatial Economy of Film: Towards a Research Agenda', *Area*, 35(1): 64–73.

Currah, A. (2007), 'Hollywood, the Internet and the World: A Geography of Disruptive Innovation', *Industry and Innovation*, 14(4): 359–84.

Desowitz, B. (2005), 'The Previs Gospel … According to McDowell and Frankel', *Animation World Magazine*, 26 September. Available at: http://mag.awn.com/?article_no=1874 [last accessed: 7 August 2008].

Eustis, M. (1937), 'Designing for the Movies; Gibbons of MGM', *Theatre Arts Monthly* 21: 783–98.

Garrett, M. (2006), 'LA Art School', *Eye*, 15(60): 18–28.

Gibbons, C. (1938), 'The Art Director', in Stephen Watts (ed.), *Behind the Screen: How Films Are Made*, London: Arthur Barker, pp.41–50.

Gil, R. (2008), 'An Empirical Investigation of the Paramount Antitrust Case', *Applied Economics*, 19 June: 1–13.

Grainge, P. (2007), *Brand Hollywood: Selling Entertainment in a Global Media Age*, London: Continuum.

Kaufman, D. (2003), 'Metadata's Impact on "Artistic Intent"', *American Cinematographer*, 84(12): 88–93.

Latour, B. (2005), *Reassembling the Social: An Introduction to Actor-Network Theory*, Oxford: Oxford University Press.

Longwell, T. (2007), 'The Creative Triangle', *American Cinematographer*, May supplement: 4–6.

Meehan, E. R. (1991), ' "Holy Commodity Fetish, Batman!": The Political Economy of the Commercial Intertext', in Pearson, Roberta E. (ed.), *The Many Lives of the Batman*, London: BFI Publishing.

Nonaka, I. and Takeuchi, H. (1995), *The Knowledge-Creating Company: How Japanese Companies Create the Dynamics of Innovation*, Oxford: Oxford University Press.

Perren, A. (2001), 'Sex, Lies and Marketing: Miramax and the Development of the Quality Indie Blockbuster', *Film Quarterly*, 55(2): 30–39.

Ramírez, J. A. (2004), *Architecture for the Screen: A Critical Study of Set Design in Hollywood's Golden Age*, 2nd edn, Jefferson, NC: McFarland.

Schorow, S. (2006), 'Hollywood Designer Urges Focus, Creativity Before Technology', *MIT Tech Talk*, 20 December: 8.

Scott, A. J. (2002), 'A New Map of Hollywood: The Production and Distribution of American Motion Pictures', *Regional Studies*, 36(9): 957–73.

Wasko, J. (2001), *Understanding Disney: The Manufacture of Fantasy*, London: Polity.

Williams, D. E. (2007a), 'The Politics of Pre-Vis', *American Cinematographer*, May supplement: 8–13.

Williams, D. E. (2007b), 'Methods in the Madness: Roundtable Q&A', *American Cinematographer*, August supplement: 26–31.

Wyatt, J. (1994), *High Concept: Movies and Marketing in Hollywood*, Austin, TX: University of Texas Press.

CHAPTER 11

Visual Continuity and Innovation in Editorial Design Practice

Sarah Owens

Introduction

Editorial design, considered by some to be 'one of the most exciting and innovative areas of design at the moment' (Zappaterra 2002: 8) is, paradoxically, also one of the most systematized and standardized design specialities. The fact that commercial magazines and newspapers require regular – daily, weekly, monthly, quarterly – production and publication has encouraged the standardization of both work procedures and the resulting printed object. Tightly scheduled deadlines thus govern the production not only of daily newspapers and weekly magazines, whose design departments rely heavily on pre-formatted page layouts, but also that of publications appearing less frequently: monthly and quarterly magazines, despite their assurances of complete creative autonomy and attempts to tailor each page to its editorial content, are nevertheless bound to highly structured production processes.

All design practice to some extent involves routine tasks and procedures. Corporate designers may, for example, spend a significant amount of time applying the principles of a design programme to various media, hence simply 'following the rules' prescribed by a company's style manual. Usually, such tasks require neither a development of, nor experimentation with, new concepts and visual ideas. What differentiates a speciality such as corporate design from editorial design is that in the former, less routinized tasks gain their uniqueness through the project-based nature of the speciality, through the fact that the corporate designer interacts with the client and responds to his/her particular needs. Editorial designers are not responsible to a client in this sense, but communicate only *indirectly* with an audience that may or may not have been clearly defined through market research. On a day-to-day basis, editorial designers instead deal with the requests of editors, marketing directors, production managers and, occasionally, the publisher. The immediate goal of this collaboration is to produce the newspaper or magazine as efficiently as possible in order to ensure a steady output; in the longer term, it aims to create a loyal readership, to increase newsstand sales and paid subscriptions, and to secure profitable advertising campaigns.

This chapter is based on in-depth interviews conducted with editors and designers, and on insights gained from the author's own experience of working in the German publishing industry. It aims to provide a detailed analysis of systematized work processes and their impact on editorial design practice. It examines the tension between continuity and innovation, exploring the way some of the risks associated with stylistic innovation are managed in practice. In particular, it shows how institutional or structural pressures to ensure regular production and brand loyalty among consumers are reflected in the development of stylistic conventions, while periodic redesigns provide the opportunity for creativity or visual innovation. The chapter concludes by suggesting that the tension arising out of the need for both visual continuity and innovation may, under certain circumstances, actually fuel creative production, even while such creativity is tightly and carefully managed.

Continuity

Although the majority of newspapers and magazines published in Germany are produced by the same few large publishing houses, titles remain remarkably numerous and diverse. In 2007, the newspaper market saw the publication of 352 dailies, ranging from tabloids to high-quality broadsheets, thus placing Germany first in a comparison with other European countries, followed by Spain with 140, and the United Kingdom with 104 daily newspapers (Bundesverband Deutscher Zeitungsverleger e.V. 2007). Over 6,200 magazine titles, including 2,450 consumer magazines, were published in Germany in 2006; the German magazine market is, however, markedly smaller than – for example – its North American and British counterparts, with totals of 19,419 and 8,558 titles respectively (Verband Deutscher Zeitschriftenverleger 2007, Magazine Publishers of America 2008, PPA 2008).

The publishing industry in Germany, like in other countries, relies in part on national editions of international publications, such as *Financial Times Deutschland* or the relatively recently introduced German version of *Vanity Fair*. These editions are often produced locally, and cater to particular tastes in editorial content and design – thus, for example, despite adhering to transnational branding specifications, *Vogue Italia* recognizably differs from *Vogue Brasil*. While such differences may be easily identified, the question of whether there exist characteristic national styles, which link publications of a particular geographic region, is more difficult to answer. On one hand, the graphic design industry might be compared to that of fashion, which occasionally discusses the concept of national style, but is generally dominated by a cross-cultural avant-garde leading the international market. Style might thus depend more on the influence of several individuals, whose geographical positions may vary, but who share similar lifestyles determined by age, class and media exposure. On the other hand, German graphic design builds on a rich *national* history of theory and practice, the latter of which 'reflects a distinctive national ability to exploit the creative tension between tradition and innovation' (Livingston and Livingston 2003: 96). Magazines such as *Twen*, for example, designed by Willy Fleckhaus in the 1960s, and the contemporary business publication *brand eins*, by Mike Meiré, have been influential both within and beyond Germany.

Conversely, the nature of working practices in editorial design depends not so much on national context as on the publication genre and frequency, as well as the size of the publishing house. At large publishers, production parameters require design work to be broken down into controllable and manageable portions; thus, work procedures are fragmented into smaller and well-defined processes, and responsibilities assigned to several departments. This results in a continuous, highly structured and regulated workflow commencing in the editorial department with the development of stories and commissioning of authors, and concluding in the production department with the preparation of the publication for print. The fragmentation of design work necessitates not only an efficient coordination of staff, but also the involvement of a large number of specialists: art directors are responsible for managing the design department and ensuring visual continuity, coherence and quality; designers lay out pages; sub-editors improve or rewrite copy; picture editors commission photographers and deal with image licensing; production managers work out schedules and prepare documents for printing. Sections of newspapers and weekly magazines are developed simultaneously by several designers, and it is usually only at monthly or quarterly magazines that a single designer deals with complete issues. The entire process, from the gathering of content to the delivery of the publication to newsstands and subscribers must, for instance at weekly magazines, be completed within a few days. Monthly magazines, which only seemingly allow more time for production, as they often contain a greater number of pages to be designed, work with a similarly tight schedule up to three months in advance – at any given moment, there is one issue in print, another one being designed and assembled, and a third one in preparation. Naturally, this has implications for the timeliness and relevance of a publication. A chief editor on a monthly magazine for instance recalled the difficulties of conducting interviews with politicians based solely on speculations concerning future events and outcomes – there was always the chance that by the time of publication, the interview would have become irrelevant (Interview Chief Editor A).

The comparatively short turnaround time of editorial design work further limits the capacity and usefulness of introducing new design concepts with each issue. Instead, these remain valid for longer periods of time, spanning several issues and evolving until a more radical design intervention, a so-called 'redesign', is decided upon by the publishing house. Apart from being more workable in terms of effort and time, this strategy also ensures the visual continuity of a publication. Newspapers and commercial magazines in particular depend on visual continuity in order to be immediately recognized amongst hundreds of other periodicals – if one assumes that most consumers will not tolerate endless searches for their favourite publication at the newsstand. Thus, commercial publications largely abide by genre conventions and publication-specific principles, utilizing instead opportunities for moderate deviations provided by special issues and sections. Periodicals which need not succumb to the commercial pressures of the newsstand, such as newspaper supplements, customer magazines, and publications positioned outside the profit-oriented mainstream, are in this sense privileged: they may choose to ignore market rules, and thus possess more freedom to experiment on a textual and visual level.

Routine

Systematization and routine permeate the everyday practice of editorial designers. The production of a magazine, for example, typically begins with an advance-planning meeting between chief editor(s), copy editors, picture editors and the art director, in which the visual and editorial direction of features and standard pages are determined. Subsequently, freelance illustrators and photographers, most of whom are well accustomed to tight work schedules and short deadlines, are commissioned. When faced with additional work in the form of seasonal or special issues, monthlies or quarterlies with a small core staff may furthermore choose to hire freelance designers and interns. Several teams – each consisting of one copy editor, one picture editor and one designer – then develop features and standard pages on the basis of the approach agreed during the planning meeting. While layouts are being completed, the magazine structure is continuously re-evaluated and changed accordingly.[1] It is only after the complete issue has been approved by the editorial and design departments that it moves into the final stages of production, which involve sub-editing, retouching, colour corrections, proofing and delivery to the printer.

The systematization of editorial design work is also reflected in the use of electronic publishing systems to administer text and design documents. These systems link editorial, design and production departments, store document versions and allow the assignment of tasks and responsibilities to users in each department. After a designer has laid out a page in a desktop publishing programme, he/she deposits it into the publishing system, which automatically creates a backup of the document on a central server. Thereafter, each time the designer works on a document, he/she will retrieve it from the system, modify and re-deposit it. With each retrieval and deposit the designer is able to change the status of the document, indicating for example whether it is currently in progress, needs to be edited or signed off, or is ready for production. All others involved in the assembly process, including the chief editor(s) and art director, copy editors, sub-editors and production manager(s), may also access the document via the system, and after completing their tasks, change the status to a further level. Thus the publishing system eases communication and shortens the physical distance between departments, aids and expedites the handing over of documents, and structures workflow. In addition, it keeps track of responsibilities by recording information concerning document modifications. This information, along with the time used for each document, is made visible to all system users via a query window. Thus, if a production manager spots a mistake, he/she is immediately able to attribute it to a specific editor or designer. Similarly, the art director is able to single out those taking a disproportionate amount of time to complete designs. Although most editors and designers view the publishing system mainly as an aid to manage their own documents and to conveniently access the documents of others, it thus also possesses a regulative function. As a consequence, assessments and criticism pertain more to the individual rather than to his/her department.

The way in which design tasks are assigned and classified within the design department relies largely on creative hierarchies, which are more or less explicitly articulated. Art directors are granted the highest level of creative autonomy. Apart from overseeing and coordinating the work of designers, they commonly deal with the most important design tasks – at newspapers, these include the design of feature pages; at magazines, the design of covers and special issues. It is further the duty of the art director to ensure that the designers are working as a team, to minimize idleness and to sustain communication with other departments.[2] Designers are attributed lower levels of creativity, as they carry out tasks assigned to them by the art director, who might guide them by elucidating content and suggesting possible ways of visual treatment. The way a creative hierarchy is played out on a day-to-day basis depends, however, on the temperament and management style of the art director. It is not unusual for senior designers to lighten the art director's workload by taking over some of his/her responsibilities, such as the commissioning of illustrators or the supervision of junior designers. Similarly, although the art director has the final say, designers' individual talents and personality may be allowed to pervade their work. Such opportunities for personal creative expression mean that 'what used to be a life of unrewarding "slog" is now a possible site for personal fulfilment. Ideologically, work is turned into a source of reward through the emphasis on creativity, no matter how irregular the earnings and regardless of how long the hours' (McRobbie 1998: 83).

Many art directors prefer working with a handful of experienced photographers and illustrators, ones who are familiar with the 'house style' and therefore able to reliably produce and promptly deliver desired images. Due to their position of seniority, these freelancers are, like art directors, granted a relatively high amount of creative freedom. In one instance encountered by the author while working at a newspaper supplement, the well-known illustrator of a regular column decided to abandon his pictorial, narrative style of drawing in favour of a more abstract, associative one. Despite initially fearing a negative response by loyal readers, the magazine's art director and chief editors chose to rely on the illustrator's experience and prestige. Indeed, even conservative readers eventually accepted the modification. Conversely, experiments of this kind by inexperienced illustrators and photographers were frequently associated with insecurity and a lack of personal style. In order to permit a gradual familiarization with a publication's preferences, illustrators and photographers with less experience are therefore commissioned mainly for standard work.

Conventions

As stated earlier, structural and institutional pressures to ensure regular production generate an intense workload that demands a high level of concentration and often calls for the implementation of routine procedures and techniques. These lead to the development of stylistic and graphic conventions – visual manifestations of systematized work processes. Newspaper articles and magazine sections thus follow prescriptions, expressed either tacitly or explicitly, regarding the style and placement of elements within the publication, while a distinctive use of format, grids, white space, fonts and colours guarantees visual continuity. Numerous design decisions are also guided by principles equated with 'good practice', which are acquired through formal education and/or several years of experience. Moreover, market research ratifies and validates visual conventions such as specific colour schemes, attributes such as clarity or accessibility, and details such as the pose of the cover model.

Covers of commercial women's magazines thus typically feature close-ups of female celebrities or fashion models, and for cover lines and logotypes employ colours perceived as feminine, such as pink, orange and red. Remarkably, even non-mainstream women's magazines frequently follow these rules, but at the same time aim to keep to a minimum the number of cover lines 'selling' the publication, as a larger number of lines implies a greater commercialism.[3] Decisions regarding the number and placement of cover lines in particular are guided by marketing considerations – a common absurdity that this leads to is the request of marketing departments to include cover lines on publications that are not even sold at the newsstand, such as customer magazines and newspaper supplements. More generally, a compliance with graphic norms demonstrates a publication's need to conform to its genre, thus it is in many ways desirable for a daily newspaper or commercial magazine not to contradict, but to resemble its competitors. 'Most identifiable genres,' Rob Waller notes, 'start with relatively unarticulated rules, and members of the genre only belong through a coincidence of purposes and constraints. But in time, rules may be articulated and, although the original functional imperatives have moved on, the genre is effectively frozen. Thus the more rule-bound genres change relatively slowly, while the less rule-bound genres change as needs, technology or fashion allow' (Waller 1999: 5). Newspapers and commercial magazines, by following 'ritualized but loosely articulated' design rules, belong to a genre that may gradually change and evolve; fashion and avant-garde magazines in contrast exemplify a genre that is even less rule-bound, and therefore more amenable to stylistic innovation.

The following of conventions established by publishing firms and market research affects not only a publication's microstructure, but also its macrostructure, by influencing the placement of features and standard pages within issues. These tried-and-tested choreographies set out important sections (such as editorials, letters, news, features, reviews and so on) in a specific order, and are employed because they are thought to best keep the reader's attention, and to reflect the relative importance of the editorial content. Most newspapers are thus structured into sections containing current and international news, commentaries, features, reviews, notices and classifieds, sports reports and, optionally, regional news. Depending on its sub-genre membership, a magazine may either be partitioned into several sections, each introduced by a feature filling several pages and followed by shorter articles, columns, reviews and listings, or it may compile larger stories in a so-called 'feature well' flanked by shorter editorial elements. A standardized structure, signposted by characteristic graphic elements, helps readers navigate, and regular readers will often know where to find favourite columns or relevant articles. As a consequence, a newspaper or magazine grows comfortable and familiar; this familiarity in turn encourages and supports brand loyalty.

Publication-specific conventions are articulated in design templates, which through grids and placeholders determine the density and placement of graphic elements on a page. These are created by art directors or external consultants when a publication is first developed, or when a redesign requires new specifications. They detail particular ways in which headlines, stand-firsts, subheads, bylines, credits, body copy, captions, pull quotes, page numbers and other textual elements are to be typeset, the way images may be incorporated and juxtaposed, and the way colour, spacing, panels, boxes, sidebars, rules or other means of typographic structuring, highlighting and signposting may be used. Newspapers rely heavily on design templates, since standard pages are often assembled by editors. Yet it is also the case in magazines that standard sections such as reviews and columns are commonly defined in such detail that images need only be inserted at the prescribed position, and accompanying texts shortened or lengthened.

Despite their ostensible rigidity, editorial design templates are not as fixed and absolute as specifications contained in corporate design or branding manuals, which must be meticulously observed. The primary purpose of employing design templates is simply to ensure that a publication visibly follows an overall design aesthetic. An interesting example inadvertently testing the limits of this strategy is the Swiss weekly magazine *Die Weltwoche*, which subjects all sections to a similar typographic style, anchored by a strict and highly functional grid, the use of only a few images and a single typeface. Thus, the magazine's editorial design alludes to the seriousness of newspaper design and its own history – it was formerly published as a broadsheet.

Innovation

Design templates and principles are not, however, always meant to be followed slavishly. When composing a page, a designer may choose to obey the grid while simultaneously disregarding more general typographic conventions, and vice versa. The degree to which a design may flout rules hinges on the editorial approach of a publication, its readership and the publisher. Visual continuity further demands that a design contributes to an overall style; all modifications must therefore be 'legitimate'. Describing the principles of Marquesan folk art, Alfred Gell argues that style:

> is the complex formed by the relationships which hold between all these transformations or modifications. That is to say, the constraints governing the

production (innovation within culturally prescribed parameters of style) of ... artworks were constraints governing the possibility of transforming a motif or form into related forms; only if such a transformation is possible can a motif or form be said to 'belong' to [this] style. (Gell 1998: 215)

The task of gauging appropriateness within prescribed parameters of style emphasizes that editorial designers do not simply 'make pages look nice', but add further levels of significance and meaning to the content. They link production and consumption as 'cultural intermediaries' (Bourdieu 1984; du Gay et al. 1997) and re-negotiate meanings between market and readership, in effect increasing a publication's cultural and economic value. Furthermore, 'cultural intermediaries' who, alongside designers, include those 'whose jobs entail performing services and the production, marketing and dissemination of symbolic goods', 'do not seek to promote a single lifestyle, but rather to cater for and expand the range of styles and lifestyles available to audiences and consumers' (Featherstone 2007: 19, 26). Thus, designers have in the past succeeded in disseminating and legitimizing 'arbitrary' forms of culture, such as fashion, cosmetics, decoration and furniture through notions of 'good' or 'tasteful' design (Bourdieu 1990).

In practice, the actual modifications and adaptations made by editorial designers are often microscopic and noticeable only to the regular reader. While a periodical may change ever so slightly with each issue and thus gradually evolve in its design, its visual continuity is systematically and more fundamentally disrupted by periodic redesigns. These are attempts by the design and production staff to continuously reinvent and reinterpret the style and perception of a publication. They aim to propel a newspaper or magazine forward in terms of visual and editorial content, and allow opportunities for creative innovation and experimentation, thus providing even highly standardized publications with a form of creative autonomy. Redesigns are essentially balancing acts between the provision of familiar content for the reader (continuity) and the development of new visual standards (innovation). In other words, a redesign should simultaneously be as similar and as different to the previous design as possible. This paradox is rooted in the fact that a newspaper or magazine aims to remain familiar by conforming to its respective genre, while concurrently seeking to establish itself as a unique and distinctive brand within this genre. Redesigns therefore give rise to the question of how far a publication can be altered without alienating its readership or risking the chance of not being recognized at the newsstand.

The redesign of one of Germany's leading newspapers, the *Frankfurter Allgemeine Zeitung*, for instance, was met with great resistance by regular readers. Its previous, rather austere design approach was characterized by large amounts of text, the almost complete absence of images and the use of black-letter fonts for some of its headlines. The earlier introduction of a small red box on the title page for many readers signalled an impending vulgarization – in spite of these fears, and due to a drop in circulation, the newspaper nevertheless decided on a change. In the end, an approach that was neither too innovative nor too cautious was implemented by, amongst other changes, introducing a colour image on the title and banning the 'old-fashioned' black-letter typeface from its interior pages (Brauck 2007).

Publications are often redesigned when they start becoming unprofitable – cancellations of subscriptions and a drop in circulation numbers are usually an indication of a gradually developing unpopularity that must be counteracted with a new visual and editorial approach. *The New Yorker* magazine for instance, which had retained and followed certain visual conventions for several decades, evolving only gradually with the introduction of new graphic elements, was only redesigned more substantially when sales dropped in the 1990s. More radical modifications in the design of a publication may also be motivated by a change in editorial direction, readership or technology, or by the wish to keep up with current stylistic movements. The importance of redesigns is reflected by the fact that most are executed by art directors or external design consultants, rather than by in-house designers. After a redesign has been completed, it is not uncommon for external consultants (who are often former art directors specializing in the redesign and development of publications) to temporarily join the design department in order to oversee the implementation of suggestions and specifications. Magazines are almost certainly redesigned when a new art director is introduced – like a newly appointed professor holding an inaugural lecture, a new head of design must make public his/her aesthetic vision for the publication.[4]

Creativity

Continuity and innovation play crucial roles in everyday design practice. Processes ensuring continuity include routine tasks, using work formulae and following design templates – they are processes that utilize previous knowledge and experiences, are reliable in terms of time and effort, and are required by the market. Processes associated with innovation create the unconventional, the new and unexpected, find new relationships between well-known elements, and may be likened to the discovery of new methods for solving problems. They further the graphic design discipline by bringing forth new means of expression, expanding or modifying existing canons and vocabularies of forms, and challenging established conventions and meanings. These processes are, however, also relatively labour-intensive, unreliable in terms of time and deterring to those who favour stability.

In order to ascertain how these processes may interrelate in creative practice, it is useful to initially examine the 'creative act' itself, the psychological aspects of which, according to Arthur Koestler, include:

> the displacement of attention to something not previously noted, which was irrelevant in the old and is relevant in the new context; the discovery of hidden analogies as a result of the former; the bringing into consciousness of tacit axioms and habits of thought which were ... taken for granted; the uncovering of what has always been there. This leads to the paradox that the more original a discovery the more obvious it seems afterwards. The creative act is not an act of creation in the sense of the Old Testament. It does not create something out of nothing; it uncovers, selects, re-shuffles, combines, synthesizes already existing facts, ideas, faculties, skills. (Koestler 1989: 119–20)

This means that if they are to function as a repository for a synthesis of this kind, facts and ideas must be learnt and internalized, and abilities and skills developed and mastered until they acquire a routine-like quality.

Henri Lefebvre (2008) makes a more general distinction between 'repetitive' and 'inventive' praxis, the former consisting of 'stereotyped and repeated actions', and the latter of the creation of novel objects or novel practice. His definition was expanded by Agnes Heller, who claims that inventive praxis or thinking may include any intentional solution of a problem – i.e. a solution 'construed as acquisition of experience, broadening of opinion, the taking of decisions' (Heller 1984: 128). Such intentional solutions may also arise out of the interaction with and experience of a situation – a notion taken into account by Carl R. Rogers: 'My definition ... of the creative process is that it is the emergence in action of a novel relational product, growing out of the uniqueness of the individual on the one hand, and the materials, events, people, or circumstances of his life on the other' (Rogers 1967: 350). Repetitive and inventive praxis do not rule each other out, but constitute necessary and complementary parts of creative practice. What drives creative practice is consequently the tension between repetition and invention, continuity and innovation. The requirement to balance the old with the new, to abide by general conventions while trying to break the rules, to conform to a genre while aiming to establish a unique selling proposition – all these provide opportunities and incentives for original and creative thought.

Such requirements need not be considered limiting, as most designers are well accustomed to dealing with constraints, such as those resulting from systematization and regulation, in their work. 'Remove these and it is like putting an engine out of gear suddenly, it returns to idling speed, or feels purposeless when accelerated' (Potter 2002: 47–8). It is the job of the designer to make the best out of limitations – and to infuse each routine activity with a dose of inventive thinking. In the case of editorial design, the fact that constraints may benefit creative practice is evident in the way in which publications create artificial limitations, which often develop into publication-specific conventions. The lifestyle magazine *i-D*, for instance, depicts each cover model with one winking or obscured eye as a visual pun on its title. Thus its art director must, for the purposes of visual continuity and stylistic innovation, for each issue devise new and clever ways of fulfilling this condition.

Other magazines derive additional creative impetus from the diversity of editorial content and/or external material. The German youth supplement *jetzt*, which was published by the *Süddeutsche Zeitung* from 1993 to 2002, was known for its emphasis on reader participation – in an effort to create a community, the supplement incorporated readers' diaries and photographs. This required a clearly defined and structured framework, thus the staff specifically requested diary entries of a certain length or images of certain topics. A higher heterogeneity of formal characteristics of the material would have resulted in chaos – the supplement was, like any other periodical, bound to the constraints and limitations set by a tight publishing schedule. However, as a former chief editor of the magazine confirmed (Interview Chief Editor B), it was the friction between routine and spontaneity, the task of balancing the required level of efficiency with unique ways of incorporating reader input, which continuously inspired the magazine makers' creative production.

Conclusion

This chapter has examined how the systematization and regulation necessitated by commercial and institutional imperatives affect editorial design practice. It has shown how efforts to meet these demands lead to standardized work procedures, which reflect departmental structures and creative hierarchies, and to the development of genre- and publication-specific conventions. Furthermore, it has explored the importance attributed to visual continuity and innovation in this field, arguing that the interrelation and tension between them may fuel creative production. Under circumstances such as those prevalent in editorial design, creative practice then involves more than traditional notions of creativity suggest. The emphasis in the latter on inventive processes and the ability to devise novel ideas and products, which is commonly attributed to artistic 'genius', is dampened by an awareness of how routine and systematized tasks contribute to creative work. As has been argued, inventive and repetitive processes do not exclude each other, but constitute complementary, related modes of thought and action. It is their interplay that can, in fact, drive creative practice. Moreover, the observation that creativity emerges from an individual's interaction with his or her environment highlights the social and collaborative aspects of creative processes. As Richard Florida notes, 'Creativity flourishes best in a unique kind of social environment: one that is stable enough to allow continuity of effort, yet diverse and broad-minded enough to nourish creativity in all its subversive forms' (Florida 2002: 35). Thus, while editorial design practice remains highly systematized and standardized, a broader notion of creativity, taking into account the contribution of routine and collaborative activities, confirms that it is, nevertheless, a genuinely creative and innovative design speciality.

Notes

1. After page designs have received the consent of the art director and chief editor, they are assembled in so-called 'bibles' (folders containing print-outs) or 'flatplans' (miniature print-outs pinned to a wall). Regularly updated and incorporating advertisement, bibles and flatplans allow the evaluation of the publication structure and strength of narrative.
2. To this purpose, art directors attend planning meetings, and often discuss and debate with chief editors the appropriateness of specific visual ideas, as well as commenting on and intervening in editorial matters. Editorial design is always a collaborative effort between departments and, more often than not, a compromise.
3. A commercial attitude, however, does not necessarily affect the visual quality of the cover, and commercial magazines with high production values are often able to reconcile a considerable number of cover lines with good design.
4. One art director at a monthly lifestyle magazine recounted having completed eight or nine redesigns to date, most of which were prompted by his appointment at various magazines (Interview Art Director A).

References

Bourdieu, P. (1984), *Distinction: A Social Critique of the Judgement of Taste*, trans. Richard Nice, London: Routledge & Kegan Paul.

Bourdieu, P. (1990), 'The Social Definition of Photography', in *Photography: A Middle-Brow Art*, Stanford: Stanford University Press.

Brauck, M. (2007), 'Ratz "FAZ" ', *Der Spiegel*, 39: 90–92.

Bundesverband Deutscher Zeitungsverleger e.V. (2007), 'Zeitungen und Ihre Leser in Stichworten 2007'. Available at http://www.bdzv.de/1826.html [last accessed 8 November 2008].

du Gay, P., Hall, S., Janes, L., Mackay, H. and Negus, K. (1997), *Doing Cultural Studies: The Story of the Sony Walkman*, London: Sage.

Featherstone, M. (2007), *Consumer Culture and Postmodernism*, London: Sage.

Florida, R. L. (2002), *The Rise of the Creative Class: And How It's Transforming Work, Leisure, Community and Everyday Life*, New York: Basic Books.

Gell, A. (1998), *Art and Agency: An Anthropological Theory*, Oxford: Clarendon Press.

Heller, A. (1984), *Everyday Life*, trans. G. L. Campbell, London: Routledge & Kegan Paul.

Koestler, A. (1989), *The Act of Creation*, London: Arkana.

Lefebvre, H. (2008), *Critique of Everyday Life, Volume II: Foundations for a Sociology of the Everyday*, trans. John Moore, London: Verso.

Livingston, A. and Livingston, I. (2003), *The Thames & Hudson Dictionary of Graphic Design and Designers*, London: Thames & Hudson.

Magazine Publishers of America (2008), *The Magazine Handbook*, New York: Magazine Publishers of America.

McRobbie, A. (1998), *British Fashion Design: Rag Trade or Image Industry?*, London and New York: Routledge.

Potter, N. (2002), *What Is a Designer: Things, Places, Messages*, London: Hyphen.

PPA (2008), 'The Number of Magazine Titles'. Available at http://www. ppamarketing.net/cgi-bin/go.pl/data-trends/article.html?uid=164 [last accessed 8 November 2008].

Rogers, C. R. (1967), *On Becoming a Person: A Therapist's View of Psychotherapy*, London: Constable.

Verband Deutscher Zeitschriftenverleger (2007), 'Der Deutsche Zeitschriftenmarkt'. Available at http://www.vdz.de/branchendaten.html [last accessed 8 November 2008].

Waller, R. H. W. (1999), 'Making Connections: Typography, Layout and Language', *Proceedings of the 1999 Autumn Symposium*, American Association for Artificial Intelligence.

Zappaterra, Y. (2002), *Editorial Design for Print and Electronic Media*, Crans-Près-Céligny and Hove: RotoVision.

Interviews

Art Director A (2005), interview by author, 14 October 2005.

Chief Editor A (2005), interview by author, 12 October 2005.

Chief Editor B (2005), interview by author, 23 September 2005.

Part III

INTERVIEWS WITH PRACTITIONERS

CHAPTER 12

Kobus Mentz

Director of Urbanism Plus, Specialist Urban Design Practice,
Auckland, New Zealand, December 2008

Kobus Mentz provides, in this interview, many views of urban design in New Zealand, which are coherent with experiences in other countries. Much of this is down to the issue that it is very much an emergent profession that, equally, does not have such a mature clientele in terms of commissioning experience as, perhaps, other design sectors. It also reveals how urban designers are involved in a range of many activities beyond site design that have to align with complex bureaucratic systems.

Guy Julier (GJ): The Urban Design Group lists 'Site and Area Design' as just one of seven areas in which the urban designer might work. What are the main other areas that you give most attention to?

Kobus Mentz (KM): I would say that at least 40 per cent of our remaining time and energy is given over to managing the implementation of urban design and then about a quarter devoted to writing design policies for development plans. And then you've got the rest, outside designing, which covers giving design advice, preparing design guidance, statements and codes and raising design awareness amongst clients and the public.

GJ: Do you use any internal or externally set procedures or practice guidelines as part of the design process, for example, the Urban Design Compendium? If so, what role do set procedures play for you?

KM: We do not formally use step-by-step set procedures based on external documents, although we have developed internal procedures and checklists for generic projects such as growth studies and regeneration projects, which often have complex workshop processes attached.

GJ: In referring to the plethora of urban design guidelines, statements and 'best practice' guidance in the UK, architect Martin Crookston has quipped, 'We've got the best guidance, but the worst practice in Europe.' Is there a danger that the production of so much design guidance ends in a 'tick-box' approach to design or as a way of cutting corners in the process? What advantages do design guidelines have?

KM: Having developed some of the first guides in this country, I have always only seen them as a guide or aide-memoire and never expected them to replace the need to regard each project as different; obviously components of activity are repeatable between projects. However urban designers are at different levels of development and will gain in different ways. [I] fully agree that ticking the boxes doesn't guarantee quality – but it may raise base standards.

GJ: If at all, how do you see the role of urban designers having shifted in the past decade?

KM: In New Zealand and Australia it has moved from general, broad 'conviction-based' advocacy – convincing the regulatory and development communities of the basic value of urban design and the need to change – to an 'evidence-based' approach with clearer strategies to deliver the outcomes. Sadly in both countries, as urban design gains prominence (and a planning/legal prerequisite), more urban designers are for hire, often twisting arguments – making good use of the above mentioned guidelines – to often support unsustainable projects, such as new developments which may have good urban features but are in inappropriate locations and will worsen travel patterns and promote social isolation etc. etc.

GJ: Who have your clients been and who do you compete with? Is there a common kind of profile to your clients?

KM: My clients vary from government or state agencies [to] local authorities and developers or landowners. The profiles vary between the public and private sectors. In the public sector areas I compete mostly with planning-/engineering-/landscape-based urban design practices and in the private sector I compete with architecture-/landscape architecture-/land surveyor-based urban design firms. There are few pure urban design firms in New Zealand or Australia, although they are on the increase. My competition comes mostly from New Zealand teams which have combined with known overseas urban designers.

GJ: Are there any ways that your interactions with clients have changed over the years that you have been working? Do they expect different things from in the past?

KM: I expect that there will be a more explicit focus on how strategic projects such as growth plans, regeneration strategies, guidelines etc. are going to be delivered in planning or legal and market feasibility terms. Urban designers are often good at creating expectations and generally less rigorous or multi-skilled to deal with implementation.

GJ: Equally, does you client relationship change as you have longer working relationships with them?

KM: Yes, if you deliver, trust builds and more opportunities are offered. The test is often whether you can translate aspirations into action plans and whether you have taken the community and stakeholders with you, especially with local authorities, which are answerable to communities.

GJ: Can you tell us a bit about how you cost projects for the client end? Are there times where non-chargeable elements, for example, extra research, or a project that could be strong for your studio profile purposes, come into a project that you either have to take into account or ignore?

KM: We always endeavour to cost projects in great detail and share this with the client. We also outline items specifically excluded. This way downstream difficulties are avoided. Extra work such as research etc. is usually readily paid for if excluded in a clearly defined scope. We do, however, at the beginning of each project, ask ourselves how we can end up with additional skills, new typologies or new methods and bid accordingly. On occasions we do carry overruns. These are usually due to oversights in our own project management.

GJ: How do you keep track of the design process? What are the practical constraints in terms of budgets, time and how long you've got to do it? Do you audit parts of the design process in order to demonstrate its cost-value relationship?

KM: The majority of our strategic urban design work takes place in a workshop environment and the issue doesn't apply as much. Fixed fee master planning projects rely on the internal discipline of checking the proportion of production progress against the proportion of fees spent; claims for extra money again relies on how well the deliverables have been defined in the fee proposal. The detail is important – how many concepts, to what scale and quality – such as CAD, 3D or Freehand etc.

Time-based projects depend on accurate, detailed recording of tasks performed on timesheets. I have found my client relationships around fees to have evolved over time. I now seldom find myself at odds and our fees are seldom questioned, although often the highest – this may be because our work is usually at the front end of the process, for example achieving a Plan Change or Court or Council approval. In other instances it may be because we specifically target the most complex projects; higher fees are usually more acceptable here and competition more limited.

I have come to believe that the most important business decision is whether one takes on a project at all. We think carefully about whether the client is reputable, [whether] we will lose money, [if] it will add to our portfolio and [if] we can do it justice. We often (politely) turn work away. We also seldom reduce our fees without reducing the scope. I would rather lose money sitting on the beach! We don't do work at risk.

GJ: Can you tell us a bit about how you apportion work within the studio? How do you allocate tasks, time, budget and aims?

KM: We do allocate tasks and review resources regularly. All projects are project-managed from mid-level staff. They have to translate the proposal budgets, where tasks are listed and costed, into a project plan (tasks, individuals, dates), which is reviewed against the budget as the project progresses. We try and keep it simple and accounts staff give support.

GJ: How have you arrived at your particular studio size?

KM: The size of our studio, which is currently ten, is really determined by a number of factors.

- As a predominantly 'expertise-based' (as opposed to 'experience-[based]' or 'efficiency-[based]', according to David Maister) practice, we are mostly focused on undertaking complex agenda-setting work. This requires a strong presence of the leadership, or in other words experts within the firm, as opposed to with more routine urban design jobs. The ratio of staff to leaders is therefore a consideration. Leaders can only front so many jobs; currently my senior associate fronts around one-third and I [front] the rest.
- Depth of market is also important. We have, for instance, undertaken all the growth plans for the four largest cities in New Zealand; they will only be redone in five to ten years' time.
- We can also afford to remain small, yet do very large projects (the

Melbourne growth strategy which we led encompassed growth for 500,000 people and involved over fifty professionals), as we operate a tight core–wide network organizational model.

- We do not want to be more than twelve as it will be difficult to maintain social cohesion.
- We need enough resources, of varying skills and seniority, to service our projects (which also vary in nature); the blend of skills includes architectural concept design, urban design site design, graphics, 3D modelling, report writing, workshop participation, project management and client management.
- In addition there is admin or finance and company management.

GJ: Do you outsource elements of your work, for example to freelances or to other specialist firms? When does this happen and how do you coordinate this process?

KM: We collaborate – as opposed to outsource – with several specialists as part of the tight core–wide network organizational model. These specialists are highly skilled at workshop processes and usually cover transport, employment, [and] town centre, environmental or open space design. In addition to the core collaborators, we often have to coordinate outside consultants – usually under our umbrella as lead consultant.

GJ: Urban design is invariably viewed as an 'in-between' discipline. Quite literally it deals with the spaces *between* buildings. It also finds itself between architecture, planning, and highways agencies ... but also in between civic demands for sustainability and social inclusion and the commercial concerns of property developers. Would you agree with this viewpoint? How would this intermediary role impact on the way you approach running Urbanism Plus?

KM: This dynamic is a cornerstone of our approach and probably our most distinguishing feature. Good knowledge of other disciplines and an ability to integrate and synthesize ensures we usually lead projects. It is a virtuous cycle: the more you work in an integrated environment, the more confident and informed you become across the disciplines, [and] the more you get asked to lead.

GJ: Do you think that urban design should be subjected to a normative professional status (e.g. be subject to professional institute recognition), as does architecture or town planning? How might this affect your relationship with clients and other stakeholders?

KM: I have mixed feelings about this. On the one hand I fundamentally believe [that] at a strategic level, professionals from any discipline should be able to be urban designers/leaders. When writing New Zealand's first guide on urbanism, *People + Places + Spaces*, for the Ministry for the Environment, I insisted on calling it a 'design guide for urban New Zealand' as opposed to 'an urban design guide for New Zealand'. I caution against yet another clique forming, with increased competition between disciplines instead of integration.

The other risk is that as a formal body it will have to accept anybody and thus, philosophically, have a 'broad church', watering down the focus on finding more sustainable approaches. Many firms will mostly be joining for marketing purposes.

On the other hand, everyone calls themselves an urban designer, often without [an] urban design qualification, and many of those who do have the qualifications cannot design. In many ways, the title 'urban designer' has become meaningless.

I think if the normative status route was pursued, it must be linked with training, with an emphasis on the fundamentals of sustainability across all disciplines, and design as a skill. I constantly see the need in this country, having delivered the National Urban Design Training Curriculum, training urban designers and other professionals under the Urban Design Protocol. It was a one-off, however, and [I] am currently, with the New Zealand Planning Institute, working towards a professional certificate in urban design. This will, out of necessity, have to focus on many basic craft skills such as general drawing and designing before progressing into complex interdisciplinary sustainable urbanism. As a sponsor of the only urban design award in Auckland I see, first hand, the poor skills levels of graduates.

GJ: Once your work is finished for a client, do you have a process for measuring the impact or success of a project?

KM: Some larger projects are peer reviewed, organized by the client; all my training courses are appraised by attendees. We do review projects internally; however, being a small practice, this is done informally and as an ongoing discussion (usually over breakfast), not an end of project event. We simply ask how we can do things better, more efficiently and more profitably.

GJ: How does your experience of private and public sector clients differ?

KM: We trade on our knowledge of both sectors. Public sector clients want best sustainability practice and guarantees that public good will be achieved. They also want resource consent processes that can be managed by low-level planners. This poses a challenge between achieving easily understood explicit planning rules versus allowing for the often complex solutions required to make good urbanism or respond to future (unknown) market needs. They seek solutions from us that reconcile these issues and rely on our private sector knowledge. Private sector clients want certainty around the yields they will be able to achieve; they also want [the] flexibility to be able to respond to future (unknown) market needs. They trade on our standing with the authorities.

GJ: Do you ever find pressure on the sequencing of urban design projects, in terms of a political or policy need, to give priority to some parts over others – for example, in the interests of securing follow-up funding support? I was thinking in terms of project delivery sequencing. Through interviewing other urban designers and planners in the UK, an issue that came up was how local authorities put pressure on the process sometimes, to ensure that the more visible elements of a scheme are done first. This is so that further funds can be drawn in to support the wider scheme but also as a public relations job with the wider public. Sometimes this results in poorly considered urban design, as detailing is specified in haste. For me this is an interesting issue, as it points to the constant compromises that urban designers have to undertake in order to align themselves with complex demands.

KM: We have not had this experience, possibly because we have far less funding from agencies outside the local authorities to draw from. We actually encourage smaller, easier – low-hanging fruit – projects to commence quickly, but this is to help maintain momentum after expectations have been raised. Our biggest issue is when local authorities break the continuity of a project; this often happens due to personnel or political changes, unrealistic concepts, poorly devised implementation plans – which good consultants should facilitate – or lack of buy-in by client body. Consultants often find strategies being tampered with, without being consulted around the original consulted and agreed logic.

Just to add ... many urban designers involved in strategic design such as growth plans, regeneration strategies etc. – as opposed to master plans for construction – seem to be letting themselves and the profession down [by] producing strategies or concepts which are not readily deliverable. So many of these projects get redone, with very little built from the previous study.

This is often because the conceptual/aspirational work is not thoroughly tested for fundability, buildability, marketability or public acceptance. Urban designers are getting good at the soft stuff but remain weak at the hard and often boring stuff. Urban design practice is often undertaken with far less rigour and accountability than the conventional professions.

CHAPTER 13

Tim Allnutt

Head of Communications Planning at Clemmow Hornby Inge (CHI), London, May 2008

Tim Allnutt was previously planning director at Initiative Media, and has also worked for Lowe London and Bartle Bogle Hegarty. In this interview he describes some of the auditing and review processes at CHI, noting the difficulty of measuring value in terms of 'effectiveness' as well as cost. He also notes that graphic designers at CHI tend, for the most part, to be involved in the execution of what he calls 'big ideas', rather than in their generation.

Paul Springer (PS): Can I start by asking whether you audit all aspects of the creative process?

Tim Allnutt (TA): Not always. There is increasing pressure on clients and agencies to prove work done will be effective and give value for money. The creative brief is normally based on research and [on] an insight [into] the brand aim, campaign purpose and the market. Data and analysis for the brief tend to be about implementation. We look at qualitative aspects of a campaign through focus groups. [For] quantitative [aspects], we look at bespoke research on sales figures, acquisition data to show how a campaign has worked ... sometimes [we have] more data than is needed. The art is to make sure you have the right research.

The tendency has been to measure things 'classically', but you can end up knowing the cost of it [the process] but not the value. You have to measure the right thing. For instance, media agencies are often measured on cost – whether they are buying resources more cheaply, not whether they are purchasing effectively. Agency behaviour tends to follow, so it's easy to drive agencies in the wrong way by sticking in measurements that lead to ineffective practices.

Media auditing has become the main measurement during the past fifteen years. We can get judged on whether we bought a page in *The*

Times as cheaply as the previous agent, but we might have bought it in a different way that is more effective. Procurement people simply want to know if the cost of your service is in keeping with a benchmark they have. So procurement is good in one sense, because it makes you focus on what you're supposed to be doing. But if you take it as an end in itself, you miss a lot around it. We also have to beware of the 'three-year brand manager' because, knowing [he/she] won't be in post for long, [he/she] wants to show [he/she] can manage costs effectively and show short-term effects. The *real* benefit to the brand is the long-term effect.

PS: Does this impact on the ultimate look of a campaign? It might be coincidental, but the most talked-about campaigns recently have [had] a strong underpinning idea and multiple, relatively cheap executions, not glossy, full-cost commercials.

TA: That's one of the things we specifically address with our 'big ideas' sessions, in-house with clients. A big idea outlasts a brand manager, and if they want to change their campaign, a big idea can mature and grow for years to come. It makes for a much stronger relationship with the customer. The relationship, how they behave – more than just an ad campaign, it can become ingrained throughout the company (just like Tesco's 'Every Little Helps'). It's difficult to measure and gain the impact of that.

PS: Is there much difference in auditing digital executions rather than traditional campaigns?

TA: It's easier to audit digital advertising business than creative campaigns. In about 70 per cent of big brand advertising digital campaigns, auditing tends to be on a quarterly basis. Brand managers look back on a campaign and review pricing and benchmarking ... so it's a more regular thing within digital media to measure. The difficulty with creative auditing is that if you try to audit the process it can stifle creativity – the processes tend not to be so linear. Also, you might crack a brief as a member of teams or individually; you might crack it instantly; it might come from a brainstorm with the client. So it's quite difficult to measure in that sense.

PS: Do you keep the brainstorming open and flexible or do you keep close reins on the development time? What if it's protracted and in danger of going over budget?

TA: Budget management and process management are down to how strong the client is and how good the relationship is between agency and client. What we tend to get is strong clients that have good agency relationships. They can use their procurement if it's part of their company's operational dictate that they need fed back and they'll use it as just another piece of information in their process, as opposed to being the thing that governs the process. That's the big difference. In my experience the auditing process on creative work is a rare thing.

PS: Is the creative method at CHI systematized?

TA: We have a loose process and we have a 'big ideas' process, which is something we try to use with all of our clients. This is a way of coming up with the initial idea *with* the clients, writ large, which becomes the governing thing that we do.

PS: And that dictates the media channels you use and market segmentation?

TA: Exactly. That hopefully channels everything and it's something we try and do. In a perfect world, with any new client where a rethink is needed, or a [there is a] major point of disruption within the client's business, we try and do a 'Big Ideas Day' with the clients – the key stakeholders. One of the important things about that is it allows us to get senior client buy-in, because they become part of the process. That is a major help if you can get the clients to be partly generating the idea. It's much easier to sell it through and that makes the process (at the client's end) take care of itself. You don't have to sell at every stage, so that is a good thing, and later, when we get more into the implementing stage of new campaigns, we have a creative briefing process.

PS: How does that work?

TA: Once we arrive at the 'big idea', we distil it into a communication brief, which describes the business problem that the client might have. We talk through in detail what the 'big idea' is and the target consumer, and we discuss what the 'call to action' (the objective) is, and specific requirements for the campaign based on assembled data. We basically try and get the brand from A to B in terms of sales, or we try to change its predisposition from X to Y. That brief will be written before any execution is determined. It won't be an advertising brief specifically, but a communications brief. We then formulate an ideas team to discuss that brief. Rather than that going into a creative department, we will get a cross-functional team of people together.

PS: How many people?

TA: It tends to be six or seven, all from different disciplines, brought to the table. It will be someone from a direct marketing background, an advertising specialism, a media, digital or data specialist, maybe a designer – depending on the brief. The idea is that we have a cross-disciplinary group of people who can bring a view on what the solutions should be, because we're all within one agency with one bottom line. There is no vested interest in selling your own idea. It might be an advertising solution, a new website, guerrilla method or an in-store-based solution. This helps to specify what the executional requirements are for the campaign, [whether] we need an ad route or a different way forward. The Big Ideas Team then clarifies the purpose and media and, as a result, trigger work for the teams to go away and refine. Once we have produced the idea in these sessions it will create subsequent work that will get us to a stage of developing, designing and refining stage. So, we have our process, but it tends to be fairly flexible depending on the size of the task.

PS: Where do graphic designers fit into this?

TA: They tend to be involved in the latter stages of the process – they don't tend to be involved in the ideas generation. Obviously they are involved in producing an expression of the 'big idea', but depending on the brief, there might be an obvious role for someone with a design element to it …

PS: Projects that require a design accent?

TA: Yes – it might be that part of what we're doing needs a graphic flavour, a re-thought logo or something and [they] can actually be involved at the beginning of that. One of the things we've seen is that as our agency staff base and discipline expertise grows, the process has necessarily become more flexible. This is relatively new. The advertising briefing process used to be really linear. When I worked with Lowes some years ago, we had approximately six weeks from brief to an answer – an advertising solution that went straight to the creative department, and you knew you would get a TV commercial or billboard ad out of it. But now, in the modern media world, it can be anything. You have to have a process that will help you avoid chaos, but still gives you the chance to create successful solutions – and money!

PS: The processes of advertising have speeded up since digital communication accelerated production times. To what extent has it impacted on the creative stages?

TA: That's an interesting question. We recently talked about this very fact –
that often we are asked for things very much more quickly then we used
to be. Clients want answers 'now', and we often have to develop strategies that have to be executed in days. Again, the 'big idea' is very good
because it allows us to take up a 'governing position' that we can hang
everything off. I think everyone is under pressure all of the time now, and
the Internet has created and motivated it, because you can create campaigns easily and get consumers and propagate them on your behalf. It's
not like the old set-piece television ads – everything is much faster now.

CHAPTER 14

Jason Severs

Senior Design Analyst, Industrial Design Department,
Global Innovation Firm, New York, January 2008

In this interview, Jason Severs gives further perspectives on the role of the design researcher in mediating quantitative and qualitative data within the design process. Severs's mediatory role is also to be found within the design studio itself, smoothing the transition of the development of a project through the studio while also acting as an important bridge between the studio and clients.

Nitzan Waisberg (NW): You refer to yourself as a generalist. You're a designer really, right?

Jason Severs (JS): You know, my undergraduate degree is in fine art – painting and sculpture – and then I kind of got to do video work, and I kind of moved out from there doing freelancing as a Flash developer in the very early days of Flash 3, 4. And I moved into thinking how new media communicates to people, and I got interested in instructional design and technology; that's when I got my first dose of what it meant to be a designer, not in the sense of a graphic designer, but to do design thinking, iterative design thinking. Which you kind of intuitively do as an artist in a lot of ways, except you are not working within a series of plans and constraints in the same way, but the creative process is the same. So I did that and got into doing usability research when I was doing my master's in inner cycles of developing education applications. I got really interested there, and I ended up going to the Bruce Mau studio in Toronto; while [I was] there we were working on this global communications project called Massive Change, and in doing that there were a lot of interesting ... ad hoc approaches to doing research that you kind of have to do on the fly ... You are almost, in a sense, a journalist in some ways – not with the skills of a journalist, but some of the approaches were similar to the way a journalist would approach a story. But at the same time we were producing outcomes and visualizing the stories in the form of a book and a website and an exhibition – communicating the complexities of the story. In a sense like building a strategic model to [give] businesses a way to think about design, but then also creating vehicles of communication to communicate the story.

NW: When you say 'design', do you mean the process of design? Or design research within design?

JS: Both.

NW: So to be able to quantify and qualify every corner radius?

JS: Exactly, yeah. I think there are still those messy grey areas that are important to have. They give you the space to think and solve problems. Because at the end of the day, we often have this kind of conflict, where the company that is working with us will start to think of us as a research firm – because we are doing design research. But we always have to come back and say, we are not just doing research, we are making things. And our end goal is to make things that are an expression of your business case or whatever, your strategic vision. And that gets lost sometimes. So they expect us to act like a research organization.

NW: How does that express itself?

JS: I think [that] thinking about design in terms of return on investment is the big thing. So it's like 'I want you to be able to tell me how this design will help me meet these end goals for the next two years'. And we spend a lot of time trying to match those two things up and it often is very hard to do; ... [we] can, to a certain extent, [from] what we know about consumer behaviour and attitudes, and needs and wants, we can design to those things, but at the end of the day, you are never really going to know. That is the beauty of design research – at the beginning it gets people, users, consumers, whatever you want to call it; it gets them involved earlier in the process. Or just in the process, period ... I love [the] model that Donald Norman thought up, [in] which you have the designer's mental model, you have the user's mental model, and in the middle you have this idea of a system image, and that is the expression of whatever you are making; and the designer has a mental model of how that thing will work, and designs to that. And the user has a mental model and that is how they will think: their perception of it, and ... their intention [of how] to use something – and it's like a guessing game on the designer's part to try and guess what the user's mental model is. Well, you know, we don't have to guess any more. We can go ... and ... figure out what that mental model is, and make a good hypothesis and observations about what that mental model is. And that informs the design of things. And that intersection is really interesting.

NW: I agree; I think it is a huge thing and historically it has happened in a fairly short period of time.

JS: Yeah. And I can remember doing some Flash work in the late 1990s – when you [got] the creative briefs ... [that were] heavily informed by market research, and those [were] very driven by these large quantifications of people's attitudes towards things, and you [were] meant to come up with some kind of creative expression of that [laughs]. It is a bit abstract and strange, you know.

NW: Very abstract and strange. Tell me a bit more about that. You've been in this area long enough, and experienced different expressions of it; how is what is going on in Frog Design, in terms of translating – if that is the correct metaphor – findings and observations and understanding people and users, how is that translated into form and function and design?

JS: The final expression? I think the big part of that is the way a researcher works within the studio. Myself, coming into the studio ... I originally started working in the digital media design department and there were a lot of large retainer clients at the time. So we were doing a lot of B2B websites when I first joined Frog. And there [are] a lot of standard usability things there. And that stuff is fairly easy to translate into design. It is a fairly task-based approach to figuring out how things work and how usable they are, and there are a lot of big practices around that. But when I started working with the industrial design team, I found the area was a lot more grey, and one of the things I felt [I had] to kind of implement at Frog is bring designers into the research process. So, designing a research programme so that designers can come in and understand the users' mental model, to benefit them, I think is part of where I saw my role at Frog, in terms of being a design researcher. And that has been a big help, actually, in making design part of design research, at least at Frog.

NW: From my experience of working in research consultancies, I found that having a background in product design was making me popular with creative clients, because they were having terrible conflicts with conventional researchers. But I was having conflicts with them as well. I'm wondering if having combined these two sensibilities, do you find you are in conflict with yourself sometimes?

JS: No, because I started as a designer. I don't have those conflicts now. I think on product design, or service design, I have that conflict less because it is very easy to translate the way an analyst would communicate ideas, and then you have on top of that the facility to visualize things, to enhance that communication. It fits very well talking about design languages, shaping strategy around projects, visioning products in terms of scenarios, and especially service, when you think about lifecycles and visioning those things and the scenario planning aspects of that. Where it became a conflict for me was when I was working in digital media design and there was a lot of intense specification and things that happen there. You start to become more of an analyst in the sense of being an information architect. It is more of an analyst's role and less of a designer's role. I feel like design research processes fit a lot easier with those guys, than [they do] into the visual media component, because you are always moving towards this intense specification. To me, that is a little different to the mechanical engineering side. Something about the industrial design process, this Bill Buxton idea of … sketching and what is generated through a sketch, and combining user experience into that; I think it is such a natural fit.

NW: You have spoken about how respondents, people, were looking at mock-ups and they were sitting with the designer and really even locating buttons, and they might draw on a mock-up. That seems like very high-resolution input. How did the designers deal with it? How did the designers use what they are saying and their input about very designerly things?

JS: In terms of – take a button for instance … the usability factor of that is easier for designers to accept. They go: 'Well, actually everybody said this was more comfortable, so that is something I can live with.' When we get more into the subjective things, like form, that is when it starts to get messy for designers. You have a style you want to communicate, and that style is informed by a culture that you understand and a history you understand, and it is something you want to project in this thing. That is why I brought in those mapping exercises in terms of the way people were perceiving things, in terms of the brand attributes, or just general formal attributes, and usability attributes. Because it was another way; instead of just looking at that sketch on the prototype, it was another way of visualizing the thinking of the group. But those were not meant to quantify brand attributes to design language to get to the client and say,

'OK, this brand attribute matches to this curve, so this is the best way to go in terms of business.' It is really to just map the thinking of the people in the room [on] that particular day. So it is another component that designers can look at to analyse their reactions to those insights that are being gathered.

NW: It was interesting to see how you were using these very visual things, which I think actually are rarely used in qualitative research. These were the types of things you might see in quantitative research. I'm wondering, how do clients react to this, and do designers use this? What do you see as the value of using these visualizations?

JS: Visualizing things in design research is so critical. Some of the exercises [make it] easier to do that. Like you take a mood board exercise and you have people sort and collect images or do collages or drawings; those things are obviously easier to visualize. But behaviours and attitudes get a bit more tricky.

NW: So, you are using these same representations to talk to designers and, say, brand managers or whatever.

JS: Yeah, and a lot of the times it is a language, especially in market research; it is kind of a language they understand, but you have to heavily caveat it, and I'm always saying it in presentations, and I'm always putting it in the text, because I had a market researcher ask me one time how can we do this on a large scale. And I was like … you can't really do that [on a] large scale. There probably could be some adaptation with final concepts, but I don't know what the value would actually be because it's the combination of what you hear in the room and what those visualizations say. It is those two things coming together that are where the magic happens. In the actual analysis and synthesis process that happens in the studio, those things are anchor points that help focus.

NW: Do you conduct any quantitative research?

JS: [Laughs.] That is the holy grail, right? To mix qualitative and quantitative. We have a few people in the office now who think about how you scale a quantitative research programme out of qualitative [research], to provide an extra layer of metrics to our clients. And that is generally for buy-in, organizational buy-in, because when they start to see numbers attached to things, they … and we want those numbers to be real numbers, but it's like this integration of a person with a particular set of skills into the way we do things as designers in the studio. So they have to understand our goals, our qualitative goals, and more importantly our design goals, and what we are actually intending to make, and then how to translate that into kind of a quantitative ... but we don't do that very often.

NW: I had a chance to work with a lot of behavioural segmentations, but what was going on in the consultancy that I was working at was they began to really think in terms of these segmentations for other clients who didn't have the budgets to do quantitative research and get these segmentations for their market sectors. We had really stopped talking about demographics and we had these kind of archetypes, almost, for different sectors. I'm wondering if that is something that is emerging in your research?

JS: Yeah. You can take those behavioural segments, and you can add variations to that. There are archetypes. In the healthcare industry you have like this idea of the mature maverick or the young [unclear]. So someone who is a risk-taker, ... in extreme sports, things like that. Segmentation could translate into product design.

NW: You were talking about stories and journalism, and I think of these segmentations as archetypal heroes who go through a user journey or experience. I'd just like to hear more [about] why you described your work as kind of like journalism, and the significance of storytelling?

JS: That is the main thing: you are always trying to communicate the essence of people. So when you are doing contextual interviews or ethnography, or whatever you want to call it, there are so many things that you observe, that aren't expressed by an individual and I think that is what a journalist does. They kind of read between the lines of what people are saying and they understand the environments and the context in which people live. It's kind of interesting what journalists do, because they walk a beat, you know. They have a territory that they kind of understand, a sector and a zone they kind of understand. And back to the idea of archetypes, I always thought that design researchers could have that as well. Like they could walk a beat, understand that segmentation; and they would react to lots of different things, to lots of different kinds of product lines, different kinds of experiences. I think in some sense you end up working in particular industries for a long time, so you do start to walk a certain kind of beat and understand a certain kind of territory a little better than others. But when I say working like a journalist, it is obviously just my assumption of what it means to be a journalist. But I think the other thing is, something we gain as designers, is we understand how to communicate things visually, whereas journalists have a real facility with ... language. They understand the nuances of words, whereas we understand the nuances of visual expressions. I think that is the new thing that design research brings; [it] is visualizing story-telling as well. Even though designers in general need to [laughs] ... their facility with language. But it is not a part of our training.

NW: It's almost a prerequisite to hate reading ...

JS: [Laughs.]

CHAPTER 15

David Scothron

Director of Product First, Product Design and Strategy Consultancy, London, December 2008

Among many insights, David Scothron shows how a turn towards more strategic work in product design has gone hand in hand with a more flexible approach towards project teams. As the firm's core membership has reduced in number, so specialist input to projects is sought outside it more frequently. As a result, the actual design office has become less important to their creative work. The interview also reveals the impact of growing and changing client use of design, so the different departments of a client with which Product First interact may now be more varied and numerous.

Guy Julier (GJ): Can you tell us about what Product First does and how it came about?

David Scothron (DS): Product First was formed in 1987 by John Boult, Graham Thomson and myself, specializing in the creation, design and development of manufactured goods. Initially a team of four people, we quickly grew to twelve, comprising 'in-house' complementary marketing, design and engineering skills. John and I are now the remaining directors of Product First and we currently operate a highly personal, 'hands-on' service, collaborating with long-term associates on a project-by-project basis, as appropriate.

The consultancy offered a total product development service – from initial concept through engineering detailing [and] prototyping to final manufactured product. Put simply, we wished to design stylish and innovative products that tackled user issues of appearance, functionality and ease of use within practical, cost-effective manufacturing parameters. 'Commercial creativity', if you like.

We have worked with companies throughout the world, with projects ranging from fast-moving consumer goods, consumer durables, industrial products, medical and scientific equipment to one-off signage systems and tea bags.

From day one we had a desire to apply creative input to corporate strategy and product planning, undertaking initiatives such as form and functional forecasting, technology communication, design research, think-tank, future concepts – essentially, exploring product futures for those clients (such as Apple, GEC, Unilever, 3M, Corus) who wished to use design as a strategic tool within their organizations, rather than using us merely to solve an immediate product design problem.

Over time, we have chosen to focus more on this strategic aspect of our work, leading us to redefine our offer. We now describe ourselves as an 'innovation consultancy based on design thinking'. We still believe the drive for great ideas, or *putting the product first,* is the starting point for successful innovative companies, but today recognize you also need to develop, in parallel, the right enabling culture. We help companies do both these things – create great ideas and build sustainable innovative cultures.

GJ: And what kind of clients do you work with?

DS: Our clients range from large multinational corporations [to] small companies, 'start-ups' and individual entrepreneurs. The common feature of our work is the clients' desire to produce successful products and recognize that design can be an agent of change within their organizations. Our FMCG work has tended to be for large, multinational brands (Shell, BP, Unilever, P&G, Coca-Cola), whilst our product design portfolio spans a range of market sectors and sizes of company (Siemens, Kango, London Transport, Lego, Racal, Filofax, Jordan, Ross Electronics etc., and numerous SMEs and technology start-up companies). Recently, our more strategic work has also involved working with organizations like local Business Links and Regional Development Agencies to national bodies such as the Design Council, NESTA and SEEDA.

GJ: Who are your competitors and how do you view your competition?

DS: Obviously, there are – and have been over the years – numerous competitors within the product design sector. I would say the consistent players have been firms like Seymour Powell, IDEO, Factory, Priestman Goode – though it's fair to say all of us have had to refine and adapt our business model over time. Interestingly, we now find ourselves competing, in the strategic market, not only against some traditional design groups (PDD and Kinear Duffort) but also new specialist service innovation consultants (Engine, Plot, Radar Station), or creative innovation consultants (What If, Via Dynamics). The market is saturated with competitors and the need to clearly differentiate your offer is becoming increasingly difficult.

GJ: What made you specialize in your sector of design?

DS: I met John and Graham at the Michael Peters Group, which was a large multidisciplinary design firm at the time. They had been brought in specifically to set up product design as a distinct discipline within the group's design portfolio – part of an overall plan to become a creative 'one-stop shop'. Within that particular brand-driven environment we quickly recognized there was a market for a more *creative* approach to product design (as opposed to the existing, traditional 'engineering'-driven consultancy model) – so decided to set up Product First. The name deliberately communicates our area of specialism.

We now specialize less in the actual 'design' of artefacts but focus more on helping companies become more innovative for themselves. We have a situation where anything is possible really – the problem lots of companies have now is 'What should we be doing, and how can we go about doing it?'

We've gravitated towards this sector because firstly we, as people, are getting older and didn't necessarily want to design another toaster! As individuals, we needed new challenges and stimulus. John and I are both active in design education, which in turn gives us an opportunity to blend, perhaps uniquely, real-world experience with academic insight and knowledge.

Design has always been about 'problem-solving' – still the same old Bauhaus 'Form follows function' mantra – it's just that now the function we're dealing with has changed. And we have reacted to that need within the marketplace.

GJ: Are there any major differences between the areas of your work?

DS: Essentially, our clients either have a specific problem or need help defining what their problem actually is. Although we see our strength now as helping companies and organizations solve the latter, we still sometimes get asked to 'design' a new product or structural pack. So, yes, there are major differences (or the skill sets needed) between the 'doing' and the 'analytical' aspects of our work.

GJ: How have things changed over the years for you in terms of the interactions you have with clients?

DS: I would say that the overall level of engagement – with product develop-
        ment issues – within organizations has increased. There is a positive
        sense of inclusiveness within development teams and an emerging col-
        lective responsibility. The introduction of design managers within some
        companies has significantly improved awareness of the power of design
        thinking – and consequently raised clients' expectations from their
        development partners. Historically, we have generally enjoyed access to
        key senior personnel – the decision-makers – in both our design and
        strategic work. Interestingly, product development is no longer seen as
        just the remit of the marketing or technical teams. For example, human
        resources is emerging as a client when issues of cultural change within
        organizations are being discussed and implemented upon.

GJ: What are the benefits to you of retaining clients?

DS: To be honest, we always strive to establish long-lasting relationships with
        our clients – rather than have a 'one night stand' affair. That way, we feel
        we become part of their team, gain mutual trust and respect for our
        capabilities, and often end up reaching further into their organization. In
        practical terms, this means we can often short-circuit the way in which
        we interact together, often enabling us to present and discuss our work
        in a less formal way. The relationship becomes intuitive and means we
        can work faster and delve deeper into their problem. Personal relation-
        ships are obviously an important factor in successful outcomes and we
        are conscious of this when we assign the team members. Of course, it
        still hurts when, after a recognized success story, the client then chooses
        to engage another consultant for the next project!

GJ: How do you manage the costing of projects with clients?

DS: Projects tend to be 'time based' and costed accordingly. All our work is
        structured in stages and is against an agreed written proposal incorpo-
        rating the client brief. The first stage is a fixed price, with subsequent
        stages re-evaluated and discussed, based upon the outcomes of stage 1
        (although 'guestimate' costings would be intimated in the initial pro-
        posal). We generally plan the project as a totality and factor into the pro-
        posal any specialist external inputs we would need to tackle the problem,
        having previously obtained costings from specialist suppliers or partners.
        There have been occasions, however, where we have absorbed additional
        costs if we believed they were crucial to the success of the project –
        though these are very rare.

GJ: And what about the management of design projects? How do you organize the design process and keep track of its costs versus price?

DS: As I say, all projects are time based and individuals are allocated a specific number of hours or days to work on the project. A director would project-manage the team and is ultimately responsible [for bringing] in the project on budget. Timesheets form an effective check on hours – but in our case the team is small [and] it is not a major issue to control and monitor. Having said that, we are not obsessive about this – we take a holistic approach, believing a task has a certain worth and value, and we strive to deliver work that matches our own expectation levels and are prepared to invest our time to achieve that – obviously within reason! We work very much as a team, bringing together individual specialisms and complementary skills. During the preliminary stages of a project, we encourage ideas and insights from everyone within the company – the fact that we have always been a small consultancy makes this a realistic option. As we work through the subsequent stages, specialist team members would then assume responsibility for specific aspects of development.

GJ: Is the way you work reflected in the layout of your offices?

DS: We have been through many studio formats and sizes throughout our existence, reflecting changes in the physical make-up of Product First, the technologies needed to meet client demands and [the] personal aspirations of the directors. Increasingly flexible working practices and the reduced size of the consultancy has meant that, over time, the office has become less important. The nature of our work means that we now almost exclusively visit clients. It's more cost-effective for us to visit them, than them sending large teams of project members to us.

GJ: Can you tell us a bit about how you subcontract design work?

DS: Yes; traditionally we have always outsourced model-making or prototyping and supplemented our technical expertise with a close-knit network of collaborators. Also, we seek specialist inputs to projects – such as market research or unique knowledge acquisition where appropriate. Whilst believing our collective experience is a key element of what we offer clients, we also recognize that alternative, younger inputs are essential to many projects. So, we have access to a wide network of challenging design thinkers to shake us up a bit!

GJ: Can you tell us a bit about how you see the differences between private and public sector work?

DS: Basically, both sectors either have a specific problem to solve or need help to identify and initiate new opportunities. Public sector projects tend to be larger, longer and often more complex in scope and delivery. More emphasis is placed upon a considered presentation deliverable in the form of a universal discussion 'document' or equivalent for extensive distribution throughout the organization. In a sense, there is a need for more accountability and recording of the process and outcomes.

GJ: How do you give your clients a sense of 'quality assurance' … that your offer has a professional value?

DS: Well, we don't follow any formalized 'standard of service'. People either 'get it' or they don't! Clients have to ultimately like something about you, or what you've done for other people and want a bit of 'it' for themselves. We obviously try to present ourselves as a professional organization based upon the range of work we have produced for an extensive range of well-respected brands and organizations. Also, collaborating with, and endorsed by, establishments such as the Design Council implies that we are serious about what we do and assumes a quality standard. The fact that we have worked for companies such as Shell International, BP, Apple, Unilever, Procter and Gamble etc. tends to position you somewhere in the professional food chain I would hope.

GJ: And on completion of a design project … what happens next in terms of measuring its success?

DS: We have always had a desire to continue the dialogue with clients after finishing a project. We tend to be quite proactive about PR opportunities, competitions etc., and often help coordinate or prepare material to this end. 'Success' can be measured in many ways. This can be through increased sales, market position, brand perception and awareness, [and] internal cultural change to quite literally 'saving the company'. We try to establish, in conversation with the client, how the project has impacted upon their business. This information enables us to then communicate our skills and services to potential new clients within a business context and so, hopefully, show how we can add value to their product development process.

CHAPTER 16

Ben Reason

Founding Partner, live|work, Service Design and Innovation Consultancy, London, June 2008

Lucy Kimbell and Liz Moor interviewed Ben Reason in London in June 2008. In this wide-ranging interview, he describes a number of live|work's projects and clients, and explains how factors such as size and complexity of client organizations impact upon the work of the consultancy. He also notes how work for particular clients (including the UK National Health Service) has led to the development of new systems and techniques for measuring value and efficiency, and about how live|work attempts to demonstrate 'value' in different areas. He goes on to describe how live|work makes use of workflow monitoring systems such as Harvest, and how these might be used in the future. Finally, he discusses the implications of live|work's 'capacity-building' work for other organizations.

Liz Moor (LM): Could you tell us a little bit about live|work: what kind of work it does, and how long you've been around?

Ben Reason (BR): It's a service and innovation design company. We've been around for coming up to seven years, and there are now twenty-five people. The work is quite broadly spread around different sectors. We do work for financial services to [the] public sector, [the] NHS and local government projects. We work predominantly with service-providing organizations, but we have done work with manufacturers. We have two core competencies: one is around customer insight, in a variety of forms, from unmet needs through to innovation. We also audit customer experiences and usability. And then the other thing is that we have a range of work around visualization. So ... some visualizing strategy work, all the way through to designing websites that work and things like that. We have an insights team and a design team, in simple terms, and a number of consultants who lead projects.

LM: Since you've been up and running, who have your clients been? And who do you compete with?

BR: We've worked quite a bit with mobile telecoms providers. I think the first ongoing client we had was Orange. We did quite a lot of innovation work for them, but then we also did work on new services that they were bringing in. Vodafone as well. So when they were developing music services for the mobile phone, we worked on that, and some of the databases, things like video calling, which was a great big failure [laughs], but we did things like that. We also now do quite a lot of financial services work, which is also B2B.

One of the things we've been really keen to develop is the public sector side of things, and that's had a pretty wide range of projects. We bring a kind of project methodology to things like rural transport, or employment services for hard to reach workless people in Sunderland, [or] housing services here in London. And then with the NHS it's been quite a range of things. We work with services for people with multiple sclerosis, and we've done a bit of work actually in hospital theatres – sort of looking for ... is there a design opportunity around work in that area? But that is not really designing in the traditional sense. It's more about design process and thinking, and bringing a rigorous creative approach to people who don't really have that in their working lives.

LM: What made you keen to build that side of your work?

BR: That's a good question. Well, we started off quite idealistic about wanting to work in kind of use design to make better public services. But we're also keen to work in areas of environmental sustainability as well. The public sector is fifty per cent of the economy – or roughly – and it's an area where they think service; they talk service. And there's quite a growing agenda now around engaging the public in consultation and all this sort of stuff. And we've been presenting in Westminster about customer insights and how we work. So there's a growing market for it in the public sector as well.

LM: And what would you say are the differences between the two areas of work?

BR: I think it is just the technical side and the content side. You have to know enough about what they're talking about. And also the organizations are structured very differently. The profit thing isn't there in the same way, although hospitals work like little businesses now. Well, big businesses!

LM: And so what is your process when you get a new client? Do you have the same process for all clients – is it formalized at all?

BR: We've started saying we do six different things: strategy; new service development; innovation; experience design; usability; and service design capability, which is more of a skills thing. So when we get a new client we talk them through those six things, and generally they want something sort of bespoke ... a kind of mix of that stuff. It also depends on what kind of [consumer] input you want into the project, whether it's [a] detailed analysis of what currently exists or insight into opportunities to do something that doesn't exist. And then that will feed into some form of ideas stage, whether it's looking at what improvements could be made, or trying to come up with a hundred ideas that feed into a pipeline. The difficult bits to describe are the bits in between, where you take the insights and use them.

We more and more try to take ideas and prototype them. It's another way of involving customers. So we try to make very light and quick prototypes. It might even be just taking a sketch and talking people through it. Or it might be simulating some aspect of the service. And then we work on whatever is needed to design the delivery, whether it's to make a business case or to specify something to go and be developed and built.

LM: And how do you keep a track on the process? What are the practical constraints in terms of budgets, time, and how long you've got to do it?

BR: Well, there's a project where we've been asked to do stuff in four weeks – and so we just try to get all that stuff done in four weeks. And then we're working with an NHS trust where it is just kind of dripping along. So it varies, partly with people's ability to use the work. Clients set the time limit and we just cut the cloth to fit. Increasingly, we'll try to give them a guide about how things will work out and what they will get but, well, it's an interesting question. We had a client who just had kind of nothing, and wanted a target of launching a certain number of things in nine months. And so the first part was just to create a load of ideas, get some feedback on them and whittle them down to ten. And then the second bit was building a set of prototypes for them. But each time we went back to it we had a new set of questions. The first time we were just saying: 'Insurance risk, what does that mean to people?' And the second time it was sort of, 'Well, we've got these kinds of ideas, what do they mean to people?' And then at the end of that we built working prototypes that we could test. So we went through a sort of beta testing phase. And the philosophy is that things should be constantly iterated ... but I think a project kind of has a certain minimum and a maximum size, and is constrained by things like how many people we need to see.

But the other thing that makes a difference is the size and the communication challenge of the client. So if it's a very big, bureaucratic organization, you have to do more to sell ideas though the business. You have to work them up in more fidelity, and put more effort into them. So with big clients like Vodafone, you have to take them on a roadshow and get buy-in and things like that. We sometimes think you could do it a lot more efficiently if you didn't have to deal with the organization, and that's actually half the challenge of the work. You know with the NHS, for example, [that] you have to do a whole load of stakeholder workshops to make sure that everyone gets their say.

LM: OK, and what are the more practical mechanisms by which you keep track of creative work? Do you have electronic timesheets, or software that keeps track of things?

BR: Well, we have to try to, or else we couldn't work out how much time we're spending. If we fix a price we need to know if we come in roughly on budget or over budget. And that's a big challenge. So we do keep time, but not to the ten minutes. I mean, the system we've got could cope with smaller or larger [than that], but I think we only ask it to account for half a day. We price in days rather than hours. The system is this thing called Harvest. It's a web-based time tool … It doesn't do enough for us, though. I mean, it doesn't make that stuff visible enough so you know how much time is available in the studio or, you know, [so you can] readily view where you are on the project. I think maybe it can do those things, but we're still getting to grips with that stuff. You can ask it to tell you everyone who's worked on X project over the last month, but you just want to log in and say, that project's on budget, and that one's over, and that sort of thing.

LM: And how does it work for your employees?

BR: Well, Harvest is a website, so they log in and track their time every now and again. It has a daily or monthly view. Our studio manager adds projects. So there's a project, like an NHS project, and it lists the different generic things we do on it, so you can just add whatever you're working on to a list. And one thing I've noticed, because we've had to do that kind of timekeeping in different jobs, is that you never see where that information goes, as a member of staff. So you're kind of scratching your head, and you're thinking, well either someone's keeping tabs on me …

But then you're always told that actually it's for management purposes so we can resource properly, la, la, la, which is now what we tell everyone!

Lucy Kimbell (LK): But are you? Since you're the manager now [laughs].

BR: Well we are, but not as much as we could do. The other thing we've got at work is a big whiteboard there with all the projects that are live, and everyone sits down and goes through what needs to happen over the next four weeks on this project each Monday morning.

LM: So how does it compare with other places you've worked, in terms of that kind of accounting for your time?

BR: It's more flexible than other places I've worked. Although it's similar, and maybe we're more flexible, but then again, we're smaller. I think those other places … when they were smaller they were pretty relaxed. Or, not so much relaxed, just less systematized or whatever. One of the reasons I left my last job was because they were getting in these guys from Andersen's [management consultants] and stuff, who were Nazis about projects.

LK: So, since you're a director of livelwork, do you have an idea that you should never be bigger than a certain size, because you want to retain a particular culture?

BR: Well, we have had that discussion. We met the other day with a company we subcontract to, who are much more of a design shop, and they do interfaces, and they were saying how, you know, they've got one big client in particular who they have to report on very carefully because they're basically on a kind of run rate. They don't have a fixed price: they can just bill what they work. But therefore they have to report regularly so that the client can say, 'Hang on a minute, it's getting out of hand.' So their guys have to account for every half an hour. And it's interesting because in a way they're much more of a design company, and they've got their juniors and their seniors and their middleweights and all this stuff. And they've also got a bit more of a kind of … 'get your head down and crank out 'X' number of screens' thing going on. And when we left that meeting we were thinking, you know, we're so badly placed to create that kind of working environment because everyone's used to having conceptual space and that kind of initiative [laughs] and things like that. I don't know; we've always had a thing in the back of our heads that there's another company out there called work|work, which is just like a factory [laughs].

LK: One of the stories about IDEO was that they only wanted the offices to be a certain size. I don't know whether that's true or not.

BR: Well there's a friend I met the other day, who has a group of about seven people at the moment. And he said [that] they had a client, the BBC, who said, 'If you get bigger than twenty-five, I won't hire you anymore.' Because there are all these myths about the size of companies, and if you get over sixty people then not everyone knows everyone. So the guy at the BBC just sort of said they were niche guys, they did one thing, and if you get bigger you start to generalize, so you become more like an agency.

LK: One of the things that came up in the Design for Services projects [at Oxford University] was that all the business academics thought that the service designers were not mentioning costs and efficiency and things like that. You're talking more about the experience, the interfaces, the quality of those, and not about ROI, efficiency and costs. Do you think that's justified?

BR: Yes, it was justified in that project. Sometimes clients ask about that. We are seeing that now and again, clients want managed innovation, but then they also want a business case created. And I mean we have done that on projects. We did this project around worklessness in Sunderland, where we needed to present back at the end, and they needed to know about that side of things. So it wasn't particularly rigorous, but we did work out a range of potential costs for our client and potential savings that would be made. I think that as a studio we're really aware of, maybe not so much the cost and efficiency side of things, but definitely the revenue side for the client. So either creating new revenue, or increasing revenue. We talk to them about reducing churn, and we make a case around those things. But we're not really doing the sums. I think when we're most effective, often, is when we have technical expertise on the client side. So in our insurance project in Norway they have this incredible actuary, and so with them it's been kind of possible to say, well this is what people might be interested in, and he can model it from an actuarial point of view. When we worked on a transport project up north they had a guy who was a transport engineer, who was able to look at the efficiency and the integration of various different services. Again he was able to model the numbers from a business side. But it's an interesting area. We interviewed someone recently, who works for Price Waterhouse Coopers, and he does that side of things, and we were beginning to think it might be good to have that in-house. I'm not sure if that kind of criticism is fair on IDEO either, because they talk about business factors.

Another thing is that we have this customer journey blueprint, and recently we've added a line in it where you could look at cost per user or revenue per user, and also map that in line with the customer journey so you can actually say, well this bit [of the customer journey] is a cost and this bit is a revenue point, and split out value like that.

LK: And you've actually added that?

BR: Yes, it was when we were working with the NHS, where we had done an experience blueprint but we hadn't put any numbers in. And their commissioning guy who we were working with said we'd like this, we could do this ... Because they have patient pathways and things, so they already look at costs in that way. He's one of those great clients who we kind of make up new stuff with. So he suggested that and we moved, [and] tested that out with him on the project.

LK: But the data, the idea for that, came from him?

BR: Yes, in a way. It was kind of how we worked on the project in Sunderland as well. One of our colleagues who works in Newcastle said that when he was designing products, you know, he'd know the cost of different production methods, different mouldings, different plastics. So it's a bit like that.

LK: So perhaps you're getting more systematic?

BR: Yes, I think so. I mean we're quite keen to. And on the measurement side, it's like it's a word that everyone's using, and we're being much more upfront about it. We're asking clients so we can understand their business requirements.

LM: So for some clients, what they'll want from you is not to think about cost, [but] just to generate ideas that they couldn't come up with, based on your insights and research? But to other clients it might be [for you] to be able to say, we can offer you low-, medium- and high-cost options?

BR: Well, if we kind of know what their business requirements are, then the ideas are more focused and more, you know, 'more better' [laughs]. But yes, for larger corporates ... they have hundreds of business analysts and stuff like that, so they don't need new people to do that.

LK: OK. What is distinctive about service design as opposed to experience design or interaction design? How do you distinguish between them?

BR: I think interaction design is more specifically around some form of computer interface, or digital interface. I think experience design is very similar to what we do. I wonder whether we have more of a focus on services than experiences. I think there's a difference between services and experiences, and I think one of the things that is particular about what we do is that we step above the experience proposition ... we kind of work a lot with creating new or refining propositions. So it's not just a case of looking at an experience and remarketing it, just giving it new things.

LK: Experience design types always quote that Pine and Gilmore book on the experience economy. So they would probably say that they are designing propositions which are experiences.

BR: Yeah, I think they probably would. The other thing I find is that I'd just rather use the word 'service' because that's what people are providing. I haven't read the book, but I think there is a thing around experiences which is kind of creating, magicking value out of an experience, the Mickey Mouse side of things, like going on a cruise ship. You know, like I'm 'buying an experience'; whereas our world is really more transactional.

LK: OK. And what is the difference between your public sector clients and your private sector clients? Are there differences, in terms of what they're asking you to do, or are there similarities? Are the public sector clients asking roughly the same sorts of things from your menu of six items?

BR: It's a good question, but I don't know if we really know, because I've been the one who has really gone after public sector clients, whereas Chris [another founding partner] has pursued the private sector. We both have a particular niche. But our private clients are much more around the web-based services, and the public clients are much more general, so we bring a process. And we've also developed a sort of skills thing, this service capability stuff. It's not just for the public sector, but they've expressed a very clear need for it. I mean [on] almost every tender or every bidding work we've done in the public sector, they've wanted skills transfer and knowledge. And they want to be able to do it for themselves at some point. Whereas I think that, well, one of the big differences – someone said – between the two sectors is that the private sector is short on capital but quite high-revenue, so they're able to outsource stuff and get stuff done for them. So ... [it's] harder to find capital to really fund something, but ... they'll outsource PR or ... design and things like that, because they've got the budget ... Does that make sense? Whereas the public sector is more likely to have a big chunk of funding come flying through from somewhere, but they find it very hard to augment their team with other people. The other big difference is that there's much more ... the whole stakeholder management thing in the public sector is more complicated. If it's in the public realm, there are more people that need to have a say in what happens.

LM: How does that impact on how innovative you can actually be? Or doesn't it?

BR: Yeah, well you can be innovative but whether it gets implemented or not is another thing. We had one project where we decided afterwards that we should have had fifty per cent of the budget for communicating within the project, because we had to sit down with different groups of people and take them through it and get their input. And almost one of the reasons for doing the more co-design stuff is that you don't come up with a bunch of ideas that they're then not able to really deal with. It's much more [about] helping them to come up with ideas that they're able to work on. And then they own it and put time into it.

LM: And in terms of capability-building, service capability, what's the economics of that? I mean, if you teach all of your clients on the first round to be brilliant service designers, where's your next commission coming from?

BR: Well, I don't think we do teach them everything. I think there might be businesses that wouldn't get into doing the other kind of work. I think there are organizations [that] might not hire you to, who might just talk about turnkey solutions. You know: here's the money and just go away and come back with something brilliant. So in a way, service capability is just a way of accessing a market [of public sector clients] that probably wouldn't buy you if you didn't work the way they want you to work ... We've got an NHS tender which I'm writing for now and ... all over it is: 'We will work with companies that demonstrate a willingness to share skills', and all of that sort of stuff. Our MD he says that this is giving away the crown jewels. So for him, there is a big kind of IP [intellectual property] premium on doing it, and the margin is higher, which means it's harder to sell.

LK: IDEO have a transformation practice, which is their equivalent of this. So they're doing it and I'm assuming they charge quite a lot for it as well.

BR: Yes, Engine are doing it, although I don't think they charge that much for it. The other thing is that we want to look a bit more at how management consultancies deal with that, because they come up with fairly flimsy things that they package up as IP. And some of them do manage to make a fortune out of some of those things. I mean someone was telling me that the consultancy that came up with the idea of a balanced scorecard makes four million a year from it, or something like that. We just really need to keep an eye on it. We haven't done enough to know how people will [react], what they do with it. For instance, the guys we worked with at Haringey Council, they've all been trained to do business process re-engineering by some training company. So in a way they've already got one improvement toolkit, and they're all saying this is fantastic, because what they don't have is a customer view, so we can mix the two things together and it will be great.

LM: I just have one more question about how you audit your work. Once your work is finished for a client, what's the process, or is there one, for working out whether it's a success?

BR: Yeah, we do have one, just about. It's 'On time, on budget, on quality': that's the three criteria. So we have a project review where we ask those three questions. Also, in response to a project going over budget, we've decided that we're going to do that upfront so that when we plan a project, we're going to look at those three considerations and how they're going to be managed.

LM: And I've read somewhere that you try to incorporate the idea of the 'triple bottom line'?

BR: Well, that's an aspiration for us. And with the work we did for Streetcar, we were able to get data which showed [that] actually from a business and a customer point of view, there was value added in all those three areas, which we've got as a slide to show people. We've also been thinking we should create a profit and loss account for that side of things as well. But it takes lots of time to do that.

CHAPTER 17

Ilona Törmikoski

Design Manager and CEO of Hahmo, a Multidisciplinary Design Firm, Helsinki, Finland; Assisted by Jenni Kuokka, Art Director and Pekka Piippo, Creative Director; January 2009

In this interview, Ilona Törmikoski reflects on her experience of client relationships and how these impact on the design processes and focus of the firm. We learn how retaining clients allows her thirteen-strong, multidisciplinary design consultancy to enjoy less formal working relationships with them. As trust between designer and client is built up through time, so the creative process becomes both more iterative and more interactive. Long-term client relationships also allow the studio to develop deeper and more complex projects that involve more strategic work. While Hahmo clearly structures and costs design work, importance is also laid on commissions – such as for the cultural sector – that help maintain the consultancy's public profile.

Guy Julier (GJ): Could we start by finding out more about what kind of work Hahmo does?

Ilona Törmikoski (IT): Hahmo is a Finnish cross-disciplinary design company with skills in design management, strategic design, public relations, graphic design, industrial design, interior design, design research and brand identity design. *Hahmo* is a Finnish word that best expresses the essence of our firm's focus: *idea, outline, sketch, character, figure, shape* and *form*. The design teams are formed according to the client's needs and goals. We often team up with architects, design and communication companies, [and] network with international specialists and researchers. We see that design management is a tool for strategic and innovative development of corporate image by using different skills together. By this, our goal is to achieve the client's business and strategic goals efficiently.

GJ: So, who have your clients been and who do you compete with? Do your clients share much in common?

IT: We have a wide spectrum of clients. They vary from cultural and public organizations (like museums, associations, educational institutions, cultural centres, universities) to commercial (like shopping centres, shops – from wholesales to single consumer products) and industrial sectors like technology and wood.

   We are very proud of our customers. With some we have cooperated over ten years, like making stamps for Finnish Post. Another long-term client, dating back to 1996, is the Theatre Academy of Finland. We have designed for them everything from new logo and visual identity to signage and web presence. Right now we are developing their quality manual and guidelines.

   A long-term cooperation is rewarding for a designer like me who likes to think profoundly, see things from large scale to the detail and with a bigger perspective. This has been possible because the environment has been open to communication and innovation, projects have been managed well and communication has run smoothly. The projects have become more challenging year by year. With many of our clients, we can use the phrase 'long-term partnership'. This is what we aim at.

   What unites our clients is that they want to use design as a strategic and tactical tool and to enhance their communication and processes.

GJ: Working across several design disciplines – are there differences in the way that you work in each of these?

IT: Because of the big variety in clients and [the fact that] some projects are design projects in a more traditional sense, some more strategic and content related, working methods and tools vary a lot in all these, but we have our own Hahmo processes for each one. The outcome shows … the maturity of [the] client in using design. It usually demonstrates well the client's understanding [of] how to use design as a tool to achieve different objectives. For example, visual design works are divided into conceptual, spatial, 3D, graphic and interface design. Working methods and tools vary a lot in all these, but we have our own Hahmo processes for each one.

GJ: What happens when you get a new client?

IT: Most of our projects are done for old clients. Adapting a visual identity to new situations and communicational purposes, the work is endless. To get new clients, we try to reach the status of being a 'household name', known by possible buyers. Also the partner designers themselves actively take part in new customer processes, finding prospects and leads, lecturing and presenting skills. We take part in competitions, actively search for work possibilities and give lectures about design – and are eager to take part in projects like this book. It is important to find customers that respect creative artistic work and understand the value of design, as well as it is important for us to understand their business and purpose. If the stars are aligned well, the cooperation can start and prosper in the years ahead – the cooperation starts and fruits, grows and stays.

With a new client, we have to claim our 'right to exist' with good communication skills and ability to understand in a swift manner the client's problematics, and even unspoken needs and wishes. The design processes must be professional and [the] end result must achieve the set goals.

GJ: Do you use the same process for all clients – is it formalized at all?

IT: Hahmo is very process-orientated. The chosen process depends on the task. Sometimes we start with research. Usually, the client lacks a clear design brief. We go to great lengths to lower the bar of buying our design services – they can just walk in and start [asking] questions. We communicate a lot what design is and how to use it to achieve results – even the text we have on our website is written in simple Finnish. We help our clients see how design can enhance their own daily processes. Good design solutions are usually a result of a good dialogue between designer and client, with [the] simple process of 'question and answer' or more structured workshops, interviews, surveys etc.

GJ: Can you give an example of a process?

IT: Let's see. A simple outline of [the] designing [of] a new identity could run something like this:
   • Firstly, we do research: with soft information-gathering methods we try to find client's needs and wishes.
   • Secondly, we have a brainstorming [session] or design workshop – with [the] client, if possible.
   • Thirdly, we try to find a solid design concept, which we test well within the client and possibly other sub-groups also.
   • Fourthly, we make sketches and start creating the form to communicate the concept. The outcome has to be communicated in an accessible and understandable manner. We use the best tools and methods [so] that the idea [is] clear to aimed audiences.
   • Fifthly, we produce the necessary material to spread (print, space,

web, digital) and make sure the final outcomes are produced with exactness and high quality.

- Sixthly, we make tools for the client to manage the identity (manuals, templates, etc.).

GJ: Can you tell us anything about how you see client relationships having changed through the years? Do they expect different things from in the past?

IT: In the beginning, our work consisted more in independent design outcomes like leaflets, brochures, event identities. Nowadays we're more into strategic design, and the design process start on concepts and [we] design more campaigns with targeted groups and messages. The identity design projects have to take into account a wider spectrum of implementations and wider guidelines, not just how to use the logo. We design more signage, the interface of space. We also guideline the right feel [for] space, selection of correct materials, [and] tone of voice. Sometimes even smell and taste. With good identity-managing tools, our client can commission and brief another design agency with accuracy.

Our clients have grown during the years – as have our design capabilities to undertake more strategic design tasks.

GJ: So perhaps your client relationships change as you have longer working relationships with them?

IT: After having worked together for some time, the clients tend to trust us more and give us more freedom but also more challenges. We also know, by then, who are the key decision-makers in the client's organization. We understand better who they are and what they want to achieve. This way our work becomes easier and faster.

With every success, the designer gains more recognition and respect. First you are a 'good designer', then you're 'expert designer', and last you're 'a trusted partner' whose opinion is taken into account with [the] client's decision-making. The cooperation becomes seamless, and traditional designer versus client roles disappear. The customer is allowed to become [a] designer and [the] designer can be like an out-tasked worker in [the] customer's organization.

During the time, the clients feel safer [about speaking] their minds, telling us their needs and aims more directly and expressing their opinions of the design and how things should be done. And surprisingly, the meetings with our old clients seem to take longer: business matters are dealt [with] between jokes and lots of laughter. The working should be also fun – not only business- and goal-oriented. The happiness and other feelings are very important when you're doing design work.

GJ: Can you tell us a bit about how you cost projects for the client end? Are there times where non-chargeable elements (e.g. extra research, or a project that could be strong for your studio profile purposes) come into a project that you either have to take into account or ignore?

IT: After the project objectives are set, we divide the work into the sub-projects with sections and goals, and resource estimates, hours and possible purchases. We make a detailed list of steps required, e.g. how many rounds of feedback, beta testing and proofreading are required. After approved estimates and project outline, the project can start. We have a dedicated person to do project management, who keeps up with [the] billing and status of each project.

   We often have different rates according to the customers: concept and consultancy work is rated [as] more expensive. Clients coming from [the] cultural sector and organizations working towards public good do often have [a] personal importance to us: we often feel it's somewhat of a responsibility to lower the hourly rates. For example, Amnesty International's Finnish section has chosen us as Designer of the Year 2008. We made a campaign for them about human rights in China and it involved designing a range of sports apparel.

GJ: How do you keep track of the design process? What are the practical constraints in terms of budgets, time and how long you've got to do it? Do you audit parts of the design process in order to demonstrate its cost-price relationship?

IT: We have done [a] lot [of] work to be sure of this! Our project proposals have an accurate list of things specifying the design tasks and outcomes of each step. Sometimes we create a project flow to an extranet [that] the client has an access to and can easily follow. During the process, our project manager keeps track of the use of the resources and status of each project. This person also manages our billing. Good documentation of our meetings, and with the help of our project management system, we stay up to date with the goings-on of each project.

GJ: Can you tell us a bit about how you apportion work within the studio? How do you allocate tasks, time, budget and aims?

IT: Every project is assigned by a project manager and a creative director; these two divide the project into sub-tasks and find the best persons to do it. Partners Pekka Piippo, Antti Raudaskoski and me – we all have different skills and strengths and industry/knowledge areas. The same applies to all 'hahmoans' – we all have our own set of skills and expertise in areas that exceed the others.

Often a partner is the creative director, or the one managing the project. People chemistry is often really important when deciding [on] the right person for the job – sometimes the client just wants to work with a person [who is in a similar] … role, like the organizer likes to work with [a] creative, sometimes [a] manager likes to work with another manager, etc.

We try to make each project's working environment as [good] as it [can] be; money being the biggest imperative and motivator won't result in best design.

GJ: How does this compare with your experience of other studios?

IT: We have quite a [bit of] experience [that allows us] to say how we compare [in] our processes to other design studios. We have developed our working method during the time and it has been [appraised] by our clients [during the] natural process of 'trial and error', but [we] also [gain information by] hearing from … colleagues or other studios [about] the best practices.

We have [received positive feedback] from our clients [about] … how we conduct our work. They value highly how we communicate the project flow and how transparent the design processes are. We do not want to keep the design work [a mystery] but open it up … We want to give [a] good insight into how we systematically work to achieve solutions for our clients. If we explain in an easy-to-approach manner how we work, it will be easy for the client to buy design from us. We are happy to communicate and consult with our client [about] how to achieve their goals by means of design.

GJ: Does the actual material layout of your office and/or the technologies you use actually reinforce or affect your working procedures?

IT: Our office building was constructed in 1908. Our office is actually an old flat, with two separate entrances. We are located near the sea, the city centre, [and] The Senate Square in downtown Helsinki. The office has a sea view and three fireplaces. We redesigned the interiors, … respecting the history of the building. Actually, our national airline, Finnair, had their office here in the past.

The entrance has a cosy lobby, easily accessible to clients from the street level. There are ... big rooms, which are like team rooms, but the teams can be easily changed if needed. We have one big meeting room and an inner meeting room (for our own meetings and workshops) that has all our books and sample library. Every person has their own individual workstation, Mac computer, programs (all licensed!), with dividing shelves dividing the space [and] allowing the person to do work undisturbed by others, if needed. The room has several places allowing teamwork, with whiteboards for brainstorming. The layout and interior design of our office is actually very simple and designed so that it enables us to do good design.

We thought it was important to create a peaceful and 'home-like' environment for working: this way the space itself enhances creativity and enables concentration. Each room has its own music system, which – quite surprisingly to some – makes concentration easier. Sometimes, after the working hours, we use the space to watch movies together and play board and console games.

By all this, our aim is to emphasize the sense of community. We are not a family as such, but a tight work community that shares values and shares the notion [of] how things are done. This is extremely important when it comes [to the] intangible work that we do.

GJ: How have you arrived at your particular studio size? I counted thirteen employees – is that all designers or does that include other staff?

IT: We like to keep our core competences – both graphic and 3D/spatial – within Hahmo. About half of the people are graphic designers with special skills in e.g. logo design, illustration, typography, photography and campaigns. In addition, we have product and spatial designers, sculptor, researcher, brand specialist, sociologist, communication manager and PR specialist. For managing the company we have a managing director – that's me, a project manager and an office manager. Right now we think that this same ratio of talent will be somewhat constant, independent of how big we are.

GJ: Do you outsource elements of your work (e.g. to freelances or to other specialist firms)? When does this happen and how do you coordinate this process?

T: If necessary, we buy complementary know-how from outside. We often do our projects in cooperation with outside talent and specialist firms like architects, animators, industrial designers etc. And productions are mainly outsourced – like film, web production and printing etc.

It's necessary for us all to communicate and work together towards a common goal without unwanted surprises. Many times we assist the client [in buying] the necessary specialist work, e.g. photography, film-making, sound design, web production, etc. We know Hahmo's limits and strengths. Everything under one roof would be too much risk and put too much stress on project management.

Sometimes we handle the total project management, though. Everything needed by the client is offered through Hahmo. This can only be done if there is [a] strong trust between our companies, their processes are flawless and we're confident about the quality of their work. Architects usually have their own commission, paid straight by the same client.

GJ: Are there notable differences between public sector and private sector clients? Are there differences in terms of what they're asking you to do or are there similarities?

IT: There are more similarities than differences. Cultural clients need to struggle for attention just the same as their commercial counterparts. Many times the private sector clients are faster in their decision-making. The design process benefits from [a] hastier pace: the creative fire is easier to keep alive. Discussions with public sector clients usually take longer – the decision-making in the organization must be more uniform. But in the end, the rules for creating an identity and a lasting experience are quite the same.

GJ: Do you ever find a conflict in presenting yourselves as a professional organization? Do you have or follow any published 'standards of service' (e.g. the American Institute of Graphic Arts uses an 'ethical code' for its members)? How do ensure your clients understand the professional value of your services and, indeed, your skills?

IT: The education [in] design is of very high quality in Finland and pro-duces professionals who are able to work on varied design tasks. But the responsibility [for] the quality of professional work is always related to designer – personal attributes, creativity and carefulness – or the design office itself.

Ethics are very important when practising design business. We want to be fair and smart partners playing by fair rules: no copying, no free work, no free workers etc. We ourselves have been very active in devel-oping our design profession and [a] better design work culture, through [the] national professional organizations the Finnish Association of

Graphic Designers, Grafia, and [the] Finnish Association of Designers, Ornamo. And we have been active also on [an] international level ... through BEDA, [the] Bureau of European Design Associations, when I was a member of [the] board. Through Grafia, we've been active in informing possible clients about appropriate buying methods – especially ... public sector clients [who] don't always understand the value of design: they tend to ask for free work while auditing design agencies.

GJ: Once your work is finished for a client, what's the process, or is there one, for working out whether it's a success?

IT: We don't have any standardized process to gather feedback, yet. We value the professional recognition we've received and [the] prizes [we've won] very highly. Direct feedback from the clients and colleagues is very important, too. But in the end, a happy client returns for more.

CHAPTER 18

Peter Higgins

Creative Director, Land Design Studio, London, January 2009

This short interview perhaps provides a counterpoint to the views expressed in other interviews. Strong formalization of the design process at Land Design Studio is avoided, according to Peter Higgins: they prefer a more flexible response to demand. In common with other interviews, however, he notes the complexity of working with public sector clients.

Guy Julier (GJ): How long have you been around and how would you describe what your studio does?

Peter Higgins (PH): We were founded in 1992. In terms of the work we do, it's difficult to define because we have to avoid being called exhibition designers. I sometimes use a Venn diagram that combines architectural space, narrative stories and the appropriate use of communication media. Wrapped around this is the need to consider destination planning, and an understanding of audience, user, brand values, revenues, sustainability, and so on. Land also has specific skills in digital interactivity, which started at The Playzone in the Millennium Dome and has been extensively introduced into our museum work. In fact, frustration at not being able to describe what we do encouraged me to help set up an MA at Central Saint Martin's, London, called 'Creative Practice in Narrative Environments'.

GJ: Are there other studios working in this domain?

PH: Our key competitors are embedded in the museum or science centre domain, [but we have] an ambition to transfer our skills to more commercial clients. Lottery funding has driven this situation; everybody is now trying to work abroad. We are presently [working] in Japan, China, Singapore and the Middle East.

GJ: What made you specialize in your sector of design?

PH: Well, I'm not really interested in interiors, or retail: [they are] too transient. Interpretive design seemed to have an inherent educational value, which is attractive to me.

GJ: Are there any major differences between the areas of your work?

PH: No, quite the opposite in fact, as we are really interested in the 'integrated solution'. Although, having said that, we have just completed a big commercial refurbishment for Christie's.

GJ: What are the processes when you get a new client? Do you use the same process for all clients – is it formalized at all?

PH: We try and match the most appropriate designer with the type of client. This can sometimes be a personality or even a gender thing.

GJ: Are there any ways that your interactions with clients have changed over the years that you have been working? Do they expect different things from in the past?

PH: Commercial clients tend to get the best out of us as there is a simpler sign-off process, and more trust in controlled risk. Museums tend to have too many people in project teams, which impacts on creativity as everybody has to have an involvement.

GJ: Equally, does your client relationship change as you have longer working relationships with them?

PH: Yes, by definition a long relationship means that they trust and like us. Mutual respect is a very powerful asset.

GJ: Can you tell us a bit about how you cost projects for the client end? Are there times where non-chargeable elements (e.g. extra research, or a project that could be strong for your studio profile purposes) come into a project that you either have to take into account or ignore?

PH: Museum projects have to be approached sensibly as there is considerable competition. We may track a percentage of the cap ex as a fee and then compare [that] with the actual time that it will take as a day rate. Without a doubt, the biggest issue is that of variations in the brief or information, and the late delivery of information from the client. It is very difficult to raise additional fees for these in a competitive marketplace. It is not good for repeat business, and clients know this.

GJ: How do you keep track of the design process? What are the practical constraints in terms of budgets, time and how long you've got to do it?

Do you audit parts of the design process in order to demonstrate its cost-price relationship?

PH: No, timesheets just do not work for us. We usually do more than we are paid for. We are in a vocational business. When projects go into delay it is always very difficult to get clients to understand the implications of this; we are expected to just stop and start as [if] there are 'taxis on the rank'.

GJ: Can you tell us a bit about how you apportion work within the studio? How do you allocate tasks, time, budget and aims?

PH: Well, we try to match the type of work and the conditions to the appropriate designer. Some do not want to travel abroad; others do not want to be involved with complex object collections. As the creative director, once I have helped set up the organizing principle, the big idea, our designers are all totally self-monitoring and responsible for their tasks. Directors step in at critical moments. Other directors manage contracts, fees [and] payment schedules.

GJ: Does the actual material layout of your office and/or the technologies you use actually reinforce or affect your working procedures?

PH: Our office is completely open, which helps with quick intercommunication, though confidential issues have to be dealt with discreetly. Good IT support is critical; also, training can be overlooked. We are constantly trying to deal with both of these.

GJ: How have you arrived at your particular studio size?

PH: We are very small; it's an organic size, so I can monitor output, which is important if we are to maintain a high profile in the industry.

GJ: Do you ever find a conflict in presenting yourselves as a professional organization? How do ensure your clients understand the professional value of your services and, indeed, your skills?

PH: Yes, [it's a] big problem. With no codes of conduct, unpaid creative pitching is an issue, with very complex pre-qualification questionnaires that are – irritatingly – always different. An issue with some clients is that they do not have fundamental skills in procuring design. There is a need to acknowledge that procurement requires specific skills: are they trained to do this?

GJ: Once your work is finished for a client, what's the process, or is there one, for working out whether it's a success?

PH: It is amazing that we rarely get involved with evaluation. This should be built into the procurement process. Lottery funding does not allow for this and often clients fail to maintain the protocols of original design concepts.

CHAPTER 19

Conclusion: Counting Creativity

Guy Julier and Liz Moor

This book has focused on the ways in which designers' work is managed, moving from a consideration of the new ways in which design is used in public sector policy to the empirical description and elucidation of contemporary design processes in more commercial contexts. This interest in the management of design comes from a relatively new set of circumstances in which design has become more central to the economy and in which design as a discipline has expanded both quantitatively (in terms of the number of agencies, turnover etc.) and qualitatively (in terms of its proliferating sub-disciplines and specialities, and areas of social and economic life in which it exerts influence). While much of our discussion has been on the British context – the area we know best – the book has also included case studies from other areas of Europe and North America and, as we noted in the Introduction, the rise of design is proceeding at a fast pace in countries such as China. The book has been interested in the management of design, above all, but rather than seeking to provide a 'how to' guide for professionals in this burgeoning area, our aim has been to take stock of how this more careful managing and monitoring of creative activity has impacted upon its daily practices and its practitioners. As we noted in the Introduction, our aim in proceeding in this way has been to 'open up' writings on design management to the messiness of the empirical, but also, as part of this, to try to draw out in a more critical way some of the forces shaping its development.

Earlier accounts of the creative industries tended to present them as involving a measure of compromise or contractual agreement between the demands of artistic freedom and commercial targets (e.g. Ray and Sayer 1998; Caves 2000; du Gay and Pryke 2002). Equally, in the world of design, the issue is invariably presented as a dualistic situation. In addressing the vexed question of design's uneasy relationship with management, Thomas Lockwood, president of the American Design Management Institute, assesses whether and how design can be measured. He quotes veteran designer

Hartmut Esslinger, who suggests that 'Business people are from Mars, and designers are from Venus', and goes on to note that, unlike business people, designers generally tend to underline their importance with anecdotes and quotes (such as 'Good design is good business') rather than with numbers. To this extent, he observes, 'Creativity resists quantification' (Lockwood 2007: 90–91).

This relationship between creative freedom and the demands of commerce may, then, be articulated at the discursive level, where professionals (including non-designers) reflect on and theorize about the practice of design. However, one of our concerns in this book has been to dissolve such dualisms of the cultural and economic, and instead to understand processes of creativity *within* and *through* the structures of everyday (largely commercial) design practices. Indeed, we have also been keen to point out that, contrary to Lockwood's assertion, creativity no longer resists quantification, and there is in fact an ongoing and strenuous effort to find ways of measuring and quantifying both the 'outputs' of creative work and the specific contributions of its component parts. Our approach therefore sympathizes with Jeffcutt and Pratt's critique of scholarly work on the creative industries, which notes that 'There is a lack of strategic knowledge about the relationships and networks that *enable and sustain* the creative process in a knowledge economy' (Jeffcutt and Pratt 2002: 228, our emphasis). They go on to argue that knowledge of this sector must be 'situated in the analysis of particular organizational fields' (Jeffcutt and Pratt 2002: 231). Similarly, Banks et al. (2002: 262) state that closer attention should be paid 'to the *contexts* in which creativity is being defined, located, valued and managed' (our emphasis).

Considerable academic work has been undertaken in exploring the locational aspect of the contexts in which creative labour is carried out. In particular, much scholarship has approached this in terms of how creative clusters might be encouraged. Here it is thought that mutually dependent and competing firms may be geographically concentrated in order that they benefit both from the opportunities for business networking and the social and cultural ambience that this creates (e.g. Landry 2000; Florida 2002; Marc and Buijs 2007; Ibrahim et al. 2006; Hospers and Pen 2008). Some work has been published on how creativity and innovation may be encouraged by spatial arrangements within firms (e.g. Kristensen 2004; Moultrie et al. 2007); we also noted in the Introduction how the layout of offices might affect internal workflows and relations. Yet in terms of the spatial distribution of creative practices, Reimer et al. (2008) vigorously contest the assumption that the kind of narrow geographical clustering model outlined above is applicable to design. They show that, generally speaking, design firms are far more interested in proximity to their clients and less concerned with the supposed benefits of geographical proximity than some policy analysts and promoters assume.

Following on from this, our notion of *context* is therefore expanded beyond this locational approach. Our interest has been in how creativity in design is structured within and between organizations – which, as we noted in the Introduction, may not be geographically close, but are increasingly proximate in temporal terms – and in forms of group interaction. Creativity in design is distributed across multiple actors and locations (Banks et al. 2002) and thus one of our interests has been in the way that it may be thought of as a relational process, in the sense of involving modes of dependence through which organizations are not only bound together but also defined and in some cases transformed. In practice, this relationality may be found in the negotiations that designers have with clients (which, again, are often defined by their *lack* of geographical proximity), in the orchestration and ownership of productive networks, in the everyday interactions of design teamwork and, in some cases, in the kinds of relationship and attachment formed with objects and socio-technical devices (see Knorr Cetina 1997).

However, while we wish to stress the relationality of design practice, we do not regard all relations that come out of this conception as being equal. The management of creativity is first *contingent*. It requires particular adjustments and configurations of material and human resources in order to exist and its qualities are therefore dependent on these configurations and adjustments. Second, creativity is *negotiated*. It involves agreement between actors as to its location and value. We have seen, for instance – in the chapters by Springer and Dorland in particular – how claims to creativity are increasingly made, by members of a design firm, more strongly at the ideation stage of a design project than in the more mundane 'form-giving' part of its materialization. Following on from this, and third, creativity is *performed*. Part of the valorization process of creative work occurs in the way that it is played out in specific organizations by specific actors presenting their work and themselves in particular ways. As such, the meaning of creativity undergoes continuous development. We have seen (for example in the interviews with David Scothron and Ilona Törmikoski) how retaining clients through time allows the design firm to develop more sophisticated working relationships with them. This in turn allows the locus of creative work to be shifted, for example, from form-giving to more strategic inputs.

Creative Labour

The structure of the book has reflected the importance we attribute to the influence of the state or various national or governmental agencies on the way design work gets done. It is precisely because design, creativity and innovation have been recognized as so important to economic success across all areas of the economy that national governments and agencies have been keen to establish parameters of 'best practice', models of effective design intervention and policies to stimulate creativity and innovation. Indeed, as we write, in the context of a widespread recession, design organizations are still able to plausibly advocate an emphasis on design as the key to future economic success,[1] while design schools in South-East Asia, for example, attract record numbers of students in part because the expansion of design capacity is seen as the key to building strong national brands that can compete internationally and developing new forms of wealth-generating intellectual property. Governmental interest in the organization of design and its relationship with other areas of the economy is hardly new, and indeed has punctuated twentieth-century history (see Woodham 1997), but it has intensified over the past twenty or more years for the kinds of commercial and policy reasons outlined in the Introduction.

The focus on policy, and on the broader social and institutional context for design, is important, therefore, because national-level policies and statements about best practice in design work have been one of the major drivers of the kinds of systematization and measurement that are at the heart of the book. Although the majority of design work in Britain, for example, still gets done by or on behalf of private companies (Design Council 2005), public sector clients make up a growing proportion of design work and the majority of design agencies now do at least some work for public sector or non-profit clients (BDI 2003, 2006). As the chapters in Part I all show, national and regional policies exert a considerable influence on the day-to-day practices of designers. They shape both the types of work that gets done in the first place (as can be seen, for example, in the continued growth of branding and graphics, as well as the emergence of new specialisms such as service design), and the formal processes through which it is organized and managed. In Liz Moor's chapter, for example, the policy context in Britain – which shows an increasing concern to 'empower', educate and 'responsibilize' citizens – has led both to a growth in the specific design areas outlined above and to a heightened role for design in general in producing particular types of political subjectivity. At the same time, the chapter suggests that these developments also raise new questions for designers and others about the appropriateness of applying commercial design techniques (e.g. branding, services marketing) to other areas of social life.

Guy Julier's chapter continues the theme of the instrumentalization of design towards civic aims, but this time in the context of the regeneration of urban centres. In particular, it highlights how certain norms and expectations of 'best practice' have become embedded into the codes and guidelines that are used both by urban designers and the many stakeholders with whom they interface. These serve both to make the design process more efficient (and, at times, faster) and clearer to all concerned. This 'scripting' of design in turn may undermine both the professional expertise of the designer and the flexibility that may be required to ensure appropriate interventions and results. In Katie Hill and Guy Julier's co-authored chapter, the increasingly complex bureaucratic infrastructure surrounding design work for local or regional authorities means that the demand for 'innovation' and creative approaches to service delivery is often in tension with the highly systematized and centralized systems for assessing and monitoring such work. At the same time, modes of local governance are often messy, attempting to combine traditional administrative systems with more entrepreneurial and open, networked approaches. Within this disorder, creative consultancies, sometimes engaging designers, are brought in to help local authorities develop creative approaches to service delivery, not least because of pressure to deliver these within tight time schedules. Thus a number of factors combine to compromise the implementation of innovative design ideas at local level.

Doug Sandle's chapter picks up on the theme of design-led urban regeneration with particular reference to the multiple roles that public art is expected to undertake. Beyond its intrinsic aesthetic value it has increasingly been folded into the pursuit of social and economic goals, through its assumed contribution to community identity and cohesion. In making a justification for its own existence, public arts commissioners and public artists are engaged in ever more complex – and sometimes questionable – systems of their impact metrics. Jane Pavitt follows with a chapter that reveals the ways by which government enthusiasms to promote the creative industries affect museum policies. Thus we see the museum evolving an alternative identity that stresses contemporary notions of 'being creative' over a former role as a repository of artefacts.

Parts II and III of the book have developed these insights in different directions. On the one hand, they provide further empirical evidence of these processes of management and systematization in practice, showing how both specific national policies and a wider normative environment of accountability, audit and measurement impact directly upon the practices of designers. This can be seen most clearly, perhaps, in our interviews with designers (such as Ben Reason), where the specific demands made by public sector clients, and their impact upon internal systems and processes, come to the fore.

At the same time, chapters in Part II of the book – which focus, for the most part, on work for or inside private sector organizations – also highlight the fact that there are in fact multiple points of origin for contemporary forms of systematization and management, as well as demonstrating their ubiquity and normalization within commercial design practice. Paul Springer's chapter traces the development of more formalized tracking and review mechanisms in advertising and communications design – a shift that has led to a greater degree of client involvement in the creative process – both to meet client pressures for greater accountability and agencies' desire to secure client approval at an early stage, and to facilitate more efficient turnaround of projects. In AnneMarie Dorland's chapter these formalized tracking and review mechanisms have already become normalized, and the focus is more squarely on the effects of such developments on everyday practice. Dorland shows that the graphic designers she interviewed had devised numerous 'routines of production' and 'occupational formulae' in order to work effectively – and successfully – within such highly systematized environments, but that the broader context was one in which time and scope for individual or collective 'creativity' (in the form of brainstorming sessions, multiple iterations and so on) was severely limited by time and budgetary constraints.

Nitzan Waisberg shows how the labour of researchers in product design is focused in a number of directions. Their core work may well be in user-centred research, discovering human needs and desires and translating these into the product design process. At the same time, they play out a mediating role, helping to both temper and show the design process as being more systematic for the benefit of both the design studio itself and the client. Finally, theirs is a symbolic role, adding to the knowledge capital of the design and innovation firm for the sake of its positioning in the marketplace against other firms and to gain further client respect.

In Lucy Kimbell's chapter, the focus on a relatively early stage in the emergence of a new design specialism allows the process of systematization and formalization to be explored from a different perspective; here, the formalization of creative practice is by no means guaranteed, and Kimbell is able to identify a number of factors that may or may not lead to the discipline's consolidation and growth. These include the extent to which its precepts and practices become accepted within other spheres (such as management and organizational theory), the extent to which the current trend towards involving service designers in public services continues in years to come, and the uncertain implications of service designers' involvement in knowledge transfer and 'capacity-building' for other sectors and institutions.

Damian Sutton draws attention to the importance of the management and tracking of workflows, pipelines and metadata in Hollywood cinema production in his chapter. It reveals the effects of subcontracting tasks and the usages of digital technologies therein. Production is distributed across networks of creative firms who work simultaneously on a wide range of aspects that go beyond the film itself into related issues such as merchandise. Design information acts as the organizing principle through these in order to maintain coherence between them. This 'post-Fordist' system therefore combines industrial pragmatism with an appropriation of the innovatory power of independent creative firms.

In Sarah Owens's chapter, the systematization of working practices in editorial design is linked above all to the commercial necessity of producing a recognizable branded product to a tight deadline. In this context, moments of 'creativity' and innovation occur in relatively structured ways, most usually accompanying the appointment of a new art director. But, as Owens shows, this does not mean that the more day-to-day work of editorial designers is formulaic or routine; rather, creativity in this context emerges out of the moving back and forth between general guidelines and specific projects and features, an insight that resonates with Ingold and Hallam's (2007) approach to creativity as improvisation, outlined in the Introduction.

The Material Culture of Systematization

Although most of the chapters in the book are empirical in focus, and indeed were intended to draw out the empirical detail and complexity of contemporary design work, it has also been our aim to develop a more critical perspective on the forces currently shaping the management of design, and to highlight some of the implications of the more systematic attention now being paid to matters of policy, regulation, management and accountability. In the Introduction we outlined a number of ways of looking at these developments, from the literature on New Public Management and audit cultures, to new ways of understanding the role of materials and technologies in the making up of creative practices and economic systems. In what follows, therefore, we seek to reflect on each of these more carefully, drawing out evidence that both supports and qualifies these broad perspectives.

One of our areas of interest at the start of the book was with the ways in which various objects and technological systems used in the design studio or agency contribute to more managed and systematized forms of practice, and create new opportunities for the measurement and tracking of people and outcomes. We noted, for example, that certain technological developments had 'speeded up' the design process, while also allowing for the dispersal of elements of the creative process across multiple sites and locations. We suggested that these developments had led to the expectation among clients of quicker turnaround times, and in some cases made the various stages involved in the development and execution of a project more visible and subject to scrutiny. This, in turn, has had very concrete outcomes in terms of dropping margins for designers, and in part explains why the continued expansion of the design field has not necessarily been accompanied by higher turnover.

But we have also had an interest in the ways in which objects and technological systems have impacted in more 'micro' ways upon creative practice, shaping the way it gets done and the extent to which it can be systematized, automated, shared and tracked over time. Perhaps most noteworthy here is the widespread, almost universal, use of technological systems such as Harvest and Oracle Workflow for monitoring the status of projects and the contribution of specific employees. Such systems are relatively new, but in most of the chapters here they are mentioned only in passing, testifying perhaps to their ubiquity and widespread acceptance. Yet they have a significant impact upon both the current organization of design work and its future possibilities. They facilitate much more detailed analyses than were previously possible of the profitability of particular clients and projects, and allow a similar logic to be applied to the contributions of individual staff members. They also allow for the almost continuous monitoring of both designers and projects, and generate new forms of data that may be either publicized (by keeping information about the status of project work on open access) or privatized (by restricting such information to management only). Of course, whether or not the capacities of particular systems are exploited to their full potential depends partly upon the inclination and competence of managers, as well as on the compliance of ordinary staff members. Yet while the actual use of such systems may fall short of their ideal or potential use, it is clear that they not only reflect the aspiration for greater transparency of operation and monitoring of workers' activities, but also shape it. By creating new types of information in some areas, and formalizing or recording it in others, they contribute to the creation of what Michael Power (2009) has called new 'organizational facts'. These facts – and their material traces – may then contribute to further and closer scrutiny of the relationship between the creative work that goes on in the studio and the ultimate profitability of organizations, a process which may, in turn, have implications for the ways in which particular types of work (and worker) are valued, both in terms of status and financial remuneration.

Technological or material developments may shape creative work in other ways, too. Paul Springer's chapter shows that in the sphere of communications design, the greater use of digital technologies to profile and target consumers has in some cases led to an expansion in the amount of work available to designers, since detailed demographic information has allowed for the creation of multiple templates for mailings based on known information about specific market segments. At the same time, the scope for individual creativity in the design of such communications is often considerably reduced, since much of the content is determined in advance, not only through established brand guidelines but also through the manipulation of information gleaned from data profiling. In this situation, clients – usually in collaboration with agency account teams – can produce very tight specifications that leave little room for imagination or experimentation on the part of designers.

Springer connects this situation to a broader trend towards the inclusion of more direct instructions within creative briefs, and a consequent reduction in creative freedom for agencies; since clients now have access to more detailed information about consumers, they are more likely to feel confident specifying the use of particular media for communications, and making suggestions about general creative direction and modes of execution. There is also evidence of this in AnneMarie Dorland's chapter on graphic design agencies, which describes examples in which general creative direction, 'look and feel', as well as copy and headlines, had all been predetermined by the client in collaboration with the account managers, with the designer simply tasked with 'making it happen'. Thus both Springer and Dorland describe situations in which the autonomy of agencies – whether in planning or creative departments – may be substantially reduced. At the same time, the use of data from digital profiles may mean that the phases of a project that appear 'creative', in the sense of creating value through differentiation or distinctiveness, are attributed not to the creative department but to earlier strategic and planning stages of the process, where what is valued is knowing how to turn data into a brief or 'big idea'. This usually involves clients as well as account planners or managers inside the agency, which may in turn diminish the 'specialness' and uniqueness of creative practitioners (with further implications for the value attached to their work) or perhaps lead to a steady reworking of what counts as 'creative' in the first place.

The Management of Design: Decoupling or Colonization?

We noted in the Introduction that whilst contemporary design work is rarely subject to the degree of external inspection that typifies audit culture in other sectors, there remain a number of ways in which the literature associated with such cultures (e.g. Power 1997; Strathern 2000) is relevant to the contemporary systematization and formalization of design practice. Principal among these is the fact that the so-called 'audit explosion' has effects not only in terms of its concrete practices but also in its contribution to a wider normative environment characterized by growing 'demands and aspirations for accountability and control' (Power 1997: 6). Most of the chapters in the book describe situations in which such aspirations are present, and are making themselves felt through the instantiation of more formalized systems, often with demonstrable effects upon practice. Yet most of the situations described here do not involve external auditors, and instead rely upon the internalization of such demands by agencies and studios developing their own systems. Some of these are aimed at pleasing (and attracting) clients, but others seek primarily to achieve greater control over the activities of employees and to measure and track their contributions more precisely. How, then, should we understand the effects of these developments? How do they impact upon the position of agencies vis-à-vis clients? How do they impact upon relations inside the workplace? And how do they alter our understanding of creative work?

As we noted in the Introduction, one way of assessing the impact of the growing formalization and systematization of practice is to think about Michael Power's distinction between 'decoupling', on the one hand, and 'colonization' on the other. In this schema, the effects of audit culture may be thought of as falling somewhere along a line characterized at one extreme by the total disengagement (or 'decoupling') of audit practices from the normal goings-on of an organization, and at the other by a total transformation (or 'colonization') of practice by the audit culture that frames it. Of course, Power's scheme suggests that no one sector or institution is likely to be totally colonized by, or totally decoupled from, audit and related accountability imperatives. And indeed this is what we have found in the chapters presented here: in the absence of a unified, external set of auditing codes, there is no need or incentive for design practice to be fundamentally altered in order to meet such demands. Yet nor is it the case that formal and informal processes of measurement, tracking and review are simply shrugged off or treated as an 'add-on'. Rather, such processes permeate the conduct of everyday work, producing particular routines (which may be formalized into proprietary systems, as in some of the communications agencies described by Paul Springer) and particular forms of behaviour. These include the types of 'performance' outlined by Strathern (2000: 8) aimed at making certain activities (typically those requiring inspection or 'sign-off') visible while others remain hidden. AnneMarie Dorland's chapter, for example, shows designers to be highly sensitized to the need for their work to be inspected and approved by multiple audiences in order to succeed with minimal revision, and that they consciously orient different stages of their work with these (sometimes competing) demands in mind. On the other hand, she shows that the entire studio may collude in 'hiding' certain types of practice from clients, in situations where time and budgetary constraints mean that advertised aspects of the 'creative process' must be abbreviated or omitted entirely. Equally, Guy Julier's chapter shows how urban designers learn the 'language', codes and systems of other professions with whom they have to collaborate in order to be able to negotiate their way through projects.

Finally, there is, in almost all chapters, a significant degree of normalization of these processes of review, inspection, measurement and auditing. Those who are subject to such processes may not like them; they may find them surprising or disappointing when they are first encountered (as in the case of one of Dorland's interviewees, who notes that 'It's not what you would think at school') and they may find ways to resist or evade them. But they are, broadly speaking, accepted as a normal aspect of the culture in which they work, and rarely subject to explicit questioning. There is, however, some evidence that smaller and/or newer agencies may have more freedom regarding the extent to which such review and tracking procedures seem necessary to management, and the extent to which their implementation intrudes upon the everyday practices and habits of staff. A related point, hinted at by Ben Reason of livelwork in his interview, is that some clients may prefer to work with smaller studios, which they imagine to be more specialized or 'niche', and which they may imagine to be less encumbered by the depersonalized and highly regulated forms of work process that they assume typify the 'agency' or 'factory' style of larger design organizations.

Systematization, Promotion and Practice

A further (related) theme that emerges from a number of chapters in the book is the way in which the presumed tension between creative freedom and playfulness on the one hand, and careful management and systematization on the other, plays out in the promotional activities of agencies and studios, and in the self-presentation of both studios and individual designers. Thus, for example, AnneMarie Dorland's chapter shows that many of the design studios she studied continue to promote their services with reference to ideas about design as unstructured and playful, even while the reality is increasingly one of 'regulation, measurement and multiple daily audit practices'. By contrast, Paul Springer's account of advertising agencies in London shows that alongside the (by now ubiquitous) performances of the 'creative workplace' – hotdesking, stylized client rooms, beanbags and so on – there now exist a new set of impulses towards the promotion of rigour and systematization, which in some cases have been developed into proprietary systems, and which clients may be invited to observe at first hand.

There is, in other words, a sense in which the actual practices of creative workers are always both more and less systematized than they appear to be, and more and less 'free' than they appear to be. This is because of the necessary element of performance or stylization in creative work (and indeed perhaps in all kinds of work), in which *both* systematization *and* a looser, more experimental type of creative freedom are required of workers at different times, depending upon the tasks at hand and the real or imagined audience for an individual's practice. What this leads to, we would suggest, is an ongoing modulation of external appearances (whether in the form of bodily presentation or material outputs), depending upon the demands of a context or task.

We might also add that while promotional materials always idealize practice, they may nonetheless contribute to an ongoing internal monitoring and reworking of actual behaviours, providing new models to aspire to, and new ideas about what is important and valuable within a creative organization. They may, in other words, be an element of what has been termed 'reflexive capitalism' (Thrift 1998), in which a range of actors reflect upon the organization and practices of firms, often with the aim of constructing generic models to embody current ideas about best practice (see also Moor 2007). At the same time, to understand how this impulse takes hold within the design industry it is also important to note that discourses of accountability, tracking and review reflect a situation in which design is considered valuable and important to a wide range of organizations and areas of social life, and in which there are new sets of external demands for accountability, but in which design as a whole lacks the norms, benchmarks and professional standards associated with related disciplines such as architecture. In this context, it is perhaps unsurprising to find that a general tendency towards formalization and systematization often takes the form of a proliferation of competing systems for establishing 'best practice' and for predicting, measuring and tracking the creative process. Nor is it particularly surprising to find that such systems often take proprietary or quasi-proprietary forms. In the situation we describe, efforts to formalize and systematize practice, and to find new ways of tracking and measuring its value, are not only undertaken in order to meet the demands of clients, but also to offer axes of differentiation and competitive advantage for the organization itself. Formal models and systems, in design at least, are often promotional as well as functional.

Design and Creativity

In this book we have sought to trace the reasons why various design disciplines have, in recent years, exhibited a general impulse towards a systematization and formalization of their processes, and towards a more careful management, measurement and tracking of their contribution to the process of value creation. Among these, we have noted the growing economic importance of design and other creative industries, the expansion of 'design thinking' into more and more areas of economic and social life (itself in part a consequence of the growing numbers of design graduates), the greater use of specific design specialisms within the public sector and its own development of a 'New Public Management' philosophy, and a more pervasive audit culture characterized by a loss of institutional trust and the normative aspiration towards a greater degree of transparency and control of organizational processes. We have also noted a number of themes that are more specific to the design industry, including its relative lack of agreed professional standards and qualifications as compared to other, sometimes competing, disciplines, the fragmentation and diversification of the discipline and the growing number of agencies and free-lancers working in the field.

We have also sought to trace how these general impulses have made them-selves felt within specific contexts. We have noted how public sector institutions seek to use design, and how this in turn has led to greater efforts among designers to account for their role in various types of value creation; we have also shown how design's involvement in public sector projects has sometimes put its innovative and visionary capacities at odds with the demands of bureau-cracy and centralized control. Other chapters have shown that the impulse towards measurement and tracking extends into areas (such as art) where it would not previously have been found, in ways that appear to demand new cri-teria for aesthetic judgement. Efforts to measure or quantify the 'value' of cre-ativity have also led to the refocusing of institutional priorities, as museums, for example, become compelled by governments and other funding bodies to find new areas of specialism in the facilitation of creative education and experience.

Elsewhere in the book, we have shown that in more explicitly commercial contexts these impulses towards systematization, formalization and measure-ment create new points of differentiation and competition between firms, while creating new opportunities and new volumes of work in some cases, but closing them down in others. We have shown that employees in design indus-tries have had to find ways to accommodate the greater intrusion of tracking and measurement systems into their working lives, even while the implications of these systems are often beyond their control or influence. At the same time, the extent to which such systems do in fact impinge upon designers' everyday practice continues to vary according to the size and nature of organizations, the extent of the demands made by managers and clients, and the cooperation of workers themselves in contributing the kinds of data and information that make such tracking possible.

One of our aims, at the beginning of the book, was to question how these changes have impacted upon current understandings of creativity. We have tried to understand, among other things, whether such developments have led to a reworking of existing or traditional notions of creativity, whether creative practice itself has changed to reflect the new priorities that circulate around it, and what the implications are of the growing centrality of design and other forms of creative industry to the delivery of both public and economic goals and outcomes. While it is unlikely that such reworkings of creative practice will alter 'lay' understandings of creativity, the chapters in this book have revealed that there is in some cases considerable debate about the locus of creative or innovative input within specific organizations or sectors. A number of chapters have noted, for example, that the traditional position and role of the 'creative' in a given agency is being challenged by those occupying more strategic and planning roles. This development is not only an outcome of systematization, for it also has to do, among other things, with a greater degree of creative confidence on the part of clients, and on the greater use of digital profiling, consumer research and tracking to specify aesthetic styles and media that are likely to be effective in achieving certain ends. It is also, at another level, to do with the rise of branding, in which there is less scope for creative freedom and innovation within specific projects, since these are increasingly produced as part of a series whose 'look and feel' has been determined in advance. Yet the discourses and materials associated with systematization and formalization do support such discussions about the location and valuation of creative work. Whether in the close and ongoing scrutiny of particular workers, or the *post hoc* assessment of the profitability of a particular project, client or designer, many of the technologies discussed here allow creative work to be more easily broken down into particular stages, for the contributors to those stages to be more easily identified, and for the content and execution of those stages to be subject to continuous alteration and modification.

Finally, we have noted throughout the book that part of the reason for the greater systematization and formalization of creative work has been its growing value to a wide range of material and social interests. This can be seen not only in the way that design and 'design thinking' has become more central to business and management, but also in its adoption by various governmental agencies in order to pursue social goals and outcomes. As Liz Moor has noted in her chapter, this governmental use of design as a kind of 'technical fix' for social problems has a fairly long history, and is typically associated with liberal political philosophies (see also Otter 2007). Its contemporary incarnation, she suggests, is characterized by its marriage to more contemporary promotional devices and techniques, such as branding and services marketing. This use of design for social ends also has to do with what George Yúdice (2003) describes as the 'expediency of culture'; that is, a perception that broadly aesthetic and/or cultural means are appropriate ways to regulate behaviour and to achieve political and social outcomes.

In Poland in the late 1980s, General Jaruzelski's communist government developed a tightly defined fee structure that designers were legally bound to follow. This specified what could be charged, for example, for the provision of a technical drawing, a page layout or a product prototype. It was an attempt to bring under fiscal control a burgeoning freelance design sector in the twilight of a command economy (Crowley et al. 1992: 87). This is probably the only known attempt at centralizing the costing and measurement of design services through government measures. Such an idea contrasts starkly with notions of the valorization of design in contemporary neo-liberal economies. Digital technologies may be vigorously applied to manage and cost the temporal allocation of design tasks. However, creative labour may also be intangible and carry symbolic value. Ideation, research and the coordination of design processes between various stakeholders, figure increasingly on the designer's task sheet. We have also seen how design, and design work, carries value in all kinds of strategic ways, for example, by signalling the regeneration of an urban centre, the reinvigoration of a brand, or the reputation of a design firm itself. The value of design may thus shift between being something that is put *into* things to something that is involved in indicating sources of future value (Lash, in Julier 2009). It is value *in potentia*, so to speak, and its measurement may therefore be bound to be an inexact science as compared with the apparently more straightforward calculations of value encoded in the fee schedules of 1980s Poland.

This notion that design may be involved in identifying and measuring intangible, potential future sources of value has some resonance in the world of financialization – a precarious and not wholly transparent realm of economic activity. At the same time, a more urgent context in which design is entwined with issues of potential future value is in its ability or otherwise to engage with the twin global challenges of Peak Oil and climate change. The role of design in meeting these challenges is clear, both in its short-term impact and its ability to address longer-term projected changes. The design of buildings and infrastructure (e.g. Shaw et al. 2007) or products (e.g. Datchefski 2001) involves a commitment to calculable carbon emissions. In these contexts, the kinds of processes of review, measurement and tracking that we have been tracing in this book may turn out to have a new social importance, even while the metrics used are bound to be the subject of debate. Identifying the details of these impacts provides the designer with data that helps him/her to target further design inputs to reduce emissions, whether this be in materials, production technologies, power usage, longevity, disposal, recycling or reuse. Eco-design is a sophisticated and complex field. But the designer's intervention in this area, in terms of reducing or mitigating the effects of climate change, or in consideration of a post-carbon economy, may also extend into a consideration of the emotional connections that we have with the objects of design, so that durability may also be founded in notions of connectivity and beauty (see e.g.

Chapman 2005). Finally, the designer's role may be found in facilitating social innovations that tap into and help develop people's potential to provide new solutions to ensure more sustainable and carbon-neutral modes of everyday well-being (see e.g. Manzini and Jégou 2005; Thackara 2005). Making the connections between design action and tangible, measurable impacts may progressively require greater imagination as we move from the consideration of individual products to complex social systems and contexts. In these new contexts, design's historical concern with 'beauty' may be perceived in many ways and may need to connect with its more recent concern with measurement and systematization in ways that are not yet easy to imagine. In these precarious social, environmental and economic times, our engagement as designers, design users and design observers with these challenges is ever more important and critical.

Note

1. The Design Council in Britain is one such example of an organization promoting the idea that it is possible to 'design one's way out of a downturn'. Its research with small and medium-sized enterprises (SMEs) suggested that a majority of such businesses in Britain intended to do so. See http://www. designcouncil.org.uk/en/Live-Issues/Can-design-help-businesses-survive-the-tough-economic-climate/.

References

Banks, M., Calvey, D., Owen, J. and Russell, D. (2002), 'Where the Art Is: Defining and Managing Creativity in New Media SMEs', *Creativity and Innovation Management*, 11(4): 255–64.

British Design Innovation (2006), 'The British Design Industry Valuation Survey – 2006 to 2007' (report), Brighton: BDI.

British Design Innovation (2003), 'The British Design Industry Valuation Survey – 2002 to 2003' (report), Brighton: BDI.

Caves, R. (2000), *Creative Industries: Contracts Between Art and Industry*, Cambridge, MA: Harvard University Press.

Chapman, J. (2005), *Emotionally Durable Design: Objects, Experiences and Empathy*, London: Earthscan.

Crowley, D. et al. (1992), *Design and Culture in Poland and Hungary, 1890–1990*, Brighton: Brighton University.

Datschefski, Edwin (2001), *The Total Beauty of Sustainable Products*, Crans-Près-Céligny and Hove: RotoVision.

Design Council (2005), *The Business of Design*, London: Design Council.

du Gay, P. and Pryke, M. (eds.) (2002), *Cultural Economy*, London: Sage.

Florida, R. (2002), *The Rise of the Creative Class: And How It's Transforming Work, Leisure, Community and Everyday Life*, New York: Basic Books.

Hospers, G.-J., and Pen, C.-J. (2008), 'A View on Creative Cities Beyond the Hype', *Creativity and Innovation Management*, 17(4): 259–70.

Ibrahim, S., Hosein Fallah, M. and Reilly, R. (2006), 'Do Localized Clusters Influence Creativity of Inventors?', *Creativity and Innovation Management*, 15(4): 410–18.

Ingold, T. and Hallam, E. (2007), 'Creativity and Improvisation: An Introduction', in E. Hallam and T. Ingold (eds.), *Creativity and Cultural Improvisation*, Oxford: Berg.

Jeffcut, P. and Pratt, A. (2002), 'Editorial: Managing Creativity in the Cultural Industries', *Creativity and Innovation Management*, 11(4): 225–33.

Julier, G. (2009), 'Dialogs: Value, Relationality and Unfinished Objects', *Design and Culture*, 1(1): 93–104.

Knorr Cetina, K. (1997), 'Sociality with Objects: Social Relations in Postsocial Knowledge Societies', *Theory, Culture and Society*, 14(4): 1–30.

Kristensen, T. (2004), 'The Physical Context of Creativity', *Creativity and Innovation Management*, 13(2): 89–96.

Landry, C. (2000), *The Creative City*, Demos: London.

Lockwood, T. L. (2007), 'Design Value: A Framework for Measurement', *Design Management Review*, 18(4): 90–97.

Manzini, E. and Jégou, F. (2005), *Sustainable Everyday. Scenarios of Urban Life*, Milan: Edizione Ambiente.

Marc, T. and Buijs, J. (2007), 'Clustering: An Essential Step from Diverging to Converging', *Creativity and Innovation Management*, 16(1): 16–26.

Moor, L. (2007), *The Rise of Brands*, Oxford: Berg.

Moultrie, J., Nilsson, M., Dissel, M., Haner, U.-R., Janssen, S. and Van der Lugt, R. (2007), 'Innovation Spaces: Towards a Framework for Understanding the Role of the Physical Environment in Innovation', *Creativity and Innovation Management*, 16(1): 53–65.

Otter, C. (2007), 'Making Liberal Objects: British Techno-Social Relations 1800–1900', *Cultural Studies*, 21(4–5): 570–90.

Power, M. (1997), *The Audit Society*, Oxford: Oxford University Press.

Power, M. (2009), untitled lecture given at Goldsmiths, University of London, 14 January.

Ray, L. and Sayer, A. (1998), *Culture and Economy After the Cultural Turn*, London: Sage.

Reimer, S., Pinch, S. and Sunley, P. (2008), 'Design Spaces: Agglomeration and Creativity in British Design Agencies', *Geografiska Annaler B*, 90(2): 1–20.

Shaw, R., Colley, M., and Connell, R. (2007), *Climate Change Adaptation by Design: A Guide for Sustainable Communities*, London: TCPA.

Strathern, M. (ed.) (2000), *Audit Cultures: Anthropological Studies in Accountability, Ethics and the Academy*, London and New York: Routledge.

Thackara, J. (2005), *In the Bubble: Designing in a Complex World*, Cambridge, MA: MIT Press.

Thrift, N. (1998), 'Virtual Capitalism: The Globalization of Reflexive Business Knowledge', in J. G. Carrier and D. Miller (eds.), *Virtualism: A New Political Economy*, Oxford: Berg.

Woodham, J. (1997), *Twentieth-Century Design*, Oxford: Oxford University Press.

Yúdice, G. (2003), *The Expediency of Culture: Uses of Culture in the Global Era*, Durham, NC: Duke University Press.

Contributors

AnneMarie Dorland has been a designer and account manager with the Canadian graphics firm, Karo Design. She currently coordinates internal and external communications strategies and media relations for the Alberta College of Art and Design. She holds a Master's in Communication and Media from Concorda University and she has maintained a research focus on the practices of creative work throughout her professional career.

Katie Hill is a researcher specializing in design processes and community participation at The Leeds School of Architecture, Landscape and Design, Leeds Metropolitan University. She has worked across the voluntary, public and private sectors on community engagement for design and public policy. She is a director of LeedsLoveItShareIt CIC, a policy research company and regeneration think-tank, and a consultant for Erskine Corporation.

Guy Julier is Professor of Design at Leeds Metropolitan University. His books include *The Culture of Design* (2008), he is an associate editor of the journal *Design and Culture* and sits on the editorial board of the *Journal of Visual Culture*. His research is concerned with political economies of design, design activism and design-led urban regeneration. Since 2002 he has been Visiting Professor at the Glasgow School of Art and in 2008 was Visiting Fellow at the University of Otago, New Zealand.

Lucy Kimbell is Clark Fellow in Design Leadership at the Saïd Business School, University of Oxford, where she teaches on the MBA course and researches design in organizational contexts. Previously, she was a tutor in interaction design at the Royal College of Art and AHRC Creative and Performing Arts Research Fellow at the Ruskin School of Drawing and Fine Art. She has led teams designing software and mobile services for commercial and non-profit organizations.

Liz Moor is Senior Lecturer in Media and Communications at Goldsmiths, University of London, and the author of *The Rise of Brands* (2007). Her research focuses on sociological approaches to consumer culture, promotion and the cultural and creative industries. She is the convenor of the MA Brand Development programme at Goldsmiths.

Sarah Owens is a Ph.D. student in Typography and Graphic Communication at the University of Reading and holds a Master's in History of Design from the Royal College of Art in London. Her research focuses primarily on the sociological and philosophical aspects of design. She has worked as a corporate and editorial designer at numerous German publishers and agencies, including the Süddeutscher Verlag, Condé Nast and Strichpunkt, and has written for the *Journal of Design History* and *Eye*.

Jane Pavitt is the University of Brighton Principal Research Fellow in Design at the Victoria and Albert Museum. Her work focuses on later twentieth century and contemporary design, and particularly on strategies for presenting design through museum exhibitions and collections. She has curated a number of design exhibitions for the V&A including 'Brand.New' (2000), 'Brilliant' (2004) and 'Cold War Modern' (2008).

Doug Sandle, a chartered psychologist, was until recently Reader in Visual Studies at Leeds Metropolitan University. His published research and consultancy include the aesthetics of sport, the psychology of art and design, public art, and visual culture. He is a founder member of RKL, a public art consultancy and was also founder, and for several years chair of the board, of Axis, the UK's leading online resource on contemporary visual art.

Paul Springer is a Head of Research in Creativity and Culture at Buckinghamshire New University. He is the author of *Ads to Icons: How Advertising Succeeds in a Multimedia Age* (Kogan Page 2007) and his research addresses brand–consumer relationships and new approaches to mass communications. Springer has written for *Admap*, *Brand Strategy* and *China*. He leads doctoral programmes on advertising research and is an advisor to Havas Media and the China Advertising Association, Beijing.

Damian Sutton is Lecturer in Historical and Critical Studies and Research Developer at The Glasgow School of Art. He is the co-editor of *The State of the Real: Aesthetics in the Digital Age* (2007), is author of *Photography, Cinema, Memory: The Crystal Image of Time* (2009, forthcoming) and has written for *Screen* and *Source*. His research includes work on cinema design as well as research into the relationship between cinema and photography.

Nitzan Waisberg is a designer and qualitative research consultant specializing in design and innovation. She holds a Master's in History of Design from the Royal College of Art, London and a B.Des. in Industrial Design from the Bezalel Academy of Art, Jerusalem. She has lectured on design in Israel, the UK and the US. Nitzan currently lives in California and teaches at the Hasso Plattner Institute of Design at Stanford University.

Index

Lightning Source UK Ltd.
Milton Keynes UK
UKOW06f0338020415

248996UK00005B/106/P